POLLY WITHECOMBE

Jewellery and Silversmithing Techniques

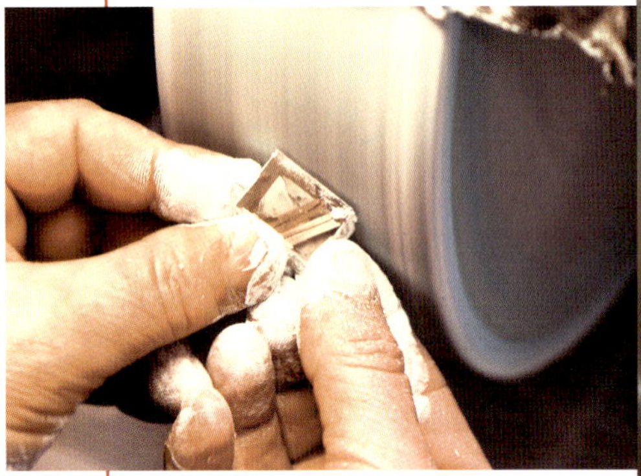
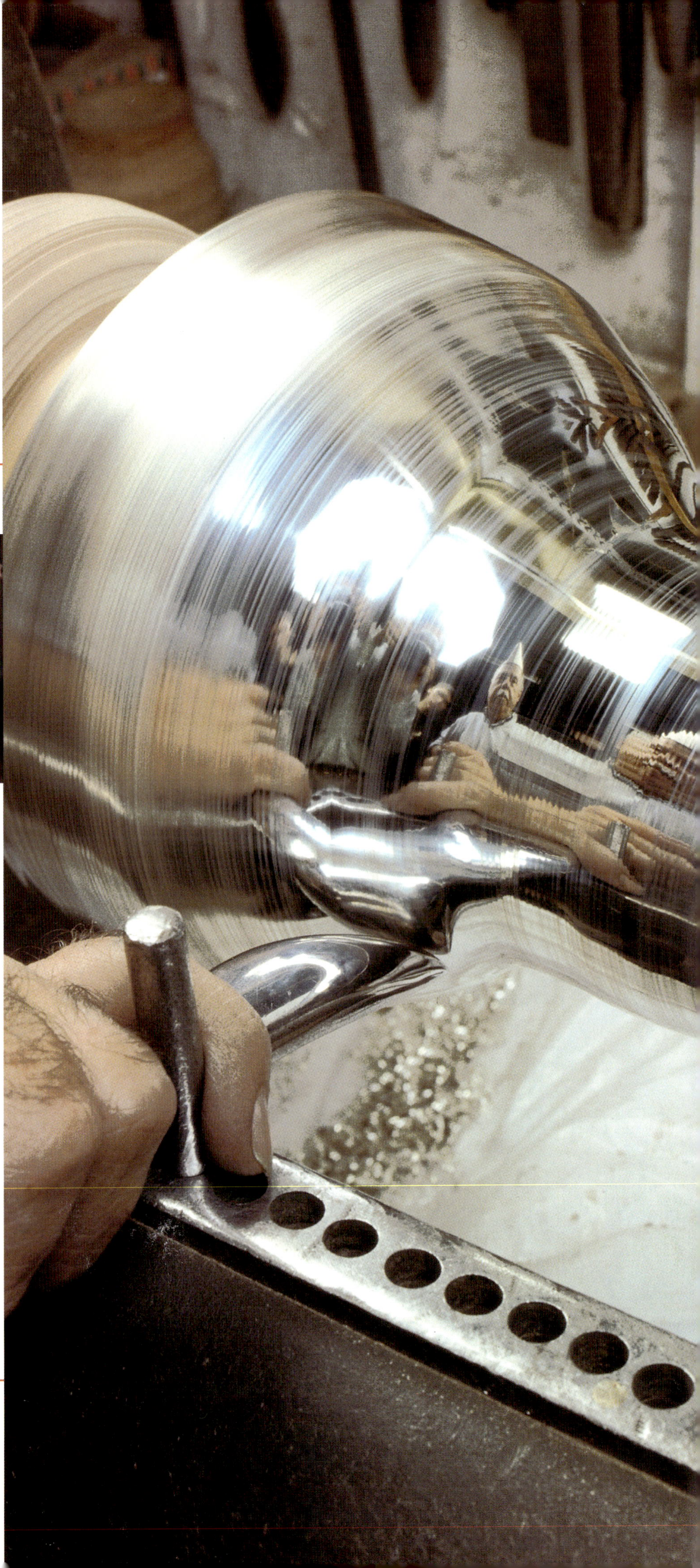

Jewellery and Silversmithing Techniques

Carles Codina

A&C Black · London

10 9 8 7 6 5 4 3 2 1

Published in Great Britain 2002 by A&C Black Publishers Ltd., 37 Soho Square, London, England WID 3QZ

Originally published under the title *Orfebrería*
Parramón Ediciones, S.A.
Gran Via de les Corts Catalanes, 322-324
08004 Barcelona, Spain
© 2001 Parramón Ediciones, S.A.—World Rights

English Translation © 2002, Lark Books, a division of Sterling Publishing Co., Inc.

Translation from the Spanish:
Eric A. Bye, M.A.

Technical Consultant:
Chris Weston

Jewellery and Silversmithing Techniques
Carles Codina

Text and Coordination:
Carles Codina

The following also contributed to the text:
Javier García Bonilla and J. Sánchez-Lafuente ("Precious Stones" and "Cutting Precious Stones"); Bagués Jewelers, Ricard Domingo, R. Puig Cuyás and Joaquím Capdevila ("Four Concepts of Creativity"); Ricard Domingo ("Image and Business"); and Joan Soto ("Photography and Jewelry")

Projects by:
Carles Codina

Collaborators include:
Pilar Cotter, Silvia Walz, Maike Barteldres, Xavier Doménech, Xavier Ines Monclús, Joaquim Benaque, Hans Leicht, Juan José López, Estela Guitart, Salima Saïd El Hadj, Oukali Saliha, Jesús P. Matamoros, Bernd Munsteiner, Joan Ferré, and Raimundo Amorós

Photography:
Nos & Soto; additional gem photography by Jordi Vidal

Illustrations:
Juan Carlos Martínez

The written instructions, photographs, designs, patterns, and projects in this volume are intended for the personal use of the reader and may be reproduced for that purpose only. Any other use, especially commercial use, is forbidden under law without written permission of the copyright holder.

Every effort has been made to ensure that all the information in this book is accurate. However, due to differing conditions, tools, and individual skills, the publisher cannot be responsible for any injuries, losses, and other damages that may result from the use of the information in this book.

Printed in Spain
All rights reserved
ISBN: 0-7136-6342-1

INTRODUCTION, 6

WORKING WITH PRECIOUS METALS, 8

Silversmithing, 10
Methods and Procedures, 18
Soldering Projects, 20
Working with Wire, 25
Stringing a Necklace, 28
Working with Platinum, 30

Table of C

SPECIAL TECHNIQUES, 32

Kum Boo, 34
Hand Engraving, 38
Electroplating and Surface Finishes for Metals, 44

Contents

CASTING AND STAMPING, 48

Alternative Casting Techniques, 50
Making Casting Patterns, 60
Metal Stamping, 65

GEMS, 72

Precious Stones, 74
Cutting Precious Stones, 84
Bernd Munsteiner, Master Gem Cutter, 88

CONCEPT AND IMAGE, 94

Four Concepts of Creativity, 96
Image and Business, 100
Photography and Jewelry, 104

STEP BY STEP, 114

GALLERY, 108

Coffee Service, 116
Square Rings, 128
Prism, 134
Earrings, 138
Hinged Bracelet, 142
Brooches, 150
North African Bracelet, 152

GLOSSARY, 158
INDEX, 159
BIBLIOGRAPHY AND ACKNOWLEDGMENTS, 160

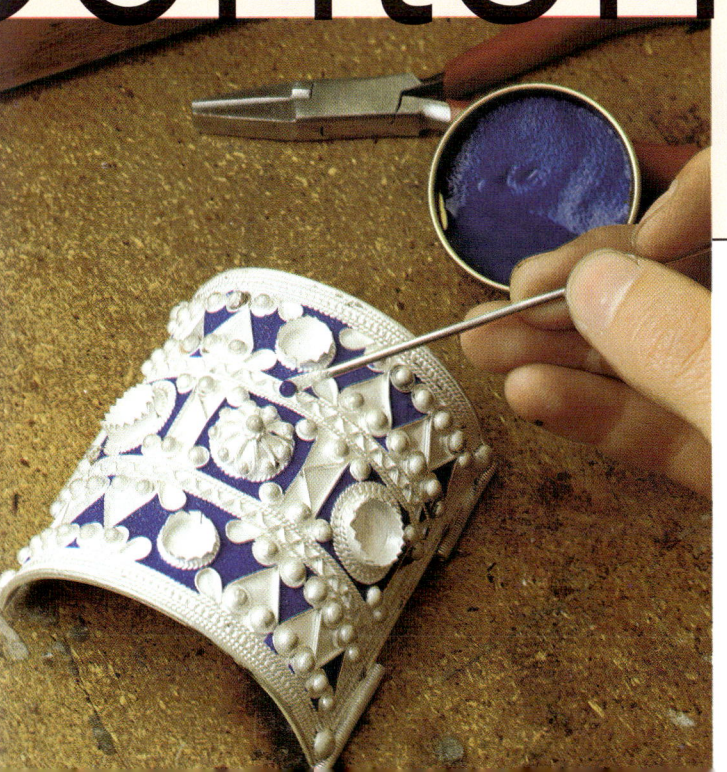

Introduction

Today, jewelry making brings together a number of different disciplines, and it requires a broad body of knowledge on the part of its practitioners. People who use gold- and silversmithing techniques to make jewelry need imagination and skill not only when designing and creating pieces, but also when problem solving; this often involves arriving at solutions that are not strictly part of this trade. Perhaps the best term for defining those of us who make these objects and are passionate devotees of the trade goes back to the Latin auri faber. This term refers to artisans who work in gold and other materials, yet use the same tools and techniques—an ancient definition that applies today more than ever. This book, my second, promotes the concept of creating all kinds of objects and applies to people who are skilled at working with any type of material that falls into their hands. This concept is somewhat nostalgic, like a contemporary reinterpretation of the medieval workshop, where in a single space and time all specialties are practiced in a natural, interdisciplinary manner. This book goes more deeply into some aspects of the trade, and presents a vision of how to conceptualize and create different pieces. It is an attempt to preserve the accumulated tradition and experience inherited from previous generations—a tradition I think is worth preserving, even if we are not bound to simply copy it.

Jewellery and Silversmithing Techniques is based on the open, social perspective that this diverse trade is a unique profession that allows different viewpoints and different styles. Those of us who have spent years making artistic jewelry and other objects know that any creative process requires relating to and learning from many people. Some of these are professionals whose work is generally little known, as they create in the shadow of large companies and more prestigious artists. Without these people, however, our craft would stagnate, and so we rely on these artisans more than ever. There are many artists whose esteemed works embody contemporary aesthetic values—I feel their artistry breaks through certain barriers of time and material. These are original and creative pieces made by craftspeople whose work is highly provocative.

The main purpose of my two books, *Handbook of Jewellery Techniques* and *Jewellery and Silversmithing Techniques,* is not practical and artistic training for the reader; nor do these books pretend to achieve any particular objective. These books were conceived more on an emotional level according to my personal sensibilities, and they are one way to relate to and understand jewelry. They are the vision of a trade that implies more than a work process and a result; rather, that this craft has a playful and human component that keeps it interesting and enjoyable.

Carles Codina i Armengol (born in Mollet del Vallès, Spain, 1961) is a practising jeweller who also teaches jewellery design at Barcelona's Massana School. His work has been shown in several countries in Europe and the Americas. He also wrote *Handbook of Jewellery Techniques* (2000), a thorough guide to basic and advanced jewellery-making techniques.

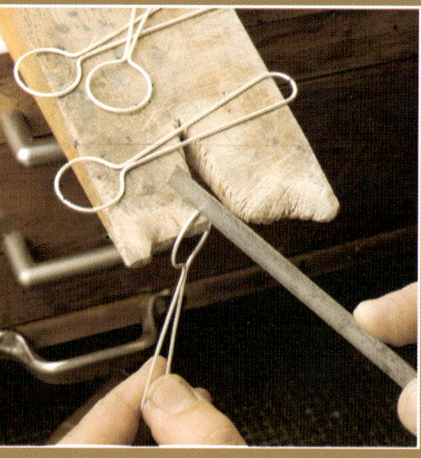

Both gold and silver have great symbolic value for many cultures. For ages, gold has cast an irresistible spell on people, provoking a deep fascination and respect. Because of its yellow color, it has been associated with the sun, the divinity, and eternal life—it is immutable through time, since fine gold neither oxidizes nor deteriorates with the years. In addition, the scarcity of these metals, which leads them to be regarded as noble or precious, has contributed to their ornamental value. Lastly, gold and silver are not suited to making tools or weapons, since they are too soft, and thus are valued primarily for their decorative properties.

The following sections will explore several techniques for working with precious metals and jewelry making, including silversmithing, construction and soldering, threading necklaces, and casting and working with platinum. Knowledge of all these skills is essential for the creative jeweler who strives to become more proficient in this beautiful and varied craft.

Working with Precious Metals

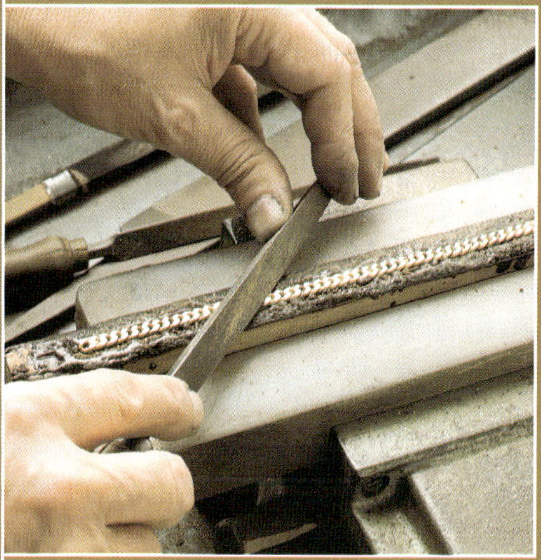

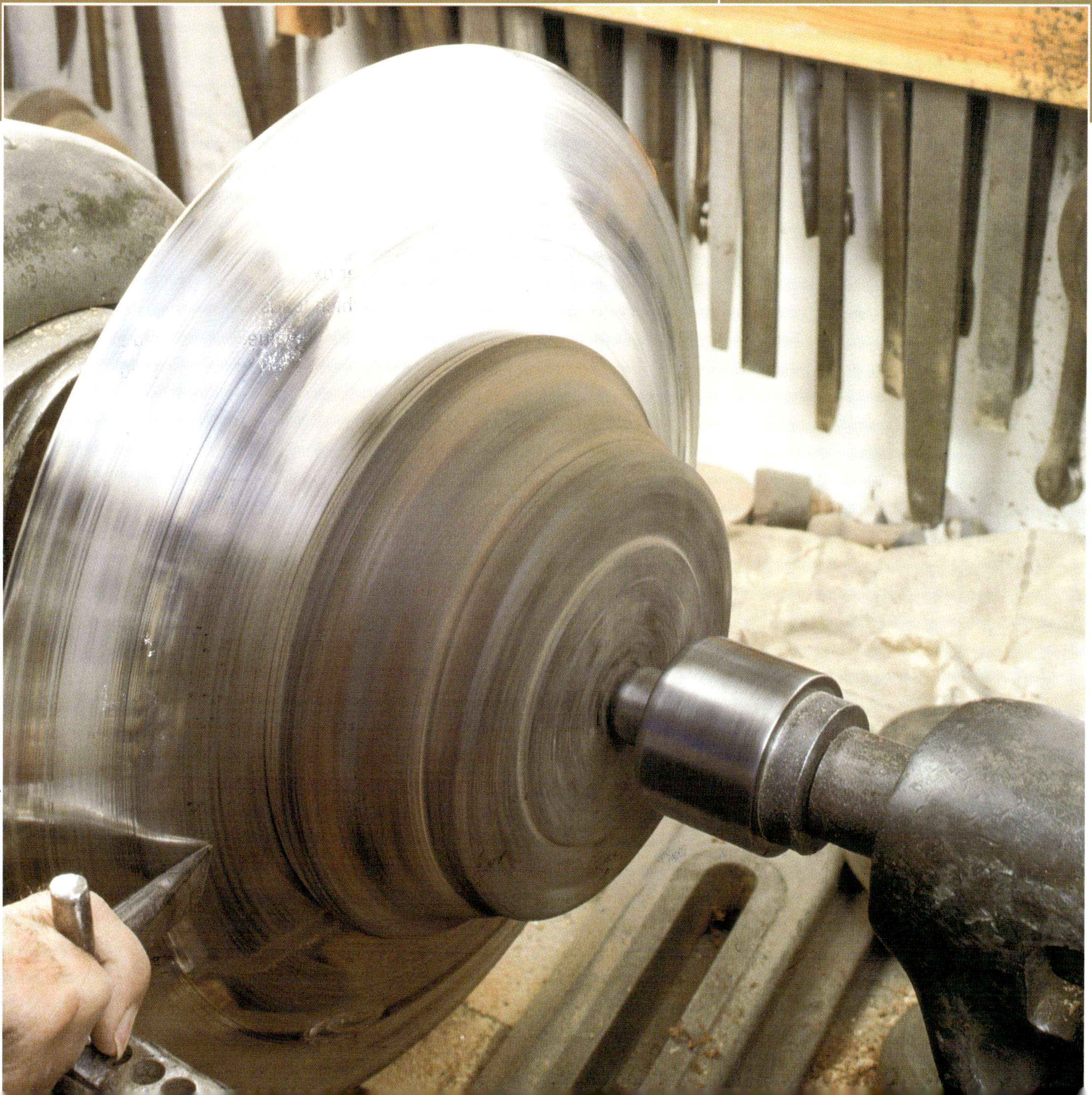

Silversmithing

Today, it's common to find silver objects that have been made using diverse techniques and processes, such as stamping, casting, and shaping on automatic lathes. Because the stamping techniques used in silversmithing are quite complex, this chapter will not address that specialized branch of the trade. Just the same, there's a lot of basic knowledge that's worth sharing and is applicable in most craft projects involving silver. These processes have been used ever since the earliest beginnings of silversmithing; examples include cold forming with various silversmithing tools, such as hammers, anvils, and spinning lathes. (The latter weren't equipped with motors, as contemporary lathes are.) The discussion of these processes will familiarize you with the behavior of this delicate metal silver and the principal ways of working it.

▲ Neck rings from Rajastan, India

Silver

Both silver and gold are very ductile and malleable metals. Silver, which is a bit harder than fine gold, is not as dense; its density varies between 10.47 for fine or pure silver and 10.31 for sterling, compared to 15.5 for pure gold. With a hardness of 2.6, silver is extremely soft in a pure state; however, its mechanical qualities improve considerably when it's *alloyed* with copper. This gives it greater hardness and durability, and improves its workability during mechanical processes such as forging and wire making. Alloying improves the durability of sterling silver, but proper construction and the mechanical process used in working the silver are also important factors in the ultimate quality of any piece.

When silver is melted in an alloy that generally consists of 925 parts fine silver and 75 parts copper, it's designated as *sterling silver*. Any silver object on which an assayer's stamp indicates sterling silver will bear the number 925; this indicates that out of 1,000 parts, 925 are pure silver, and other metals used in the alloy comprise the remainder.

Most silversmiths buy sterling silver in laminated sheets of the desired size and thickness. Different types of wire and hollow tubing are available also. These materials can be purchased in prefabricated form, and they can be drawn or laminated to the desired dimensions. The sheets are excellent for the craftsperson; they cut down the time required for preparing the material and avoid the costs and problems associated with heavy machinery. Just the same, though, the silversmith should know how to cast and prepare certain elements, and how to alloy pure silver to create sterling.

Copper is the metal commonly alloyed with pure silver; however, it's also appropriate to improve the color and durability of silver by adding other metals, as long as the proportion of 75 parts per thousand for sterling is respected. There are a number of ready-made alloys that can improve the hardness of the final alloy and that are satisfactory for some types of clasps and fittings. There are also alloys that are suited to *investment casting*, as well as oxidation-resistant silver alloys, and alloys that have enhanced conductivity.

It's easier to melt silver by using a *flux*, since it dissolves metallic oxides that form from the contact of the oxygen in the air with the heated metal. Borax is the most commonly used flux.

▲ Niclaus Manuel, *Saint Eloy Working in the Shop*, 1515.

▶ David Huycke, *Ovalinder 2*, 2000. 10 x 13 x 17 cm. Container in sterling silver.

Soldering Silver

Most construction projects involving silver require the joining of various elements or pieces; sometimes rivets, inlays, and screws are used, but generally, they are soldered together. The *solder* used is an alloy made of silver with a lower melting point than that of sterling; as a result, when it melts in the heat of the flame, it unites the two metal pieces and produces a strong, durable *join* or *solder seam*.

The two metals to be soldered together must have the same internal structure. A strong bond is created by soldering silver to silver, or to gold or copper, since these are non-ferrous metals with similar structures. (In contrast, joining such metals as silver and iron does not produce a strong bond.) Good solder should be malleable and able to withstand forging, for as the piece is worked, it will be subjected to constant expansion and shaping by hammering. Solder also has to flow properly when it's melted, without forming lumps. It mustn't corrode or perforate when it's hammered, and its color must be as close as possible to that of sterling.

Solder should be bought from sources that deal in precious metals, so that you can be confident that it will perform properly. It's a good idea to ask about its technical characteristics, especially its melting temperature, and to investigate its quality and color. If you prefer to make solder from commercial alloys intended to be added to pure silver, these can produce excellent results when melted properly in a clean crucible.

Solder can also be made using the proportions indicated in this chart:

Hard	82 Silver	14 Copper	4 Zinc
Medium	77 Silver	17 Copper	6 Zinc
Soft	67 Silver	24 Copper	9 Zinc

The alloys to be added to the fine silver to form solder are composed of 60 to 70 percent copper and 30 to 40 percent zinc. This is also the composition of brass, but never make solder by adding commercially manufactured brass to silver without first knowing the exact alloy of the brass. Brass normally comes in sheets that contain small traces of other metals, which can lead to serious problems in soldering silver.

Prepare solder in a clean crucible that's used exclusively for the purpose of melting solder. After fluxing and preheating the crucible, melt the silver, then add the other metals used in the alloy. When adding an alloy specially prepared for producing solder, avoid overheating the mixture of metals in the crucible, since some of these metals are volatile and the solder won't behave properly when it's used subsequently.

After forming sheets .3- to .4-mm thick, clean the solder with abrasive paper and store in a sealed, airtight container with a label indicating the type, generally hard, medium, or soft.

▼ David Huycke, *Untitled*, 1998. 32 x 32 x 7 cm. Dish made of sterling silver.

Annealing, Pickling, and Soldering Silver Objects

When silver is worked cold (through forming, forging, or *repoussé*), it hardens considerably, and it becomes difficult to work because the crystals in its structure have been deformed. At that point, it's necessary to *anneal* the piece, which returns the crystalline structure to its original state.

Annealing is an essential step, and it has to be done properly. Since most silversmithing objects are large, and are often made out of delicate sheets, they are more difficult to anneal consistently than pieces of jewelry. When heating the piece with a torch, apply a soft, uniform flame to bring it to a temperature of about 600° C, and then cool the piece quickly. It's generally preferable to anneal large pieces on a charcoal block. First, apply a broad flame with light air pressure, rotating the piece for a few seconds and moving the torch with your other hand so that the flame reaches all parts of the object. Once the piece is heated adequately, increase the gas pressure to produce a long, gentle flame that likewise is moved uniformly over the entire piece. Maintain this temperature for a few seconds, and then submerge the piece in water, as long as the project is in the early stages (as with wire or ingots). In general, sudden cooling from a high temperature softens silver, but it may also completely deform the piece; as a result it's a good idea to let pieces cool gradually before putting them into pickling solution, not only to prevent distortion, but also to avoid splashing the solution.

Applying heat causes the silver to *oxidize*, and this layer of oxide has to be removed before continuing to solder or shape the metal. This process is called *pickling*, and it's usually done with a hot solution of water and sulfuric acid, in a concentration of 10 to 15 percent acid to water. Today, it's also possible to get substitutes for the acid that are less dangerous and easier to recycle, and they work well for removing oxidation from silver and gold.

The processes of annealing, soldering, and pickling require special care, since they have to be repeated several times in the creation of any piece. Most solder contains zinc and copper, and these metals are more

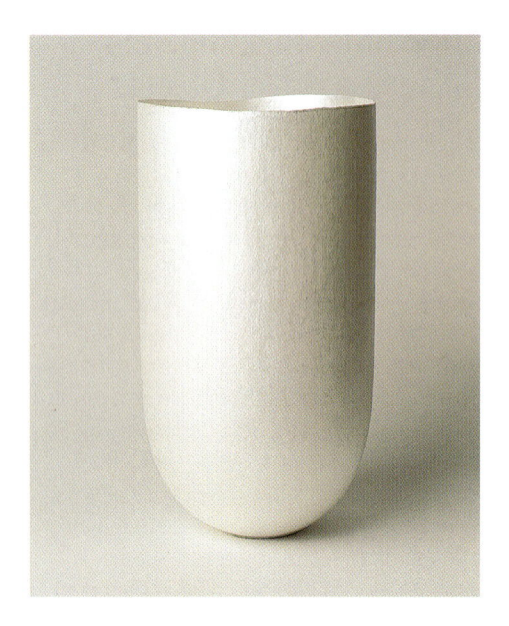

▲ David Huycke, *Bolinder I*, 1999. 17 x 17 x 31 cm. Vase.

susceptible to corrosion than sterling. Metals like these tend to dissolve; specifically, zinc is very volatile when it's overheated. For that reason, when solder is heated and pickled repeatedly, it becomes porous and fragile, and appears burned. To keep that from happening, avoid overheating the piece; don't pickle it unnecessarily; and try to keep the metal from oxidizing as much as possible. One way to do that is to protect the surface before applying heat. You can use a specific anti-firescale coating that's sold in specialty stores, or you can coat the surface with a very diluted borax paste.

Joining the Surfaces

A good join or solder seam depends on a perfect fit between the parts to be soldered, good quality solder, and proper surface preparation. The surfaces to be joined have to be clean of oxidation and grease, and the solder has to be bright and free of grease and dust. The same applies to the heat-resistant surface on which the parts will be soldered, and to the soldering tweezers—in general, all the items that are used in the process. Also, the surfaces to be joined need to be roughened up with a fine file or abrasive paper, which will clean and lightly score the areas and greatly improve the bond.

To begin, apply the diluted or liquid borax and then the solder *paillons* or *snippets*; otherwise, solder with commercial wire solder or paste solder. Gently heat the piece so that the paillons of solder remain in place, and apply uniform heat until the solder melts. The heat makes the solder flow and run into the *joint* through capillary action, forming a bright line. Silver solder is delicate; sometimes it may appear to run perfectly, but if it doesn't, it may not get into the interior of the mass. In that case, when the piece is bent or manipulated, the solder may separate easily and suddenly. If that happens, don't use solder to fill in the gap.

Solder

Like other metals, silver expands when it's heated and contracts when it's cooled. In soldering, the application of heat and the subsequent cooling may produce changes in shape that interfere with the work. Heat the largest piece or part first in the way previously described, making sure that the flame envelops the entire piece and only later is concentrated on the smallest part. It's preferable to equalize the temperatures of the two pieces to be joined, since solder always flows in the direction of the hotter piece. Since smaller parts heat up first, distribute the heat by constantly moving the torch to heat the larger pieces as needed.

Once the soldering is complete, pickle the piece to remove the oxidation, and then rinse in water containing a little dissolved baking soda to neutralize any leftover acid. After it's dry, proceed with subsequent shaping and soldering.

Binding with Wire

The wire that binds together the parts that are being soldered must be used with care. Silver has a greater coefficient of expansion than the wire, so binding wire that's too tight may produce marks on the surface because of its greater resistance to expansion when heated. One way to solve this problem involves leaving a little room for expansion when the wire is tightened on the piece. (See step 2 on page 20 for a demonstration of this technique.)

Fire Stain and Tarnish

After silver is alloyed or soldered, oxidation can appear as purple spots or gray areas on the surface, commonly known as *fire stain* or *firescale*. These spots can usually be eliminated by carefully polishing the piece, but it's better to avoid them in the first place. Keep these spots from appearing by utilizing the following: sheets melted by induction in a controlled atmosphere; pure electrolytic copper or specific alloys; or anti-oxidizing products that prevent surface oxidation in soldering and annealing. With proper handling of the silver and use of these methods, the spots will be minimized and therefore easier to remove.

Silver is attacked directly by nitric acid and sulfuric acid (if the latter is very concentrated); sulfur and sulfates also attack it and remove its shine. There are small amounts of sulfates in the atmosphere; even domestic gas contains a certain amount of hydrogen sulfate (H_2S) that can affect silver, due to the formation of black silver sulfate (Ag_2S) that tarnishes and blackens the surface.

▼ Silver bracelets from eastern Tibet

A Silver Bowl

Making a small bowl from a disk of silver is a good basic exercise for subsequent silversmithing projects. With a little skill and practice, all kinds of shapes can be created with these techniques. In fact, you can continue the work until the bowl is almost completely closed or you produce a totally different shape; those variations would take a little experience with choosing different stakes and hammers in respect to the desired shape.

One very interesting aspect of this project is that it is reminiscent of an old way of working silver, a method that's not used much anymore because it takes so long; however, your labor is compensated with the satisfaction of creating a unique piece with an inimitable surface quality.

▼ David Huycke, *Tweebol*, 1999. 40 x 40 x 15.5 cm. Bowl.

Tools

To begin with, you will need a small lead shaping form or a concave wooden form; a lead one will be used in this project. It's important to keep the lead from adhering to the silver before annealing it; any possible traces of lead have to be cleaned from the surface of the silver. Also, make sure that no lead mixes with the gold or silver used in the workshop.

▲ The basic tools are hammers, usually made of steel with different shapes, weights, and profiles; the different tools will allow access to interiors, let you create flat surfaces, and so forth. Wooden mallets and horn hammers are also used for closing up metal without stretching it. Silversmiths make most of their own hammers from steel or iron.

▲ It's a good idea to keep the forms and hammers well polished for all projects; that way, the smoothness is transferred to the silver without producing marks on the surface.

▼ The only way to create a bowl from an .8 mm silver disk is to use a silversmith's stake and a double-faced hammer, as shown in this photo.

◀ Most stakes of different shapes and steels are made by the smiths themselves, and the surfaces are polished smooth. These are often modified to suit the particular project.

Making the Bowl

Since you may not own silversmith's stakes, here is how to make a simple container using nothing but a few common hammers and a lead block made by melting leftover pieces of lead in an old circular pan. This is a basic procedure that will allow you to understand how to work silver on this material. The following photos will demonstrate the creation of a bowl made from a silver disk that is .6 mm thick. The bowl will be shaped entirely by hand, using the most basic and common silversmithing tools. Start with a clean, annealed disk without any holes or cracks. In this project, the hammering begins immediately, but if you wish, you can use a compass to mark off several concentric circles to serve as a guide in striking with greater precision and convenience.

▲ 1. Raising hammers all have blunt striking surfaces and convex profiles to avoid marring the silver. Start with this hammer, using concentric blows around the outer edge of the plate so it begins to close up.

▼ 2. To create greater depth, shape the lead by striking it with a hammer; this will create the necessary profile to allow you to close the edge inward toward the center.

13

Silversmithing

▲ 3. Continue to hammer the inside concentrically, increasing the force and modifying the lead block with the angle of the blows. As the metal becomes hard, it will need to be annealed and cooled quickly; but first, remember to scrub the surface with a stiff brush to get rid of any traces of lead.

▲ 4. Now, using a broader and heavier hammer, smooth out any wrinkles inside the bowl and continue working on the curvature; leave the center a little flatter than the outer edges.

▲ 5. Modify the lead block once again and beat the inside edge with a highly domed forming hammer; proceed with less force but greater precision. Keep working in the same way, using light but accurate hammer blows and moving in concentric circles.

▲ 6. After another annealing, it's time to start hammering on the silversmith's stakes. Choose one with the desired inner profile—in this project, the shape of a ball—and clamp it tightly in the vise jaws.

▲ 7. This stake is adequate for the present project, but if the work were to continue with tighter curves, you would need to use a specially shaped stake that you would insert in the piece and hammer from the outside.

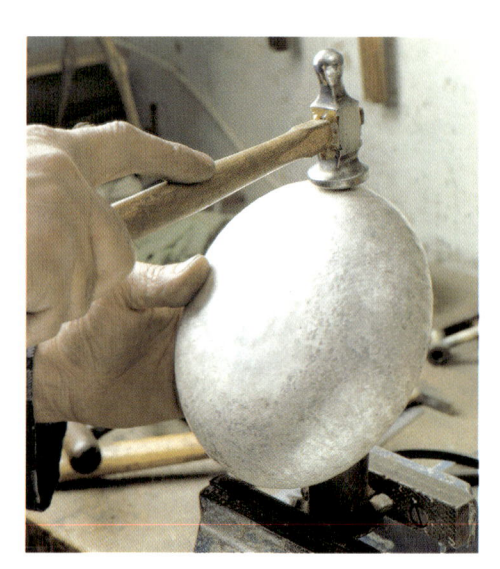

▶ 8. Use a planishing hammer to smooth out the piece; be sure the striking surface is perfectly polished, and hammer against the stake placed inside the bowl.

▲ 9. Once the hammer work is done, take impressions from three pebbles and sand-cast them; solder them on to serve as legs and provide stability for the bowl.

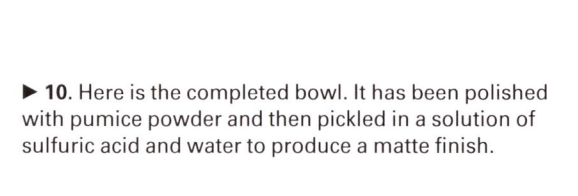

▶ 10. Here is the completed bowl. It has been polished with pumice powder and then pickled in a solution of sulfuric acid and water to produce a matte finish.

Working with Precious Metals

A Centerpiece

The following project shows how to make a centerpiece by combining the technique of repoussé with hammering or planishing. It's possible to complete the dish with nothing more than a few hammers and the appropriate stake, but using a spinning lathe simplifies the process and is a common practice in silversmithing workshops.

To make this piece, start with a silver disk .8 mm thick and about 35 cm in diameter. The final weight will be 1.25 kg of silver.

▶ 1. Prepare an initial or rough chuck or pattern out of wood. It needs to be turned with the precise inner shape desired for the dish.

▲ 2. Secure the disk to the wooden chuck by using a small piece of wood known as a follow block. Center the disk and shape it on the lathe using a spinning tool.

◀ 3. Next, adapt the metal to the chuck, first using a well-polished spinning tool known as a flat spoon. Press hard from the center toward the outer edge with the flat side of the tool, using the pin on the toolrest as a fulcrum.

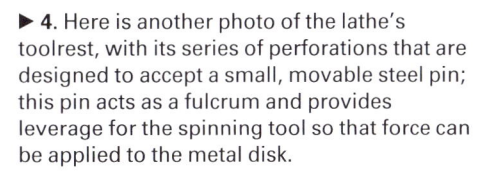

▶ 4. Here is another photo of the lathe's toolrest, with its series of perforations that are designed to accept a small, movable steel pin; this pin acts as a fulcrum and provides leverage for the spinning tool so that force can be applied to the metal disk.

▼ 5. Now, anneal the disk uniformly to stabilize the metal. To perform the hammering process without stretching the metal, use a large piece of wood that's concave on the inside and very close in shape to the silver disk. Fill the inside with hot chaser's pitch, making sure that there are no surface bubbles.

▲ 6. While the pitch is still hot, press the disk down into it without forming air bubbles between the pitch and the silver disk, because any bubbles could collapse and produce serious defects when the silver is hammered.

▲ 7. When the pitch is cool, begin in the center of the silver and hammer concentrically, using a hammer with a domed head that's well polished on the striking face.

15

Silversmithing

◀ **8.** Apply regular, short hammer blows, but try to keep the surface as uniform and even as possible. Once you have finished the entire surface, use low heat from a torch to remove the tray from the pitch, and use acetone or alcohol to eliminate any traces of pitch.

▼ **9.** Here is a close-up of the texture produced by hammering.

▲ **10.** Next, anneal and pickle the metal again, and return it to the same wooden chuck used in spinning; then smooth it out with a broad, heavy planishing hammer. Hold the hammer as indicated in the photo, and press down on the surface in a rhythmic forward and backward motion.

▲ **11.** The inner face of the tray also needs to be smoothed out; place the piece on a large, smooth anvil or steel plate, and work the surface with a raising hammer whose head is smooth and slightly smaller than that used in step 10.

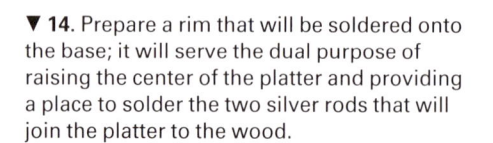

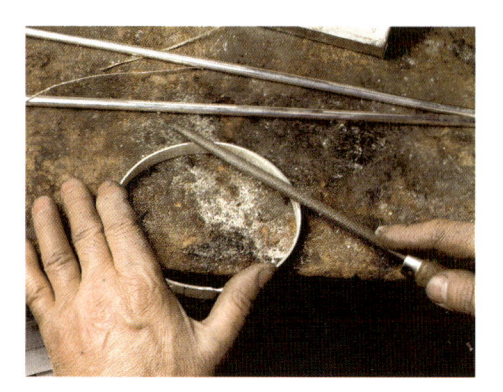

▲ **12.** The platter should be smooth and well balanced after the previous step. Now, anneal the piece to stabilize it and relieve the stresses in the metal.

▶ **13.** Prepare two 8-mm rods to secure the silver platter to a base of two strips of bobinga wood, which have already been cut out, sanded, and treated with wax.

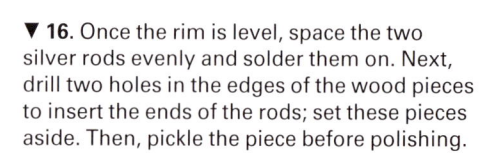

▼ **14.** Prepare a rim that will be soldered onto the base; it will serve the dual purpose of raising the center of the platter and providing a place to solder the two silver rods that will join the platter to the wood.

▼ **15.** Solder the rim to the base and file it level.

▼ **16.** Once the rim is level, space the two silver rods evenly and solder them on. Next, drill two holes in the edges of the wood pieces to insert the ends of the rods; set these pieces aside. Then, pickle the piece before polishing.

Working with Precious Metals

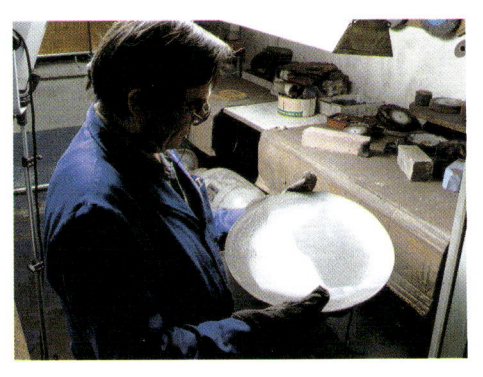

▲ 17. Once the construction is complete, begin to polish. In the first step, eliminate scratches by using a coarse, abrasive paste, different buffs of varying grades, and a powerful polisher.

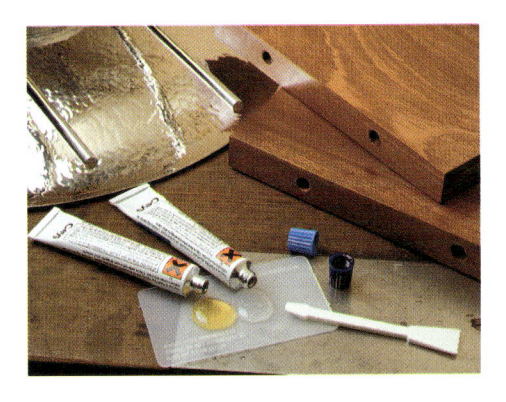

▶ 18. For the second step, use cotton buffing wheels and red rouge to brighten and polish the silver.

▶ 19. Silversmith Joan Ferré checks the surface of this piece for uniformity, making sure that the scratches have been completely removed.

◀ 20. Glue the piece to the wood, using a two-part epoxy that's suitable for this type of bond.

▶ 21. Close-up photo of the dish

▼ 22. This centerpiece was designed by Carles Codina and produced by master silversmith Joan Ferré in 2001.

17

METHODS AND PROCEDURES

The following section will focus on several methods, procedures and construction techniques that are frequently used in creating jewelry, including setting gems, preparing surfaces, soldering, and working with wire. Some discussion will be devoted to working with platinum, as it has some special requirements. This is essentially an overview of how most jewelry items are constructed, including the steps to follow and the criteria to consider in their manufacture. While utilizing some of the materials common to this trade, several accomplished professionals will demonstrate how they carry out their work.

Soldering

▲ Ingres, *La Princesse de Broglie*, 1853. The Metropolitan Museum of Art, New York.
  A mastery of many different techniques is required in constructing pieces of jewelry. Necklaces, bracelets, rings, etc., require remarkable interdisciplinary skills.

Soldered joins or seams are used in most construction processes involving precious metals. As discussed on page 11, solder is an alloy of metals similar in nature to the metal being joined or soldered, but solder has a lower melting point due to a different proportion of metals. Good solder is malleable, flows perfectly when it melts, and creates a perfect, strong bond; it also has a color that blends with the metal used for the piece of jewelry.

There are many types of solder available commercially. They have excellent fusion and color, and they are free of cadmium, which gives off toxic vapors in the soldering process.

Correct soldering also requires the use of a flux that acts as an antioxidant and protects the surface from tarnishing when the metal is heated in the soldering process. Fluxes dissolve metallic oxides and retain the heat in the area of the joint, and that is advantageous in making the join. With gold and silver solders, different mixes of boric acid and borax are used as flux; you can also buy commercial products that contain these ingredients.

The solder flows in response to the heat provided by the torch; however, because of the uneven expansion of the different parts of a piece, some distortion may result during this procedure. The better an alloy conducts heat, the less likely it will be to suffer distortion; an alloy of gold with a high silver content generally is more resistant to deformation than a white gold alloy. The risk of distortion also increases when working with flat sheets and objects with large surface areas. In these cases, first heat the piece indirectly until it reaches a uniform temperature. Then, concentrate the flame on the solder so that it flows properly. Try to avoid heating the piece unevenly; to produce a uniform temperature, use the appropriate clean soldering pad or block.

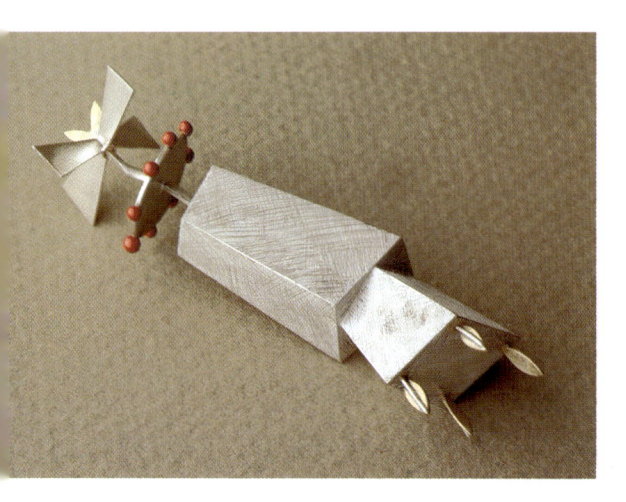

◄ Piece constructed by joining different silver plates and soldering on small gold elements. The finish has an interesting texture, created by filing the surface. Pendant created by Jimena Bello, from Colombia.

► In order to assure a good join, the pieces to be soldered together have to be dry and free of oxidation, grease, or oil.

Working with Precious Metals

▲ 1. All the elements of the main structure that can be assembled separately, such as the setting or mount in the photo, should be soldered together in advance using hard solder; then soldered to the body of the piece using solder with a lower melting point.

▲ 2. The various pieces are carefully fitted together. Do not use the solder to fill any voids; since the solder is softer than the surrounding metal, it could develop grooves when the piece is polished. Apply a little liquid soldering flux with a fine brush, and add a paillon of solder dipped in the liquid flux before applying heat from a torch.

▲ 3. To protect joins that have already been soldered, apply a commercially prepared heat-shielding product to any solder that might be susceptible to melting again. There are many very effective products for this purpose; they don't become diluted by the soldering flux, and they are easy to clean off.

▲ 4. Solder is usually prepared in thin sheets about .3 to .4 mm thick. Once the solder has been made into sheets, it has to be polished clean and free of oxidation. To apply, cut the solder into small squares or paillons; put these into place using fine tweezers dipped in soldering flux.

▲ 5. The uniformity of the flame is very important, since solder always spreads toward the hottest area when it melts. Choose a good surface for soldering that uniformly absorbs and spreads out the heat from the torch, dependent on the type of flame and the piece that's being soldered.

▲ 6. Surface oxidation is produced with every soldering; remove this in a 10 percent solution of sulfuric acid. You can also use a specific pickling solution, since that will yield better results without the dangers associated with the use of acids.

Using Wire in Soldering

Wire is frequently used to bind together different elements of a piece so that they remain in place when they are soldered. This has to be used with caution, since the wire and the piece of gold or silver consist of different alloys and expand differently under heat. As a result, you should avoid tight knots; it's better to twist the wire together, especially with large pieces, in order to compensate for the different rates of expansion between the wire and the piece. If the piece expands before the wire does, the wire could bind against the piece and severely deform or damage it.

▼ Choose the right gauge of wire with respect to the thickness of the metal and the shape of the piece to be soldered, and remove the wire before pickling the piece.

Soldering Projects

Most construction projects involve joins held together with different types of solder. There are an infinite number of possibilities; the following section shows just a few applications that can be used in constructing pieces of jewelry. In some of these segments, different artists will demonstrate how they design and execute their creations, though experience and inspiration determine much of the creative process.

A Hollow Ring

Solder is used in three main forms; perhaps the most familiar forms are paillons or small metal squares, but it's also common to use commercial paste solder, or to buy or make solder in the shape of flat or round wire. This is all the same material, even though sometimes one form or another is much quicker and easier to use, as this section suggests.

Two important questions are addressed in the construction of the following ring, made by Carles Codina: the method of binding the piece together for soldering, and the way in which the solder is applied. In this case, wire solder is applied to the piece once it reaches the right temperature. This type of construction is fairly common in jewelry.

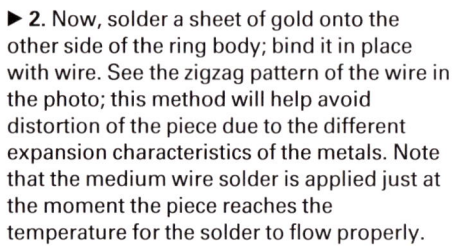

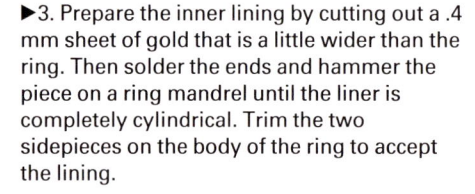

▲ 1. First, make the outer walls from .8 mm sterling silver sheet, incorporating the desired angles and slants. After truing up the two edges with a file, solder on a sheet of silver; after that's done, saw off the excess.

▲ Xavier Ines Monclús, *The Precious Stones Factory*. Piece made using various types of solder, predominantly silver sheet and wire.

▶ 2. Now, solder a sheet of gold onto the other side of the ring body; bind it in place with wire. See the zigzag pattern of the wire in the photo; this method will help avoid distortion of the piece due to the different expansion characteristics of the metals. Note that the medium wire solder is applied just at the moment the piece reaches the temperature for the solder to flow properly.

▼ Ring made by soldering together numerous pieces of white gold wire. Work by Aureli Bisbe.

▶ 3. Prepare the inner lining by cutting out a .4 mm sheet of gold that is a little wider than the ring. Then solder the ends and hammer the piece on a ring mandrel until the liner is completely cylindrical. Trim the two sidepieces on the body of the ring to accept the lining.

▶ 4. Solder the inner liner, and file and polish all remaining surfaces before adding the other features.

▶ Ring with precious stone. Work by Carles Codina.

Working with Precious Metals

A Pendant with Concealed Solder Seams

There are very high-quality solders with good physical properties and colors to match every need. However, when constructing pieces from sheet and various wires, try to keep the soldered joins in places where they won't be visible, especially in very smooth areas, or places where you want to preserve a certain texture or decorative feature.

When the surface is highly textured, the process is a little more complicated. First, you must find the right color solder. And once the joint has been soldered it can't be filed and polished, because that would totally destroy the surrounding texture. To prevent that, you have to bevel and fit the metal sheets and wires properly, as this project demonstrates. It's also a good idea to finish the inside of the setting or mount with abrasive paper; in this case, it will hold this unique stone, and then a simple braided steel cord will be added.

▲ 1. Prepare a sheet of textured gold by running the sheet and a piece of soft paper towel through the rolling mill. (This process is demonstrated on page 134.) Next, anneal the sheet and flatten it out by hitting it with a plastic mallet on a steel anvil. Cut out a rectangle equal to the perimeter of the gem, and then bend it oval by using an oval ring mandrel.

▲ 2. Shape a small rectangular wire, about 1.2 mm thick by 3 mm wide, to fit inside the form made in the previous step; this will serve as a seat for the stone.

▲ 3. Gently wrap the setting with wire so it doesn't open up when it's soldered; use hard solder and apply a uniform flame on a charcoal block.

▲ 4. File the backpiece and the inside rim of the setting to a 45° angle, so that the backpiece will fit flush with the edge when it's soldered in place; that way, it won't be necessary to file the exterior, and the surface textures will be preserved.

▲ 5. Once again, bind the main piece of the setting without exerting too much pressure. Apply medium solder so it pools evenly inside the previously prepared beveled areas of the setting. Next, put on the back and bind it in place, as shown in the photo. To finish, heat the whole setting again, using the torch to draw the solder outward and toward the top, creating a clean, precise join.

▶ 6. To suspend the setting and the stone, drill two holes with a ball bur to accept a braided steel cord.

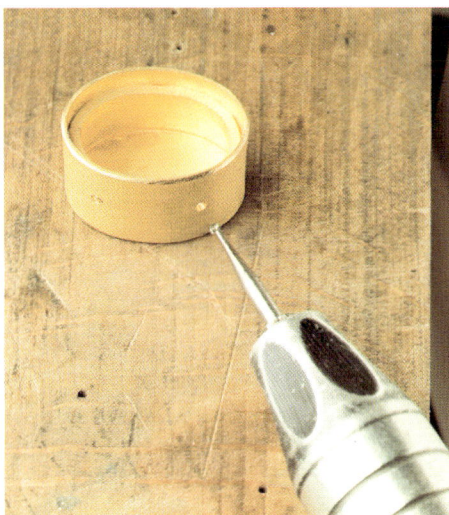

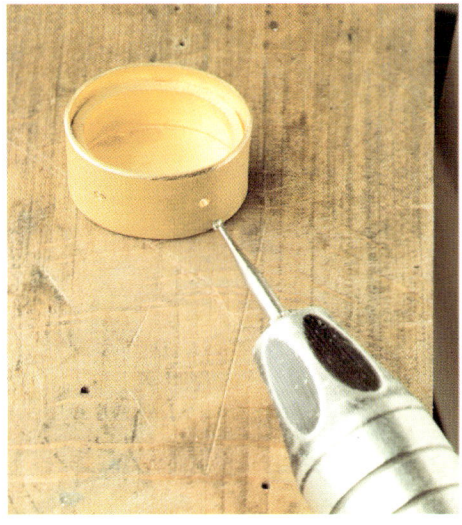

▶ 7. After the stone is set correctly, manually polish the edge of the setting. Smoky quartz pendant by Carles Codina.

21

Soldering Projects

Hollow Tube Construction

Many projects can include hollow forms; the pieces are much lighter and more appealing to wear, and the resulting weight reduction lowers the price of the jewelry. Most hollow forms are manufactured by industrial die stamping, but it's common to use hollow tubes for constructing chains and creating structures to hold pendants, like this piece.

The first step involves making a round tube; to begin, prepare a .6 mm sheet of gold and use a hammer and a grooved forming block to shape it into a round tube. Then join it using hard solder, and keep drawing it through a round drawplate to produce a perfectly round tube of the desired length.

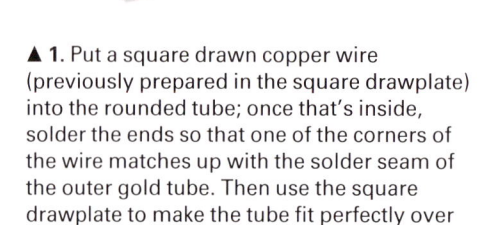

▲ 1. Put a square drawn copper wire (previously prepared in the square drawplate) into the rounded tube; once that's inside, solder the ends so that one of the corners of the wire matches up with the solder seam of the outer gold tube. Then use the square drawplate to make the tube fit perfectly over the inner core.

▲ 2. Use a three-square or square file to bevel a 90° angle, leaving very little metal; the deeper and cleaner the cut, the cleaner the corner will appear once it's bent over.

▶ 3. After making the notch, anneal the piece before bending it or it will snap in the process. After bending it over and checking the angle with a square, solder the joint.

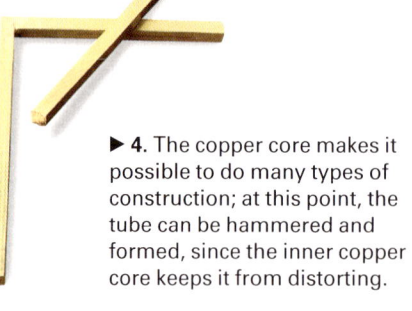

▶ 4. The copper core makes it possible to do many types of construction; at this point, the tube can be hammered and formed, since the inner copper core keeps it from distorting.

▶ 5. Once you have decided on the shape of the piece—in this project, a pendant with a silver decoration—remove the core by immersing it in nitric acid for several hours. This eats away the copper without harming the gold of the outer tube.

▲ 6. After the piece has been rinsed and cleaned out, solder on the additional features. From this point on, handle the piece with extreme care, since it no longer has the inner core. The exterior gold is extremely thin, so be careful not to dent it or bend it. A light polishing is all that is needed.

▲ 7. Make supporting brackets from two pieces, sawn from a .5 mm sheet of gold; solder the pieces in place, adjusting for the thickness of the silver to be placed inside the frame.

◀ 8. Finally, texture the surface of the silver and attach the various features to the pendant with rivets.

▶ 9. Use a chain made of steel wire, with a special braiding that allows the pendant to hang attractively. Work by Carles Codina.

Making a Frame

Hollow gold tubes with inner copper cores can also be used to make frames and brackets for various types of jewelry, including enameled pieces and cameos. Here is a frame for a piece of silver; the square gold tube and the beveling work has been done as described on page 22.

▶ **1.** Use two bent 90° bevels to construct a rectangle that is exactly the same perimeter as the piece of silver to be mounted. Join the frame with hard solder, clean, and then polish with abrasive paper up through 1200 grit.

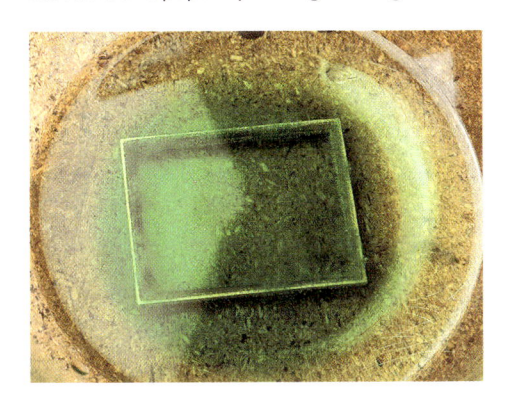

▲ **3.** Place the assembly into a bath of nitric acid, which removes the copper but leaves the outer gold shell untouched. From this point on, as with the previous project, the structure is delicate and will need to be handled with great care.

▶ **4.** After rinsing, use a scraper or a graver to remove any traces of copper that have been left behind.

▲ **2.** Start with a coarse file, and then change to a smaller file with medium teeth as you file the entire inner angle as it appears in the photo; keep filing until the copper is visible inside the gold tubing. Carefully file along the edges of the gold, so that only the gold remains after the copper is removed in step 3.

▲ **5.** At this point, the silver piece should fit nicely inside the frame.

▶ **6.** Solder a few pieces of tubing onto the frame to create a pendant.

▲ **7.** The piece inside the frame is a thick sheet of textured silver, surface-treated with niello; attach it to the frame through the back, using tiny watchmaker's screws.

▶ Pendant by Carles Codina

Working Safely with Nitric Acid

Take the necessary precautions when working with acids and other potentially harmful chemicals; handle and store them carefully as well. They must be clearly identified, kept in a safe, well-ventilated area out of children's reach, and stored so they cannot be spilled accidentally. Avoid breathing any vapors, and don't let these substances come into contact with your skin or mucous membranes. Use proper gloves when handling acids, and wear a respirator to protect against breathing in vapors. When you must mix acid with water, do so carefully; if necessary, it can be neutralized with baking soda.

Making a Brooch of Different Wire Shapes: Xavier Ines Monclús

Pieces like this are based on a planar concept. Normally, such jewelry would be made using a flat sheet as a base, then adding various structures made with techniques like repoussé or *lost wax casting*. They also can be constructed from different shapes of wire or silver sheet.

Here, Xavier Ines Monclús constructs a brooch using a .7 mm sheet of silver, adding various elements and finishes that are characteristic of his work.

▲ **1.** The main structure is composed of a repoussé-worked silver cloud and various rectangular shapes in silver, all soldered onto a flat sheet .6 mm thick. The cloud and rectangular pieces constitute the main body of the piece.

▲ **2.** Prepare separately several other elements, based on different types of round, square, and rectangular wire; use a small piece modeled in wax and cast, if desired. All these elements will be soldered to the main structure.

◀ **3.** Solder the elements and trim off the excess metal. Next, file and polish the surface, using different grades of abrasive paper to create a fine surface free of scratches.

▶ **4.** Solder a copper tube across the inside of the cloud; it will hold a crank made by bending round silver wire. Several pieces of wood (from ice cream sticks) will be used also.

▼ **5.** Fit the pieces of wood inside the piece and glue; finally, file and polish the entire piece.

▼ **6.** Prime and paint the wood and the metal surfaces. Use acrylic paint on the wood, and colored resin on the metal. Brooch entitled *Cel*, by Xavier Ines Monclús.

Working with Wire

A common way of shaping objects involves bending wire and sheet stock with various tools. With the right ones, it's possible to bend various materials into all kinds of shapes.

There are many ways to bend material, including the use of *mandrels* for shaping rings and bracelets. Jewelers also make specific tools using special steels and folding templates. One of the most commonly used tools in the workshop is a pair of pliers; make sure they are good quality. You'll want to have several pairs in different shapes.

Any work involving pliers, a ring shank bender, or a mandrel has to be done with great care to keep the work piece from being damaged or scratched. Any marks will have to be removed later using files and abrasive paper, which will distort the piece and waste time. Keep tools in good condition, and make sure the inner surfaces are clean and even. When you are working, bear in mind that bending metal significantly hardens it, which requires subsequent annealing to soften the metal.

▲ Close-up of a piece by Mikala Djorup, made of various forged silver wires

The Classic Method of Making a Chain

Making a chain from links is a classic construction project; many variations are possible by filing or by alternating decorative motifs and links of different widths. The following is a simple exercise that nonetheless requires the correct execution and a certain amount of experience.

As with all chains, the initial step involves soldering together numerous links, which are made of round wire and coiled on a specially designed winder.

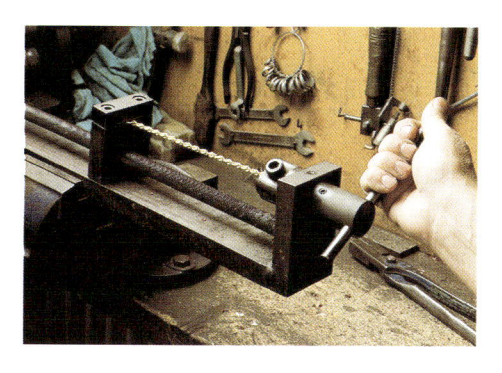

▲ 1. Arrange the links so that all the solder joins are on the inside, where one link meets another. In a hand lathe, secure the chain tightly at each end using brass wire. (An alternative method is to secure one of the ends in a stationary motor-driven lathe and the other in a clamp.)

▲ 2. Keeping continual tension on the chain, manually turn the lathe in a clockwise direction until the twist in the bands is flat. Once you reach this point, go another half-turn. This is an important detail, since it makes the chain hang uniformly.

▼ 3. To improve the uniformity of the chain, gently roll the chain through the rolling mill, keeping it taut throughout.

▶ 4. File or cut the chain. For this procedure, secure the necklace to a board that has been treated with a light coat of lacquer; that helps secure the chain so it can be filed uniformly. Then, polish the chain using abrasive paper glued to a flat strip of wood.

◀ 5. Here is the polished necklace, made by Juan José Lopez.

Making a Wire Brooch: Xavier Doménech

Using nothing but .8 mm round silver wire, Xavier Doménech creates an interesting brooch that incorporates a repeated shape into the design.

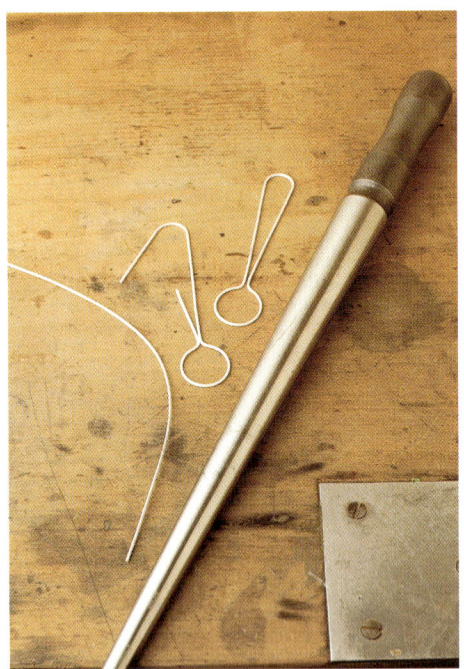

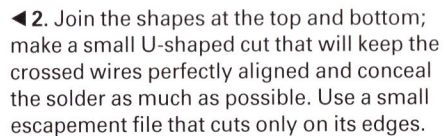

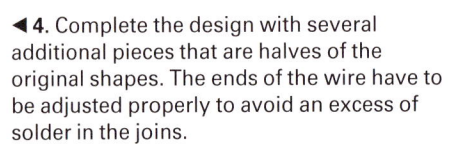

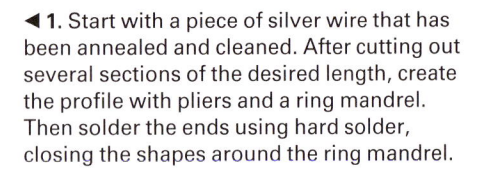

◄ 1. Start with a piece of silver wire that has been annealed and cleaned. After cutting out several sections of the desired length, create the profile with pliers and a ring mandrel. Then solder the ends using hard solder, closing the shapes around the ring mandrel.

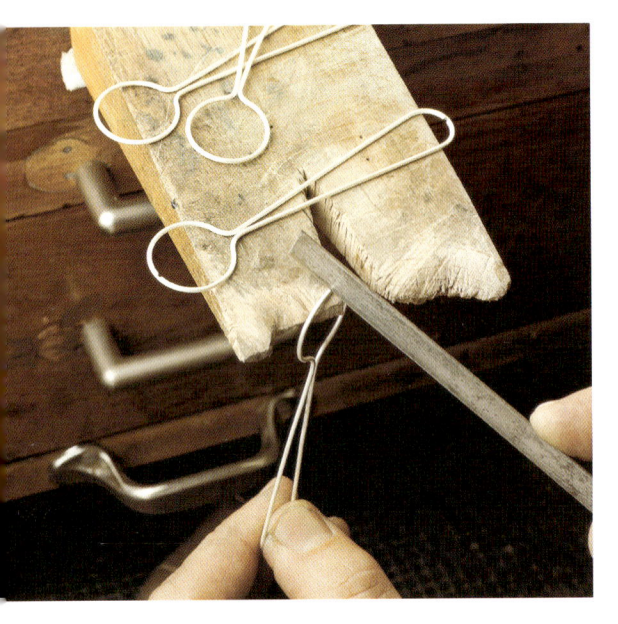

◄ 2. Join the shapes at the top and bottom; make a small U-shaped cut that will keep the crossed wires perfectly aligned and conceal the solder as much as possible. Use a small escapement file that cuts only on its edges.

▲ 3. Fit the shapes together and solder them in place with medium solder.

◄ 4. Complete the design with several additional pieces that are halves of the original shapes. The ends of the wire have to be adjusted properly to avoid an excess of solder in the joins.

► 5. Finally, adjust and solder the additional pieces. Then, pickle the brooch several times to create an intense white color on the surface of the metal, a process called "bringing up the silver." Brooch by Xavier Doménech.

Working with Precious Metals

Making a Ring Out of Wire

Rings are generally made from wire of various shapes, or from cross sections that have been bent round. This is how engagement rings are made, as well as more complex designs.

To make a simple, round wedding ring, make two marks that correspond to the size determined by measuring the finger in a numbered ring gauge. Apply the usual formula to determine the linear equivalent.

▲ 1. Bend the ring until the two measuring marks line up; don't dent or scratch the surface.

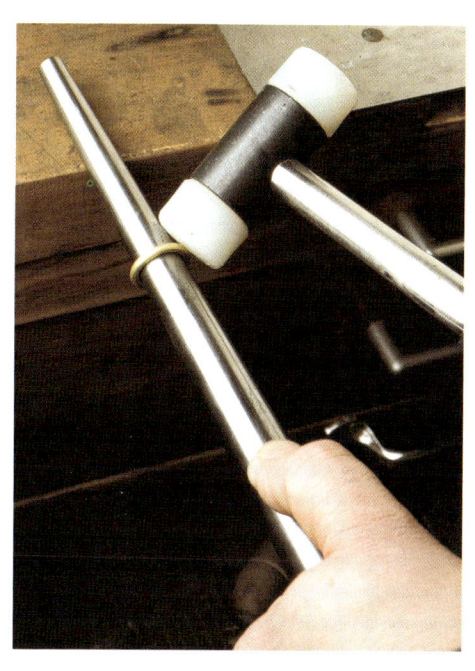

▲ 2. Continue closing the shape at the two marks and adjust the size. Then, use a saw to cut it to length and assure a good joint before soldering. After soldering, hammer the ring on a ring mandrel with a plastic mallet as shown, taking great care to avoid marking the surface.

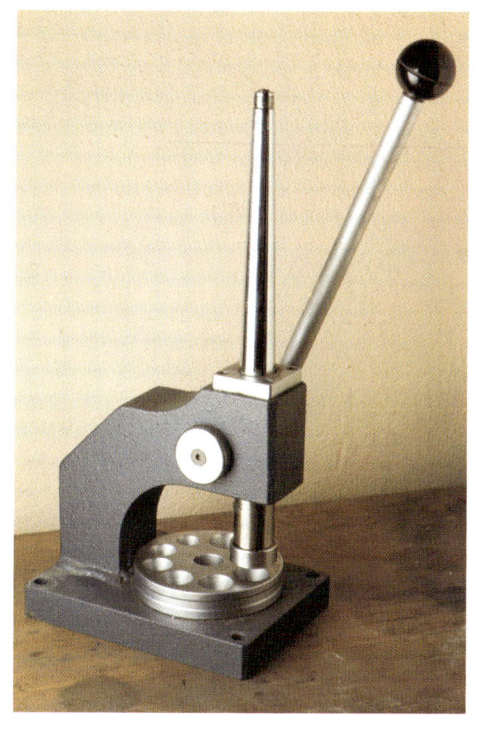

▲ 3. The ring can also be rounded with a ring sizer. Place the ring onto the cone of this tool; it will expand and round the ring from the inside.

▲ 4. At this point the ring should be perfectly round. To complete this project, sand and finish in the polisher, as long as the drawplate is in perfect condition so no marks are produced on the surface of the metal when it is worked.

▲ 5. The wedding ring could be considered finished after step 4; however, you can also add a simple setting if you wish. Merely take two pieces of the same wire, bend them into a U, and use a diamond bit in a flexible shaft to fit them to the body of the ring.

▶ 6. Solder the wires with hard solder, then set the stone.

▶ Ring by Carles Codina, using a gem cut by Tom Munsteiner

27

Stringing a Necklace

There are several ways to string a bead necklace; in fact, this is a specialized branch of jewelry making. This section will show one reliable method of stringing necklaces that's quick and easy to learn. Use high-quality beading silk with a fine copper wire at the end to thread the beads. You will also need a metal spiral to protect the part of the wire that comes into contact with the clasp, and some small pliers.

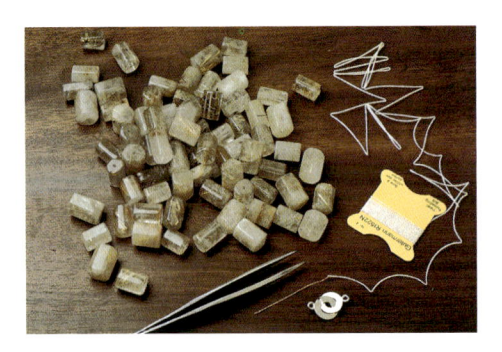

▲ **1.** Prepare the beads—in this project, smoky quartz beads—making sure that the clasp is properly polished and that the beads have no internal ridges that could catch on the silk.

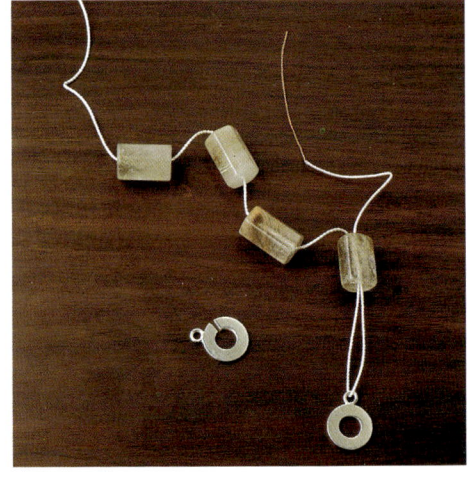

▲ **2.** String three or four beads on the silk. In general, when working with pearls or smaller beads, these first pieces have to have a slightly larger hole, since the wire passes through them twice.

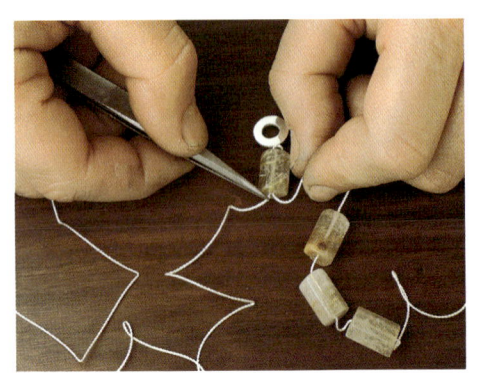

▲ **3.** Take the first four beads and thread the length of the silk, then add the clasp and a little spiral tube protector. Then, pass the needle back through the first bead in the opposite direction; pull all the silk through and use pliers to tie it off.

▲ **4.** Now, pass the wire through the second bead and tie another knot in the same way. This same process is done with the third and fourth beads as well.

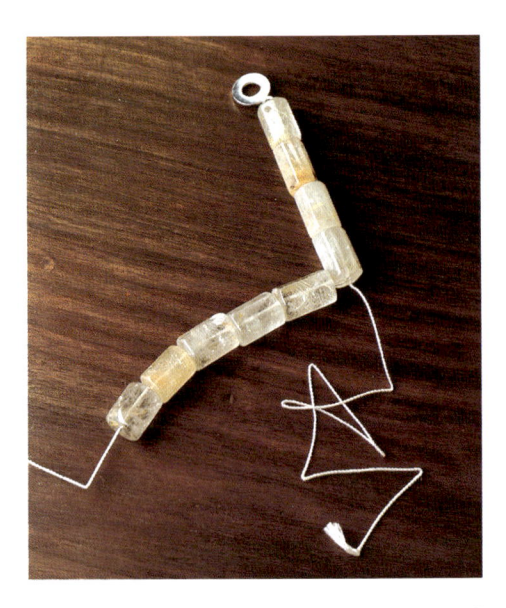

▶ **5.** When the last knot is done, string on individual beads or groups of beads, depending on your design.

▼ Ceramic bead necklace by Carles Codina

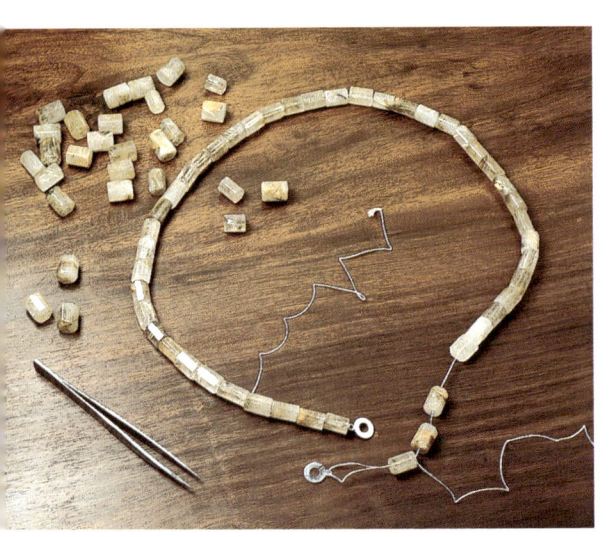

▲ **6.** Save four beads with larger holes to string on last; thread on the other part of the clasp and put on a spiral tube protector. Then, pass the wire through the last bead again and knot it tightly where it comes out. Repeat this process with the next two beads until they are close up against one another.

Working with Precious Metals

Disk Clasp

This clasp is simple in design and easy to make. It's a good choice to use for beaded necklaces.

◀ 1. Start with 1 mm silver sheet and saw out two washers like the ones in the photo; solder a small ring on one edge.

◀ 2. Saw a notch in one of the pieces to let the other one hook into it.

Preparing a Lobster Clasp

Lobster clasps are a fastener that's often used on bracelets and chains; this section illustrates how they are made.

▶ 1. Like many clasps that have an internal spring, lobster clasps operate with the tension from a small bent wire that springs the hasp to its original position after it's been opened.

▶ 2. Insert the steel spring inside the hasp so the longer end pushes against the inner body of the lobster clasp. When the hasp and the spring are put into place, squeeze them into the body of the casting with a pair of flat-jawed pliers.

Forged Clasp

This is a clasp made from nothing but square gold wire; it can be used to secure wire necklaces and bracelets. Here is how to forge a wire and create the right tension so that the clasp functions perfectly. This is a cold forging process that can be used for other interesting applications.

▲ 1. Start by preparing a 1.5 mm square gold wire; anneal and pickle it.

▶ 2. Cut a 2.5-cm long section (based on the size of the clasp desired), and hammer both ends on a flat anvil.

◀ 3. With combination flat/round forming pliers, shape the curves as shown in the photo.

◀ 4. Once the curves are closed up, forge their ends to create breadth and improve the tension in these areas. Then close up the ends with the pliers, and clean the entire clasp with abrasive paper before polishing it.

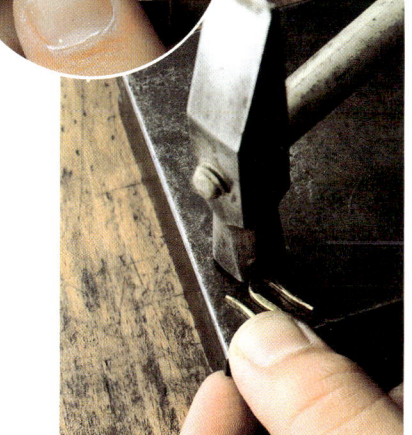

▶ 5. This clasp is easy to make and functions very well; it can be used on all types of necklaces and bracelets. It works through the tension created in the forged arms.

Working with Platinum

Platinum has many uses in the chemical, electrical, and aerospace industries. Since it has a fairly high melting point of 1772°C and expands very little when heated, it has to be worked in special ways. This metal is used less frequently than gold and silver, mostly for fine jewelry. Even though it's rare and costly, it has excellent ductility and malleability that is appropriate for all types of shaping, extruding, and forging.

Platinum has a light silvery color and a specific gravity of 21.45; it's more dense than gold, is inert, and is resistant to corrosion, even though it can be dissolved very slowly in *aqua regia*. Once it's polished, this metal shines beautifully, so it's ideal for setting precious stones, especially diamonds.

Along with rhodium, palladium, osmium, iridium, and ruthenium, platinum belongs to what's known as the platinum group of metals. Because of its usefulness in industry, it may be alloyed with other metals in the same group. But in jewelry, it's usually combined with iridium or ruthenium to take advantage of their hardness and durability, since pure platinum is soft, and only a few parts per thousand of another material are needed to harden it and improve its mechanical properties.

Casting a Platinum Bead or Button

Because of its high melting point, platinum should usually be melted in an induction furnace, especially when any quantity is involved; even so, jewelers occasionally melt small amounts of platinum with an oxypropane torch. This type of torch needs to be equipped with a special nozzle with twelve orifices and adequate pressure regulation. To melt platinum, wear special platinum casting glasses with an appropriate filter, and a respirator. The crucible needs to be made of high-quality fused silica for platinum, in which nothing *but* platinum is melted, since any remnant of gold, no matter how small, might have a negative impact on the malleability of the platinum. No flux is used when melting platinum; the torch flame should be slightly oxidizing.

When melting platinum, start with metal that's at least 99.95 percent pure. Similarly, only pure metals should be used in alloys with platinum. The right proportions for an alloy are 95.2 percent pure platinum alloyed with iridium or ruthenium. It's probably best to get a platinum alloy from a precious metals dealer.

Platinum comes in sheets or small, sponge-like pieces. The latter is very pure—grayish with a slight green tinge—but it must be melted in advance and made into sheet form to prepare the correct alloy. If it's not melted first, this powder may experience losses or reductions varying between .2 and .5 percent; the result is that the percentage of alloyed platinum would be lower than permitted by legal precious metals standards.

One method of alloying platinum is to melt the powder and then form it into very thin sheets; take a small sheet and roll up the iridium or the commercial alloy inside it; melt the two of them together; and then forge and laminate the result. Cut the remaining platinum sheet into small pieces and melt again. Once the pieces have been melted, add the *button* or *bead* of iridium alloy, stirring the metal with the pressure from the oxygen torch.

A torch tip with twelve orifices will melt platinum completely. Next, cool the button a little so it changes color; then use a steel wand to stir it, and melt it again. A second melting is almost always advisable.

▼ Platinum ring by Jörg Munsteiner, using a 1.26 carat yellow beryl and a 14.54 carat aquamarine cut by Bernd Munsteiner

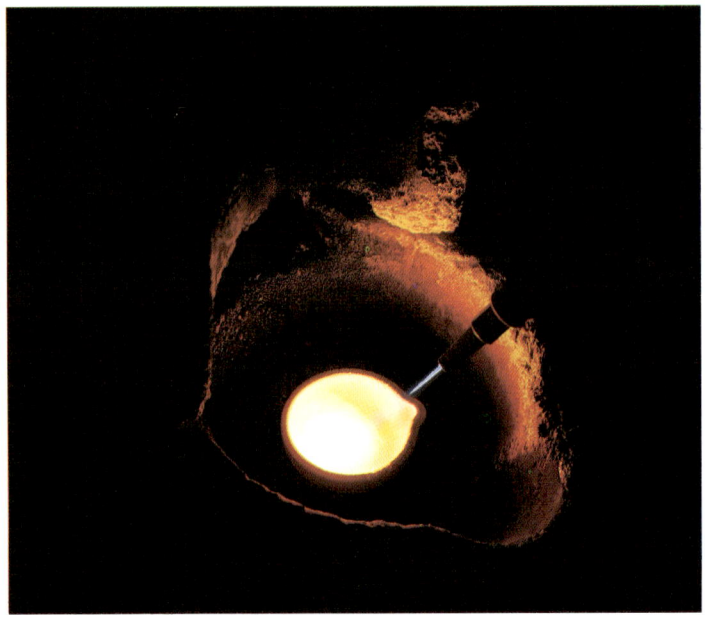

▲ It's common practice to melt platinum powder that is a result of refining processes; it is very high in purity. The protective glasses and respirator are extremely important for safety reasons; be sure to use a twelve-orifice tip and a proper crucible.

▶ Platinum behaves differently from gold when it melts. The mass of metal appears to float, and it can be stirred with the pressure from a slightly oxidizing flame.

Working with Precious Metals

Forging the Button

Platinum is hard to pour into an ingot mold; it requires an intense forging process to compact the metal perfectly. Good forging is a prerequisite to obtaining high quality metal that attains an excellent finish in the polishing process. After the second melting discussed on page 30, cool the button inside the same crucible; when it changes color, remove it with a rod. After it's pickled, the button can be forged.

To forge the button, grasp it tightly with parallel-jaw pliers and strike it with a heavy, flat hammer to create a square or rectangle, according to the desired result: plate or wire. As the metal is worked, some longitudinal scales and small openings will form that need to be re-melted with the oxypropane torch, using a tip with a single orifice; after this step, continue with the forging process. The process of melting and forging will probably have to be repeated several times, even if no scales are produced, since platinum needs great compression in its internal structure.

Once you have forged the button properly, make it into sheet or wire in the rolling mill. After reducing it by 50 percent in the rolling mill or draw plate, anneal it. Use a bench-top torch for the annealing process; bring the metal to an orange color and keep it there for at least 15 seconds, depending on the thickness of the metal.

◀ 1. Forge the button by gripping it tightly at one end with pliers and hammering it on an anvil with a flat hammer. As the button develops a rectangular shape, turn it and hammer it on all sides.

▼ 2. The process of melting and forging should be done two or three times; lightly melt each face of the ingot.

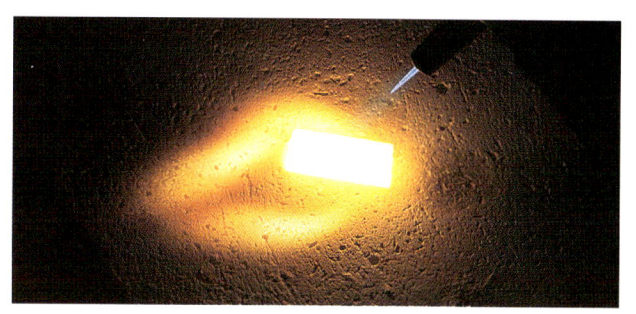

◀ 3. Continue the forging process until you produce a square or rectangular ingot, as shown in this photo.

▶ 4. To eliminate any traces of iron or other materials that might stick to the surface in the forging process, it's wise to degrease and submerge the piece in a 10 to 20 percent solution of hydrochloric acid before annealing.

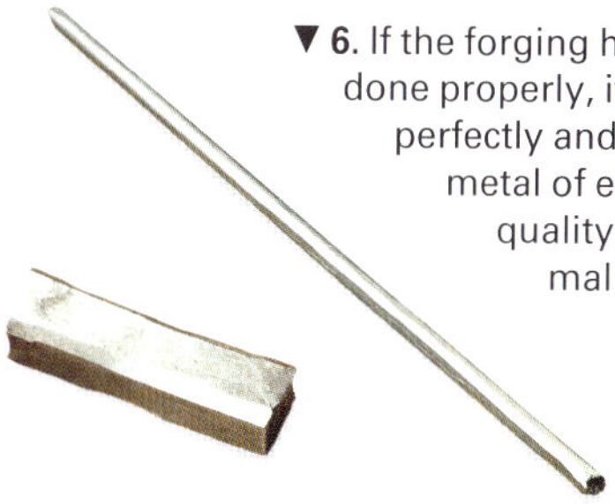

▶ 5. This ingot has also been hammered along all of its corner edges, as shown at right. This compacted ingot can be rolled or drawn using different types of flat or wire rolling mills.

▼ 6. If the forging has been done properly, it will draw perfectly and yield a metal of excellent quality and malleability.

Soldering Platinum

There are some specific requirements for soldering platinum, since it must be done at high temperature. To prepare the seams to absorb the solder, score the mating surfaces with a coarse file or a saw, as shown in photo 1. Solders are generally prepared in different grades, and they must not be mixed or confused with solders for white gold. In projects joining platinum and gold, you have to be very familiar with the properties of the two metals, since they behave differently and they require special preparation when they are united.

▶ 1. Soldering platinum requires the right preparation and treatment, not to mention polishing; joins between platinum and gold are particularly delicate. The photo shows a platinum piece in which the mating surfaces have been roughened.

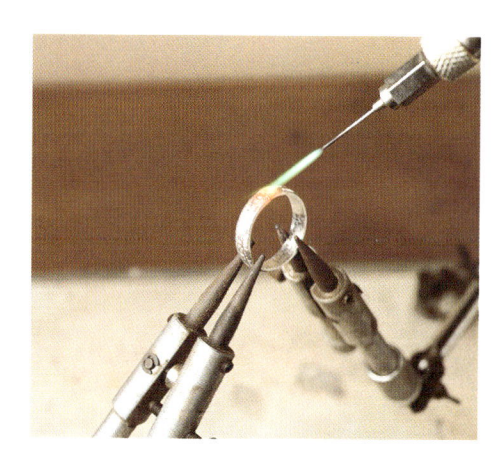

Silver 730	Platinum 270	Low
Silver 667	Platinum 333	Medium
Silver 226	Platinum 620 Palladium 154	High

▲ 2. Adjust the joint, apply a paillon of solder, and then join the seam. In this kind of project, an electronic water torch may be adequate.

31

Contemporary jewelry makes use of all kinds of materials, whether precious metals or less traditional materials, such as plastics, resins, papers, and fabrics. Increasingly, jewelers and other craftspeople who want to create decorative objects need a thorough knowledge of numerous disciplines, and a familiarity with many different materials will foster success in any creative field.

It was impossible to include every technique in *Handbook of Jewellery Techniques*, and it would be equally impossible to do in this second volume. Some techniques deserve special attention, however, and they are included in this chapter. For instance, engraving and electroplating are presented as they relate to metalsmithing and jewelry making. The first section in this chapter presents a fascinating technique that may be interesting for many goldsmiths; this is Kum Boo, which uses both gold and silver.

Special
Techniques

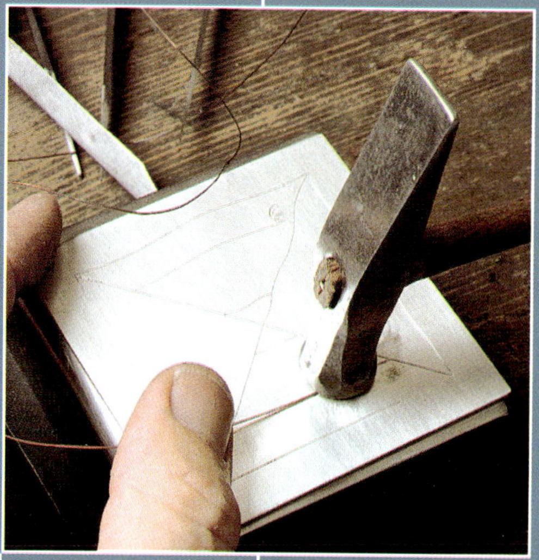
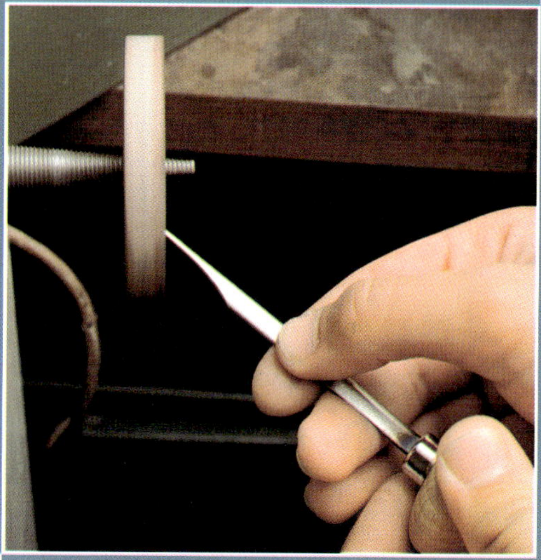
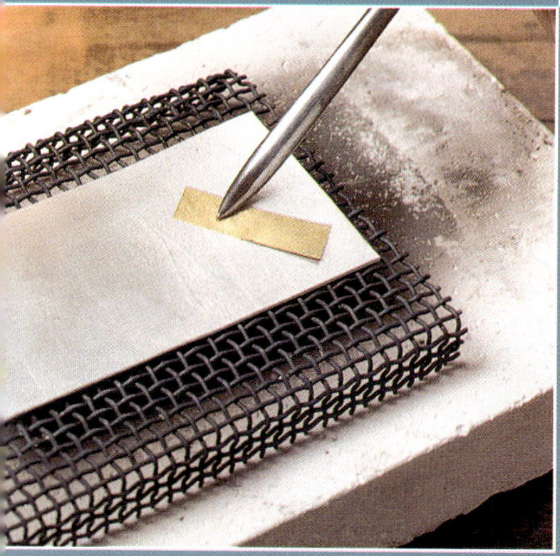

Kum Boo

This Korean technique fuses fine sheets of gold onto silver, creating beautiful decorative motifs. In ancient times, Kum Boo was used to decorate objects for both daily and ceremonial use, especially kitchen or table utensils such as spoons and bowls. It also embellished objects that expressed wishes for health and prosperity through characters and drawings. The metal was applied to the inside of the utensils because it was believed that contact between the gold and the food transferred some of the metal's precious properties to the food before it was eaten. This tradition highlights the importance of precious metals in Asian culture.

The term is derived from *Kum*, which means *gold*, and *Boo*, which can be translated as *added* or *applied*. Given the extreme delicacy of the pure gold sheets, traditional solder can't be used. Instead, to apply a 24-carat gold sheet, you have to thermally fuse it onto a silver alloy under the right temperature and pressure.

◀ Brooch with Kum Boo by Carles Codina

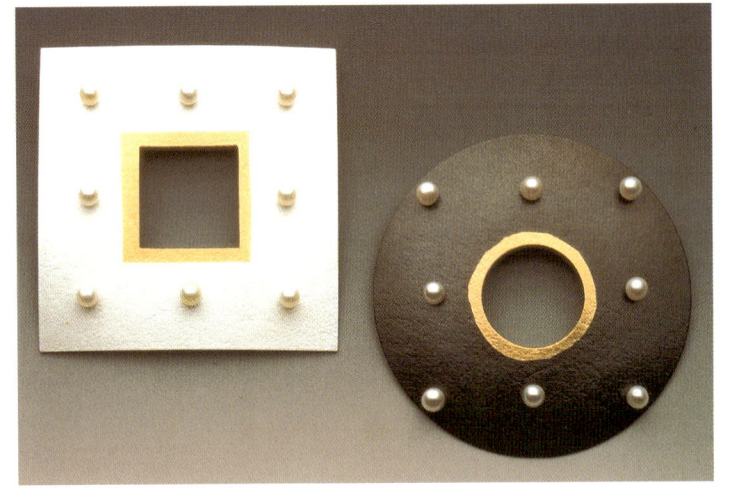

◀ Brooches with Kum Boo by Clara Inés Arana

Preparing the Gold Sheet

Buy the gold sheet ready to apply, or prepare it by rolling a fine sheet of gold between two sheets of pure copper to produce an extremely thin sheet, thicker than gold leaf, but thinner than a piece of paper.

Cut the pieces from this 24-carat sheet using clean, sharp scissors or a scalpel. Set these pieces aside and then heat the silver item on a hot plate or some other support until it reaches the right temperature for application.

▲ **1.** Prepare two sheets of copper that have been annealed; they have to be pickled, clean, and dry.

▼ **2.** Roll the sheet of fine gold as thinly as possible in the rolling mill. Then place it between the two sheets of copper and repeat the rolling process.

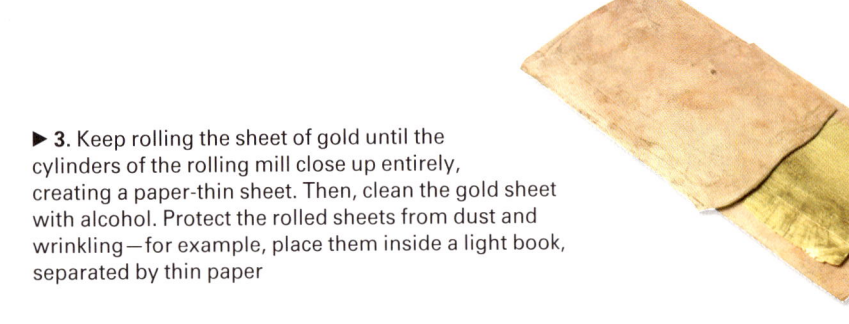

▶ **3.** Keep rolling the sheet of gold until the cylinders of the rolling mill close up entirely, creating a paper-thin sheet. Then, clean the gold sheet with alcohol. Protect the rolled sheets from dust and wrinkling—for example, place them inside a light book, separated by thin paper

Special Techniques

▶ 4. The sheets can be annealed again, but do so with extreme care. Next, flatten and clean the sheets; handle them with clean cotton gloves to protect the surface from the oils on your fingers.

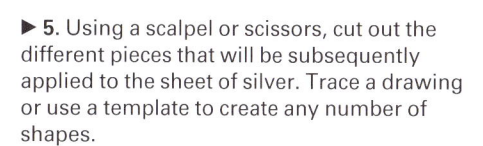

▶ 5. Using a scalpel or scissors, cut out the different pieces that will be subsequently applied to the sheet of silver. Trace a drawing or use a template to create any number of shapes.

Preparing the Surface of the Piece

The surface is prepared as follows, in a process that is repeated up to six times. First, heat the surface until brown spots appear from superficial oxidation of the metal. Then, immerse the piece in acid or pickling solution; rinse in water; and lightly rub the surface with a bronze brush and little baking soda.

The piece needs to be perfectly dry before applying the gold leaf to the surface of pure silver. (If the silver piece is to be soldered, this step must be completed before the gold leaf is applied.) Avoid touching the surface with your fingers, since any trace of dirt or oil will interfere with a good bond.

▶ 3. Clean the surface by rubbing gently with a bronze brush and a little baking soda.

▶ 4. Repeat these three steps a minimum of five times until the surface is white, clean, and free of oxidation. In the successive heatings, apply the flame indirectly to the underside of the area where the gold leaf is to be applied.

▲ 1. Heat the silver sheet, whether flat or shaped into a finished piece, until the layer of oxide appears on its surface. It needs to reach a yellowish shade—not very dark—similar to the shade resulting from annealing.

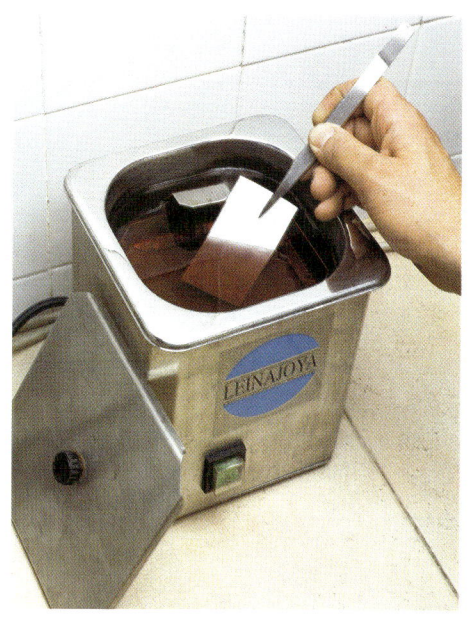

▲ 2. Put the sheet into a pickling bath of new acid, or a high-quality pickling solution, until it's perfectly white.

35

Applying the Fine Gold Leaf

Although the Kum Boo technique is simple, it's also very exacting. It requires perfectly clean surfaces and very careful handling of the gold leaf, which must never come into direct contact with the fingers; instead, work with tweezers and gloves. It's a good idea to rinse the fine gold leaf in alcohol before applying it to the silver.

The application temperature varies; it ranges from 260° to 370° C. A small electric furnace, a gas burner with an iron plate on top, or a soldering torch can be used for this, but it must be an indirect flame that will not oxidize the surface of the piece.

Once the proper temperature has been reached, use a steel *burnishing* tool to rub the gold leaf onto the piece until the molecules of the two metals fuse, producing a permanent bond between the two sheets.

▲ 1. Place the sheet onto a steel grill like one used for enameling. Put the grill onto a refractory brick so the flame can be applied from underneath, avoiding direct contact between the flame and the application surface. For greater convenience, use a hotplate that's capable of reaching from 300 to 350° C.

▲ 2. Keep the silver base hot while the fine gold leaf is applied. Use tweezers to place the pieces of gold leaf.

▶ 3. Once the pieces are put into place, use a clean, smooth burnishing tool to rub the surface until the gold adheres perfectly. Keep increasing the pressure until you're sure the bond is complete. Then, cool the burnishing tool by plunging it into water.

▲ 4. The bond should be perfect, as shown in the photo. Though it has some limitations, it can be worked like normal leaf; roll it or even stamp it carefully, if desired.

◀ If possible, avoid using any solder after the gold leaf has been applied. The ring in the photo was embossed and the special elements were soldered on before the fine gold was added. Kum Boo ring by Carles Codina.

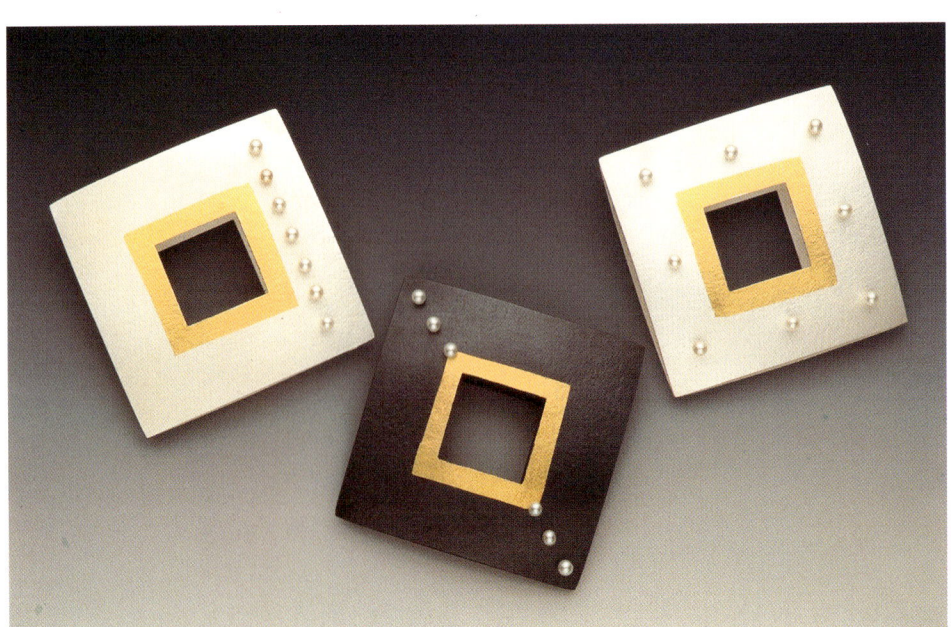

▶ Finish the pieces made with this technique with processes that are appropriate for silver. Kum Boo brooches by Clara Inés Arana.

Special Techniques

A Kum Boo Bracelet

The next project is a bracelet made from a sheet of silver about 1.3 mm thick. The leaf, in irregular shapes, is applied as previously described.

▶ **1.** Apply the Kum Boo to a flattened piece of sterling silver before you begin to create the shape of the bracelet.

▶ **2.** Use an oval bracelet mandrel to bend the metal. Shape the piece on the mandrel by striking it with a rubber mallet, first covering it with a paper towel to avoid scarring the surface.

▼ **3.** Placing the bracelet on a slightly rounded silversmith's stake, use a hammer to strike the entire circumference; this produces a bright edge that adds to the aesthetics of the piece.

◀ **4.** As shown in the photo, use a scraper to deburr the edge and create another finely polished area.

▼ **5.** Here is the finished bracelet. Work by Carles Codina.

37

Hand Engraving

This is a technique that is commonly used in jewelry making to decorate surfaces, create letters, drawings, and various inscriptions. *Engraving* is also used to create different textures, and simply to fill in and decorate spaces. There are several ways to engrave, including the use of acids, photogravure, steel engraving, pantographs, and sophisticated devices that use scanning to do precise, fast engravings and inscriptions on metals as well as other materials.

Hand engraving using a *graver* or *burin*, as explained in this chapter, is not a quick process; however, it's an essential skill for all jewelers, for there are some pieces of jewelry that can only be engraved in this fashion because of their complexity. But that's not why this technique remains vital; the character of the cut made by hand and the resulting surfaces have a quality that distinguishes them from any other type of engraving. In this technique, the metal is cut and lifted from the surface; it is not stamped or scratched in. This process creates brilliant pieces of an unequaled quality.

Even though the technique appears simple, it takes years of practice and experience to master. This chapter will be an introduction to this process, focusing on preparing the tools and engraving some basic lines, as well as explaining inlaying.

◄ Pendant made from silver wire and several engraved gold plates. Work by Kerstin Östberg.

Preparing the Gravers

Engraving with a graver or burin requires lots of preparation, since the tool has to be shaped in just the right way. The graver is a steel implement that's been treated and tempered to a high degree of hardness; there is a wooden handle on the end. Gravers are already hardened when you buy them, but you have to prepare them properly to produce the desired cut and obtain good results.

New gravers tend to be too long for most uses. To shorten a graver a little, clamp it in a hand vise and give a sharp blow on the side against the edge of an anvil, breaking it at the desired spot. The shortened graver can be fitted with a wooden handle, and then you can shape the proper cutting angle, taking great care to avoid affecting the temper of the steel.

Once the graver has been fitted with a handle, you have to shape the cutting face properly; this is a delicate operation. Since the graver is already tempered, the shaping must be done with a grinding wheel. To keep the graver from getting too hot, cool the wheel with water, or frequently dip the graver in cold water before touching it to the wheel.

It's important that the angle on the cutting face of the graver be about 45°; if it's greater, more force will be required in engraving, and that will produce an excessively deep cut. If the angle is less, the graver will cut better, but the point will dull more easily, and it won't remove as much metal.

After the graver is shaped, dress the flat point with an *Arkansas stone* and light oil. In sharpening, press the flat face of the graver onto the surface of the Arkansas stone and move it forward and backward. Use this stone to create the additional inner angles or heels on the graver. Once you have finished sharpening the faces, and before beginning to engrave metal, it's wise to rub the tool lightly with a cloth moistened in oil.

◄ Fourteenth-century engraved silver chest, with tracery arches and the coat of arms of France and England

Special Techniques

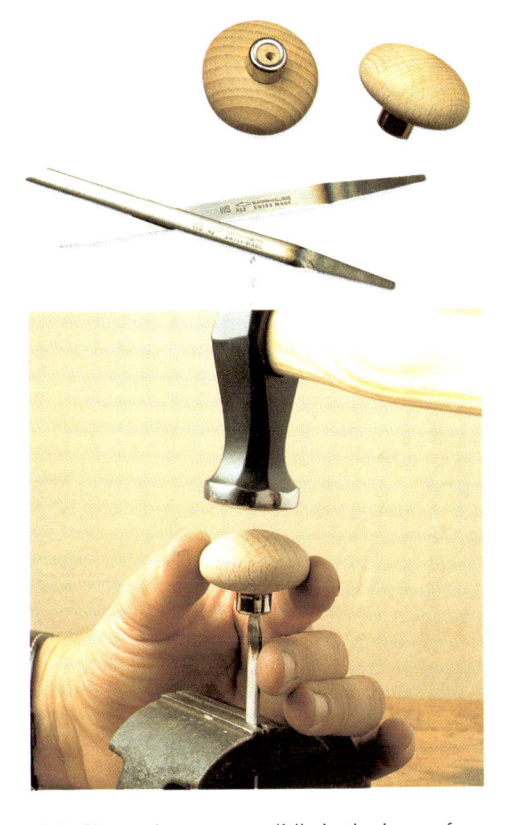

◀ 1. Anneal the graver on the end where the wooden handle will be fitted. Handles come in various shapes.

▶ 2. To get the handle to fit onto the graver, shape the annealed end on the bench grinder, using a coarse grindstone; create a point to help secure the graver in the wooden handle.

▲ 3. Clamp the graver solidly in the jaws of a bench vise and put the handle into position; hit it on the top using a plastic mallet or a hammer until it's firmly seated.

▲ 4. Before creating the angle, remove a section of the graver to create a smaller cutting face. Using a coarse wheel, hold the graver with both hands and move it from the center of the wheel to the outside.

▲ 5. It's essential to cool the graver continually with cold water. Otherwise, the heat generated by friction against the wheel could anneal the point and render it totally useless.

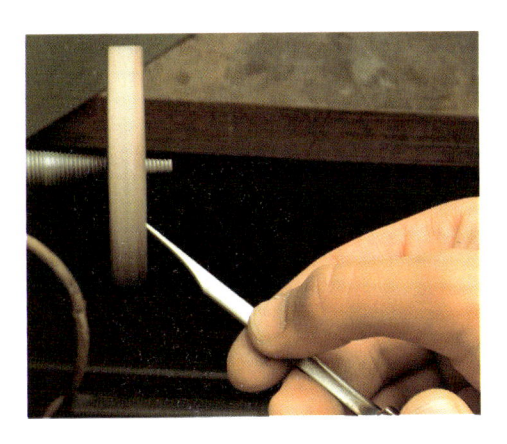

▲ 6. Then, using a finer wheel, create the 45° angle, continuing to cool the graver.

▲ 7. Sharpen the cutting surface of the graver on an Arkansas stone coated with light machine oil; press and rub back and forth, taking care not to round the face. It's common to create a slightly asymmetrical angle on the cutting face, so the metal extracted from the cut will curl and be expelled on one side of the graver. (See the photo on page 40.)

▲ 8. Use the same stone against the underside to produce the heels and faces shown in the picture.

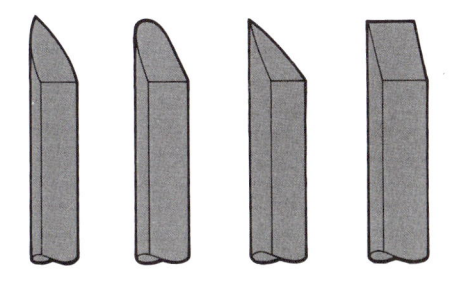

▶ 9. Here is a completed graver—an onglette—ready for work.

◀ Common graver shapes

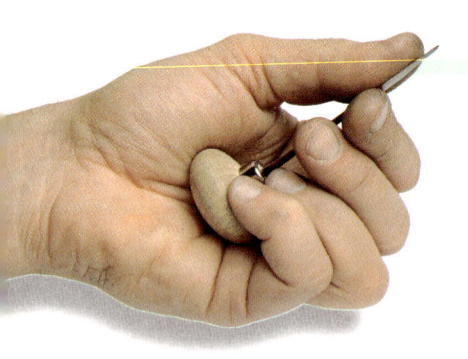

Hand Engraving

▶ Gravers are controlled by pushing against the handle with the fleshy part of the hand, placing the thumb alongside the blade with the point of the graver held tightly against the piece. The index finger rests along the opposite side of the graver, and the other fingers stabilize the handle.

How to Engrave

The metal has to first be annealed, pickled, and free of grease. To begin, secure the piece to be engraved. There are many ways to hold the piece down; an engraving block, for example, makes a perfect holder, but you can also glue the piece to an engraving ball. If the piece has a flat surface, glue it to a board with some pitch or a gum lacquer mix. Another method is to mount the sheet onto a block of wood clamped in a movable bench vise, using screws to hold the plate in place; just be careful to avoid puncturing the sheet.

It takes a certain amount of practice to control the graver; first, hold it correctly and orient yourself properly to the work. Apply force to the tool using the hand muscles; this pressure is what drives the graver into the metal in a single, smooth action, avoiding fits and starts and uneven lines. Make the *entry* or first cut by placing the point of the graver very close to the thumb of the engraving hand; then, pull the thumb back a little, and without changing position, alter the angle of the cutting face. The cutting angle should be around 10 or 15° to the plane of the piece.

▶ The proper position for using a graver

◀ If the face has been sharpened properly with the Arkansas stone, the metal will be driven out to one side, and the cut will be clean but deep.

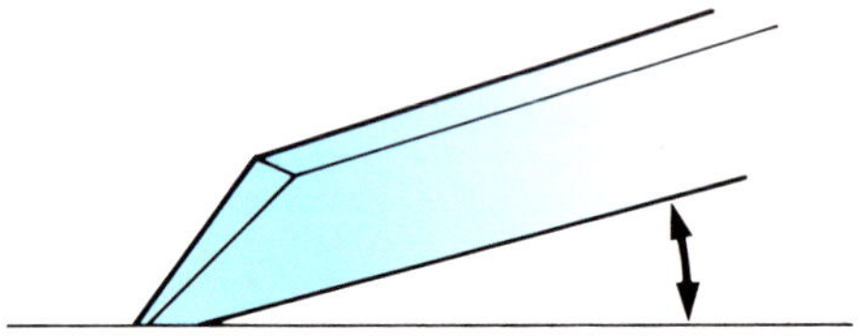

▲ The proper angle is about 10° from the work surface.

▲ Use the same technique with a flat graver, and the cut will be like the one pictured above.

▶ Using lateral movements, gravers can also create textures and backgrounds. Textured silver brooch by Kerstin Östberg.

◀ This piece is decorated with lines created with an onglette graver. Gold necklace and pendant by Teresa Capella.

40

Metal Inlay

Historically, metal inlay has been used in the technique of *damascening*, which involves inlaying soft metals such as gold and silver into harder surfaces, normally iron, steel, and bronze. The term comes from Damascus, the capital of Syria, where artisans used to create elaborate works using this technique. It's difficult to determine when craftspeople began decorating metal by inlaying, and it's hard to imagine that this method spread to many parts of the world without some exchange of knowledge. Work of this type was done in China in the first millennium B.C., and then later in eleventh-century Spain. It was in general use in the Arabic world, where a distinctive style of damascening developed. It was used in decorating armor, arms, and small metal objects, especially those produced in Toledo and Granada, Spain.

The inlaying presented in the following pages originates from linear damascening.

◀ Jewelry box with Arabic decoration

This technique has several variations, involving gold, silver, or bronze wire; to begin, start with a base or a sheet of metal in which a flat, deep groove is cut. Next, form some undercut interior angles along both sides of the groove. (The incision can be done with gravers, or fine chisels, struck at a 30 to 40° angle.) Then, take a fine, annealed wire in another metal, place it into the groove, and lightly tap it with a flat-ended cushion punch, forcing it to fill the groove and create a permanent solderless bond.

Gravers

To obtain satisfactory results when inlaying, proper tool preparation is necessary, just like hand engraving. During this process, use slightly re-shaped gravers suitable for each operation.

Make oblique cuts with a slightly modified onglette; don't remove any material from the top of the tool. After the face of the graver has been shaped to about 45°, sharpen it on the Arkansas stone; repeat for the two faces and the base of the heel. This heel needs to be fairly short if you intend to cut curves, but fairly long for straight lines.

Although you can hold the graver in the normal position, it may be preferable to drive it by striking the handle with a small hammer. To prevent damage from the blows, prepare the handle as follows: Make a circular hole in the center of the handle and glue in a small piece of brass or copper rod that enters as far as the shaft of the graver inside the handle. Use two-part epoxy to glue in the brass; once it's dry, file off any excess metal.

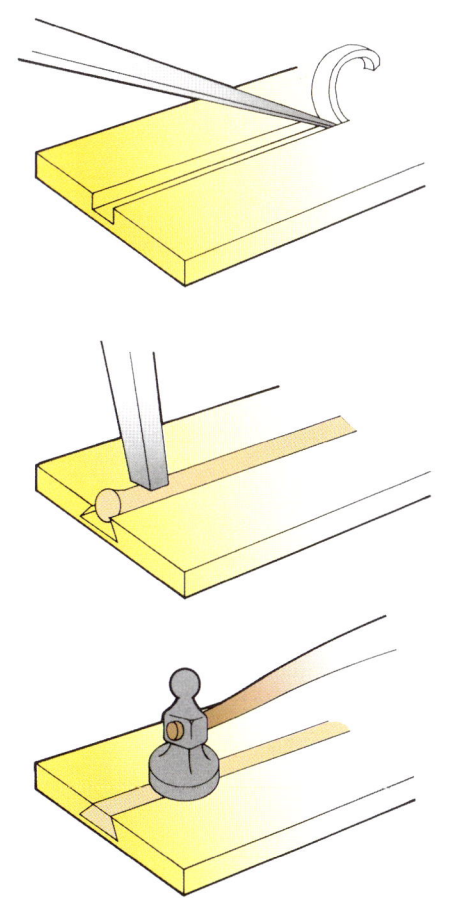

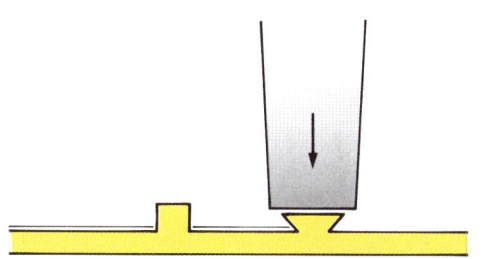

▲ To inlay a plate, cut away the surface where it will be installed; chisel out the edges of the remaining metal; and strike it vertically on an anvil.

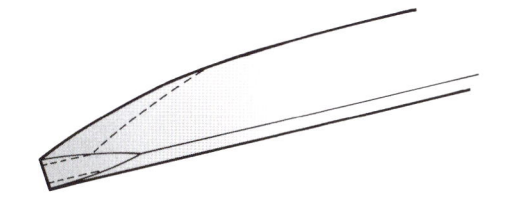

▲ Shape of the graver

◀ Steps to inlay wire on a flat surface

41

Hand Engraving

Metal Inlay: Hans Leicht

In the following project, Hans Leicht has prepared a 1 mm sheet of sterling silver, along with a fine gold wire and a .3 mm sheet of 24-carat gold that will be inlaid into the silver sheet.

▶ 1. Mark the design on a silver sheet placed on top of a sandbag. Note the position of the graver and the support shown in the photo.

▼ 2. Use an onglette engraver to remove the metal from the lines, creating the space for a mechanical bond between the gold wire and the silver sheet.

▼ 3. Next, take a piece of annealed gold wire and insert it into the grooves; strike the wire with a hammer until it is forced into the sheet.

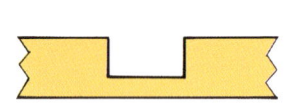

▶ 4. To inlay a sheet, use the same process: cut out a sheet of gold, mark off and cut out the space where it will fit, and then undercut the entire perimeter of the recess.

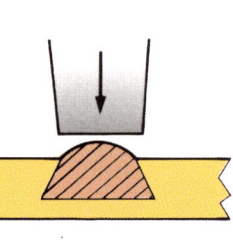

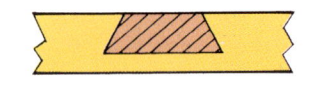

◀ The stages of the metal inlay process

Special Techniques

◀ 5. Set the sheet of gold in place and strike around its perimeter until it is perfectly seated in the recess.

▼ 6. Next, polish the surface with abrasive paper, using successively finer grades until all excess wire is removed and the surface is flat and smooth.

▼ 7. Here is the finished project.

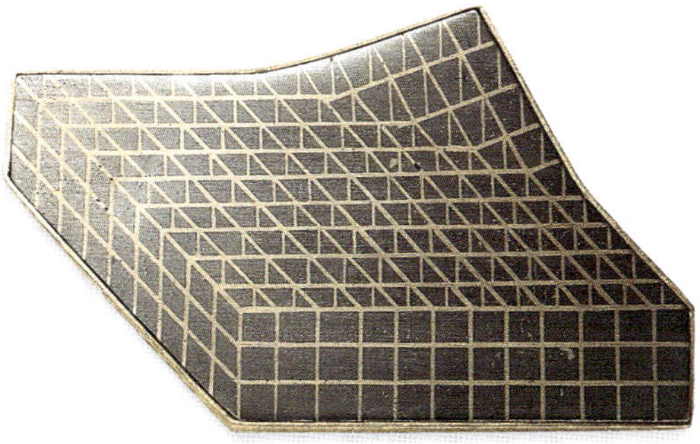

▲ Brooch made of oxidized silver sheet with gold wire inlay by Hans Leicht

▶ Box made of oxidized silver with gold wire inlay by Hans Leicht

Electroplating and Surface Finishes for Metals

In jewelry workshops, it's common to use electrical current to create surface finishes for metals. It is often used in plating with gold, rhodium, and silver baths to improve the final appearance of objects.

This chapter will demonstrate the essential processes from a functional viewpoint; these include *electroplating* and *electropolishing* with gold, rhodium, and silver baths. It's possible to use these processes in a small workshop with the aid of an inexpensive *rectifier* and some products that are found in specialty shops.

Electroplating

When compounds are broken up, they split into ions, some with a positive charge and some with a negative charge. These ions with opposing charges conduct electrical current under certain conditions. When voltage is applied to an ionized compound, as in a gold or silver bath, a chemical reaction is generated. The introduction of a potential difference by connecting a source of direct current modified in a rectifier causes a movement of ions: positive ions go to the negative electrode, and the negative ones to the positive. When they arrive at their respective electrodes, there is a corresponding gain or loss of electrons and a resulting transformation into neutrons—in other words, particles with no charge.

The action of electrical current in a compound can be understood in the following example: If a salt such as silver nitrate is dissolved in water, it breaks up into positive Ag ions and negative NO_3 ions. When a potential difference is applied between the electrodes submerged in a solution of $AgNO_3$, the positive Ag ions move toward the *cathode* and are discharged in the form of metallic silver. The nitrate ions move toward the *anode*, become oxidized, and are eliminated in the form of O_2. It's really not common to use an $AgNO_3$ solution as a silver bath, however. The baths used instead have a silver anode bar that is consumed as electrical current passes through it and is then deposited in metallic form on the piece to be plated, located on the cathode.

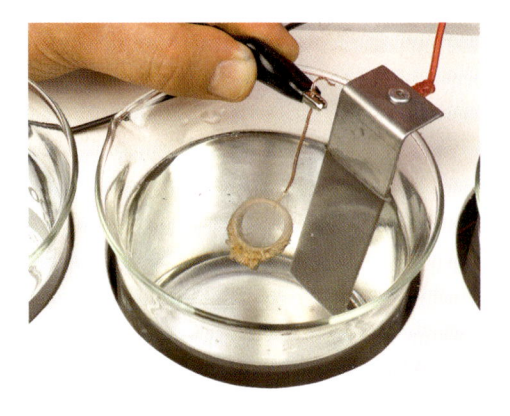

▲ The electroplating process uses an anode and a cathode. The cathode, which is black in the photo, holds the piece of jewelry; a sheet of stainless steel is suspended from the anode, which is red. Other metals can be used, depending on the nature of the procedure and the type of metal used to plate the object.

A metallic salt or gold bath is used for pieces made of gold. The salt is put into a glass tray containing a positive anode bar of stainless steel and a negative cathode, which is the object to be plated. The application of a continuous low-voltage current causes the gold ions to be deposited on the cathode in the form of metal. In this process, the cathode object is the piece that's being treated in the gold bath and is connected to the negative electrode by a copper wire.

Since all the chemical changes involve a regrouping of the electrons in the affected substances, there must always be a balance between the metal that's deposited on the cathode and the metal that originates in the anode. With silver, the spent atoms are replaced by the fine silver inserted into the plating bath and connected to the anode; with gold, the plating bath has to be replaced by a new one that contains more dissolved gold.

▶ This is one basic setup. It includes a rectifier that regulates the strength of the voltage and the amperage. These devices make it possible to do basic operations involving rhodium, gold, and silver plating, and in some cases, even electropolishing.

Equipment

Electroplating produces very fine layers of metal; the voltage applied has to be very precise and carefully regulated, requiring a direct current rectifier. The thickness of the plating depends on the voltage, since the metal deposited on the surface of the electrodes is subject to *Faraday's law*. This states that the quantity of material deposited on each electrode is proportional to the strength of the current passing through the electrolyte. And, given the same quantity of electricity, the weight of the transformed elements is proportional to the equivalent weights of the elements; in other words, to their atomic weights divided by their valences.

A rectifier is the basic device for providing the controlled potential difference that is necessary for any plating process. For plating, you need to use a rectifier that converts alternating current to direct, since alternating current intended for domestic use continually changes polarity and has excessively high voltage, from 110 to 220 volts; for galvanic use, a charge of 10 volts is rarely exceeded.

The jewelry supply market offers many kinds of devices that are capable of multiple functions, and that can be used for large pieces as well as small. An inexpensive device will be used in this chapter for the finishes that are most commonly done in jewelry workshops. These mainly involve rhodium plating, which is used for the final finish of white gold pieces; flash or gold plating, for finishes that are unavailable in yellow gold; silver plating; and electropolishing.

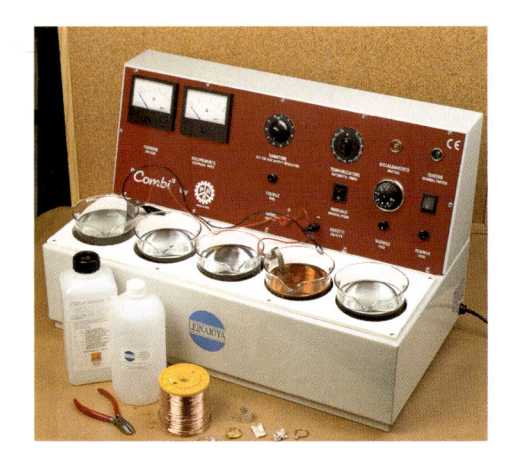

44

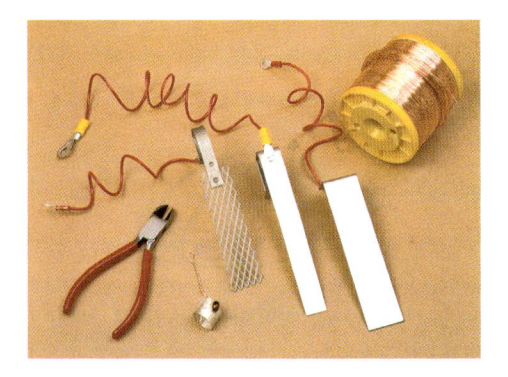

Special Techniques

▲ Use different types of material as anode bars, depending on their function; also use a spool of copper wire to hang the piece from the cathode.

▲ An ultrasonic cleaner is a very useful tool. It's frequently used in the workshop for degreasing and cleaning, before starting the plating process with the rectifier.

▼▼ There are some small devices, like the one in the photos below, that are designed for rhodium plating or dipping small pieces like rings; these are equal in quality to larger machines.

There is an advantage to the smaller machines—they allow parts of the piece to be rhodium plated without having to block off areas with special protective lacquers; instead they use a special pen connected to the anode. The point of the pen absorbs the solution for rhodium plating, and after the piece is connected to the cathode, the pen is used to plate the desired part of the piece.

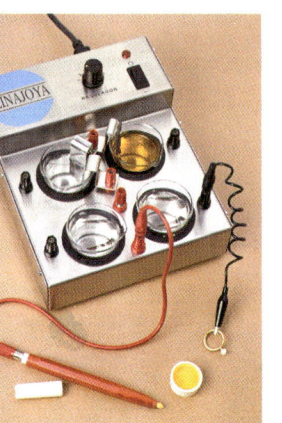

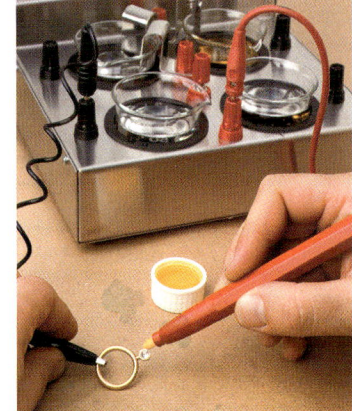

Rhodium Plating

Eighteen-carat white gold is an alloy that contains 750 parts pure gold and 250 parts alloy, the alloy being mainly palladium and lesser quantities of silver and copper. When it's melted, this alloy takes on a white color, with a slightly yellow hue imparted by the 750 parts of pure gold. There are also many other alloys of white gold, with or without palladium, that reduce the price of the eighteen-carat alloy, since the palladium content can be limited. Some of these alloys have excellent color and scarcely need rhodium plating, but in any case, it's preferable to improve the color of white gold with a thin plating of rhodium. Rhodium improves shine and color, since this metal is harder and much more reflective than silver, and is also corrosion-resistant.

Rhodium Bath

1. Clean the piece with ultrasonic cleaner and rinse in running water. Then rinse once again using distilled water.
2. Perform electrolytic degreasing in special salts, using a stainless steel anode as the positive pole. Apply about 5 V, depending on the size of the piece, for at least a minute.
3. Rinse with distilled water.
4. Rinse a second time using distilled water.
5. Rinse with water in a concentration of 5 percent sulfuric acid for one minute.
6. Immerse in the rhodium bath at 1.5 to 2 V for one minute. The anode bar should be platinum-coated titanium.
7. Rinse with distilled water.

▶ 3. After the two rinses, immerse the piece into the rhodium bath by hanging it from the cathode. The anode bar is platinum-coated titanium; platinum is insoluble, so it can be used continually. Finally, do one last rinse in distilled water.

▶ Earrings with diamonds, made of white gold and plated with rhodium by Carles Codina. Note how the shine of the rhodium highlights the pavé-mounted diamonds.

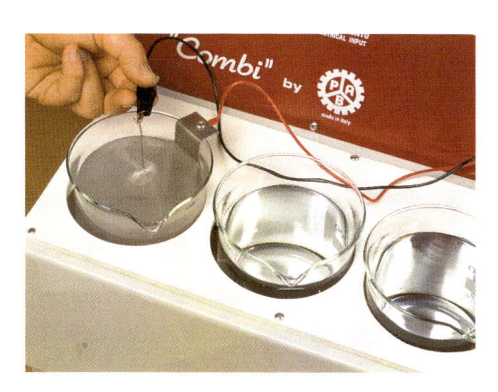

▲ 1. Rhodium bathing first requires electrolytic degreasing in special salts. Suspend the piece of jewelry by a copper wire and connect it to the cathode by an alligator clip. Immerse the stainless steel anode bar in the salts for degreasing.

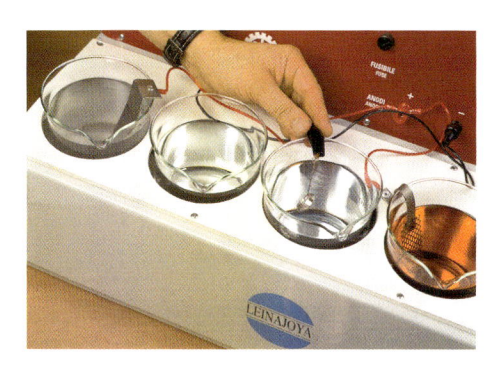

▲ 2. Do two consecutive rinses of the piece in distilled water, and then a third with water to which 5 percent of sulfuric acid has been added to make a pickling solution.

Gold Flash Plating

Gold flash plating produces a very light coating; it is not to be confused with true plating, which is thicker and is created using different equipment.

In jewelry, a gold flash plating is often used to give the appearance of polishing in the parts of a piece that are impossible to reach with a polisher. With alloys, jewelry boxes, and certain pieces done in relief, there's no way to reach into tight corners using traditional methods. So, use electropolishing and then apply a flash plating. Then, polish the exterior or the most accessible part in the polisher. That way, if you used a bath with the same color as the alloy used in the piece of jewelry, there won't be any visible difference between the parts treated with the polisher and those plated with the bath. The piece will have a perfect finish.

The color of the plating can vary as a function of the strength of the current: a weaker current will produce a more yellow tone, and a stronger one will produce a darker color.

Gold Electroplating Procedure

1. Clean the piece in an ultrasonic cleaner, rinse with running water, and then with distilled water.

2. Apply electrolytic degreasing at about 5 V for at least a minute. (The power will vary in accordance with the type of piece.)

3. Rinse with distilled water.

4. Suspend in the gold plating solution at 2.5 to 3 V, and even up to 5 V, for a minute. Use a stainless steel anode bar.

5. Rinse with distilled water.

Silver Electroplating Procedure

The silver process is similar to the preceding one. The difference is that the anode must be made of pure silver of a specific thickness; as items are plated, the silver anode bar is used up, for it is deposited in the form of metallic silver on the cathode where the piece of jewelry is located.

▶ The process for silver electroplating is similar to gold flash plating; the differences are in the solution used for the bath and the anode bar, which in this case is pure silver.

▲ **1.** After cleaning the piece with an ultrasonic cleaner, rinse it in running water and then in distilled water. Next use salts to degrease it in the first dish, for at least a minute.

▲ **2.** Clean the piece in running water, and then in distilled water, before putting it into the electrolyte bath.

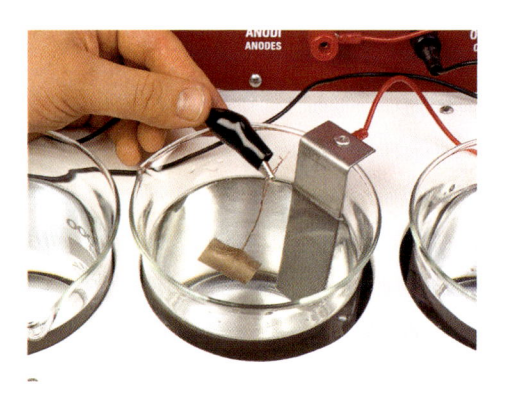

▲ **3.** The piece is attached to the cathode and suspended in the electrolyte bath; agitate it a little to even out the solution. Small bubbles will rise from the surface. Too much voltage will produce an undesirable color.

Electropolishing

Sometimes, it's not possible to use the buffing motor or polishing machine to finish pieces. You can use electropolishing if you have time-related constraints, or if the piece you are working on has areas that are impossible to reach by any other method. This procedure is very useful for professionals who do jewelry repairs and for jewelers who need to shorten the time they spend finishing pieces. Electropolishing dissolves, so to speak, a little of the surface; if buffing is done subsequently, it produces a truly brilliant surface.

To start the electropolishing process, the piece has to be entirely degreased and free of oxidation. Electropolishing can be done using the same rectifier as was used for plating, if the amperage is adjustable; in any case, reverse the anode and the cathode. Connect the piece to the anode, and use a stainless steel dish or pot as the cathode, as long as it's at least ten times larger than the anode. Generally, in this process, the current should be stronger and the immersion time longer than usual; the latter varies in proportion to the size of the piece and the equipment used. Conducting salts for this technique can be bought in a specialized jewelry supply shop.

Surface Finishing

To achieve the best results, the jeweler must spend a lot of time on the final finish—more specifically, on surface polishing. A buffing motor is the best method for polishing jewelry today. It produces the best shine and surface quality in metals such as gold, silver, and platinum, but it also requires dedication and experience.

There are other processes that can be used as alternatives to the buffing motor; these involve using highly specialized machines that can still be incorporated into any small shop. These processes can be used to improve the phase prior to buffing and can also be used to achieve the final polish—reducing the time required for the last finish and increasing shop productivity.

Special Techniques

Some of these techniques involve utilizing rotary, centrifugal, vibratory, or magnetic tumblers, all of which are probably practical for a small shop. Choosing the right machine and procedure depends on the type and quantity of jewelry to be treated.

In general, these procedures are done in two phases. The first phase involves smoothing the piece; various types of ceramic polishing media are used. When they are mixed with water, they have an abrasive effect on the piece, and as a result, they even out the surface. In the second phase, the pieces are first cleaned, and then they are buffed bright. Nowadays, there are a great many metal burnishing materials and products that are used wet or dry, but this process is usually still done with a combination of different-sized steel shapes, including small spheres, and rods. These have to be clean and bright. It is possible to burnish the pieces without metal damage or loss by combining these materials with the pieces of jewelry and a soapy solution.

◄ Different types and shapes of materials used in polishing or burnishing processes. The proper combination is selected from an assortment like this.

◄ Vibratory tumblers produce better results, permit varying the size of the pieces, and shorten polishing time. The photo shows a vibratory tumbler in the first phase of polishing.

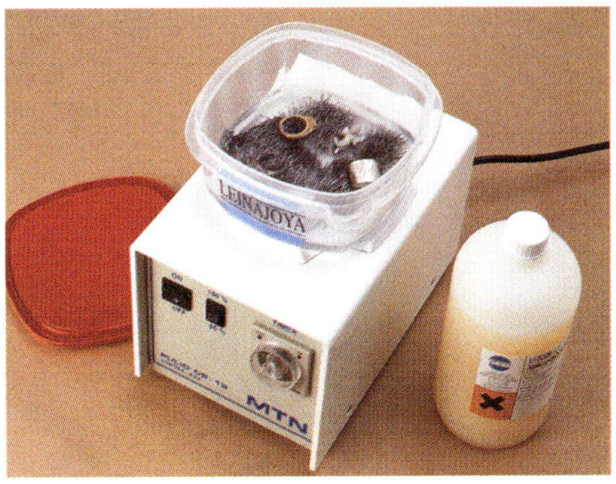

▼ Rotary tumblers use the effect of friction produced by falling steel balls after being lifted by the rotating drum. The spheres are in a solution of water and special soap; they burnish the surface of the piece as they hit it repeatedly over the course of time. The photo shows a tumbler performing a final polishing operation.

▲ This type of machine is a good choice for a small shop, as it polishes a small number of pieces in a container that contains a combination of steel shapes and polishing solution. It works through rotation of a magnet that causes the metal polishing media to rub against the precious metal pieces, which are not affected by the magnetism used in the device.

▼ Here's the result from polishing two pieces in a magnetic tumbler/polisher for 20 minutes at medium speed. Using small steel rods or very fine shot makes it possible to polish the most inaccessible parts of the pieces.

Sandblasting

There are other types of machines and tools that provide alternative finishes to the brilliant polish that is generally applied to precious metals. One is a *sandblaster* that prouces a fine, uniform pitting on the surface. It has a closed metal cabinet that contains tiny glass spheres with the consistency of very fine sand. An air compressor forces air into the cabinet, causing a drop in pressure that propels the sand forcefully toward the piece through the same valve or piston that expels the air. This same valve also accepts a handpiece that increases the sandblasting pressure; this allows the grit of the sand to be changed and produce different types of surface textures.

► Basic sandblasting equipment, excluding the air compressor

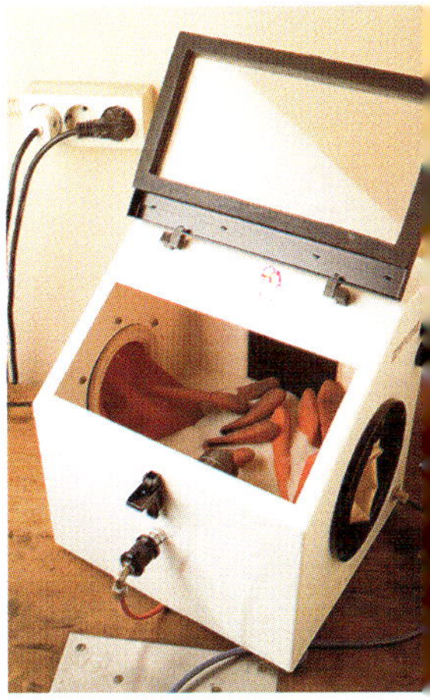

▼ Note the difference in the finish of the sandblasted piece on the left and the one that was polished on the right. The piece has to be polished first with abrasive paper to obtain a good sandblasted finish. Earrings by Carles Codina.

47

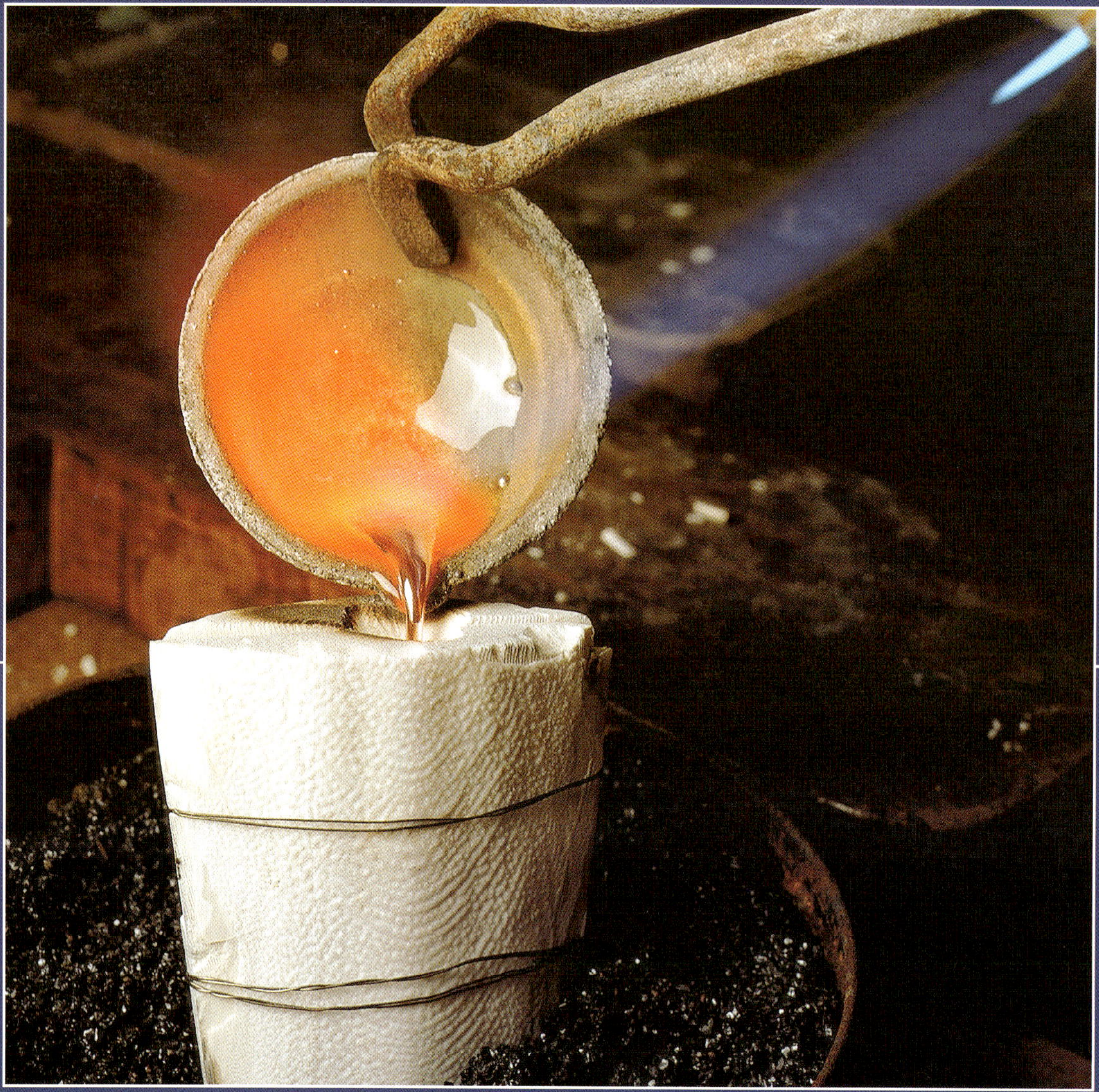

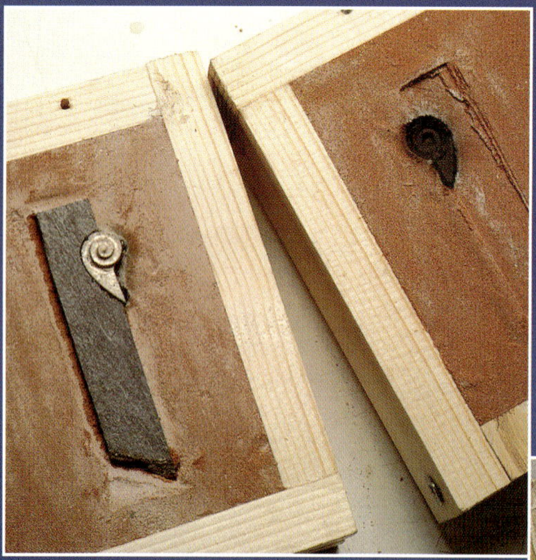

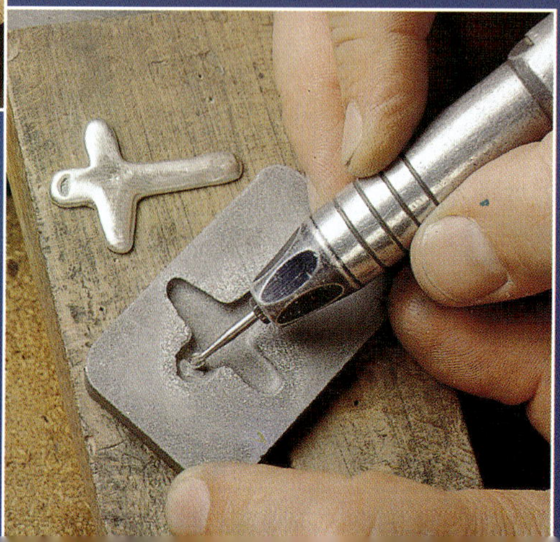

Casting and *Stamping*

Gold, silver, and especially copper and its alloys such as bronze, are all malleable metals, and they are fairly easy to extract and alloy. The Stone Age ended when humankind observed how easy it was to change certain metals from liquid to solid—and vice-versa—through the use of heat. Thus, metallurgy appeared independently in most cultures partly because of these very properties. Ancient peoples discovered how to cast metals such as copper, bronze, and iron to make arms and various utensils.

However, once pure metal was cast, it remained too soft to be workable. To produce greater hardness and improve color and shine, different alloys were created by melting together pure metals. The search for greater hardness and durability in cast metal also involved a hammering process; primitive peoples learned that cast tools and arms acquired durability and strength if they were forged, hammered, or stamped. In fact, the minting of coins as valuable objects originated with stamping.

The following chapter describes how to cast and stamp metals, and how to use these processes intuitively and quickly, utilizing new products and tools as well as some primitive techniques.

Alternative Casting Techniques

When temperature increases, metal quickly changes state and acquires the capability for new functions. Temperature control and the evolution in furnaces have been historical keys to metallurgy, making possible these changes in state, from solid to liquid and back to solid once the metal cools. For this process, you need an appropriate heat source, a furnace, and a mold for producing the desired shape. In the following pages, you will learn how to cast and produce quick results using common, simple resources, not complicated machinery. You will also pick up some knowledge from antiquity, since some of these techniques have their origins in Roman times, but the methods nonetheless convey the essence of casting.

These methods are very direct and easy to carry out, and with a little imagination, they can be adapted to specific needs. Even if these simple techniques don't produce an exact reproduction, as modern investment casting does, they offer many sculptural and aesthetic qualities, like texture, and they allow improvisation. The results are especially attractive because of their immediacy.

▼ Ring made by casting silver directly in the cavity of a small piece of slate; this technique was used by the Romans. Made by Maike Barteldres.

◀ Bronze ring from Mali (Dogon)

▶ Rings made by casting silver directly in fabric pockets submerged in water. Works by Regina Schütz.

Ashanti Casting

This is an ancient technique from Ghana that is still used today; it involves casting metal pieces based on a model crafted in wax. This primitive method is incredibly simple and logical, and helps clearly explain the concept of lost wax casting.

For the following piece, demonstrated by Silvia Walz, begin with a model created in a soft wax that is easily shaped. Once the model is complete, add a long, conical sprue from the same wax. Then, cover the wax model, and melt the wax inside it to form a compact, closed shape that functions as a mold and crucible. Prepare a very simple oven that's capable of withstanding 1300° C; this is a simple structure made by interlocking refractory bricks together with small spaces between them. Place some charcoal and coal inside to create a high temperature as it burns.

▲ **1.** Prepare a liquid, homogenous mass by mixing equal amounts of pulverized charcoal and potter's clay moistened with water. Apply a thin layer of this mixture over the wax.

▲ **2.** Once the first layer is dry, apply a second, thicker coat consisting of 40 percent charcoal dust, 25 percent horse manure, 25 percent potter's clay, and 10 percent chamotte (refractory clay). Cover the entire piece with this mixture, especially the hollows, so that it produces a mold similar in thickness to the one in the step 3.

◀ **3.** When it is thoroughly dry, apply another thick coating made of horse manure, potter's clay, and chamotte only (no plant charcoal), and let it dry. Next, remove the wax inside by heating the mold with a torch so that the wax melts and runs out.

Casting and Stamping

◀ 4. Make the crucible from the same mixture as the outer covering of the mold: 45 percent potter's clay, 45 percent horse manure, and 10 percent chamotte, without the charcoal.

▶ 5. This is the right quantity of metal to add to the crucible to fill the cavity; see the instructions in step 6.

▲ 6. To calculate the weight of the metal, first weigh the wax and multiply by 20 (for silver). This will yield the right quantity of metal and produce the right pressure so that the mold will fill properly.

▲ 7. The crucible with the metal is sealed to the body of the mold; first score the edges of the two pieces with an awl and then cement together. Use a little of the previous mixture, brought to the consistency of paste.

▲ 8. Before casting, make sure the mold is free of all moisture; otherwise, it could crack when it's heated rapidly. The photo shows the crucible joined to the mold before casting.

▼ 11. Remove the piece from the mold and cut off the sprue button.

▲ 9. Construct the oven by interlocking several refractory bricks and adding a mixture of charcoal and coal. Place the mold upright inside the oven on the mixture of charcoal, and leave it there until it reaches an orange-red color. One advantage of this process is that the crucible and the mold form a single unit and they simultaneously reach the same temperature, which is very helpful when casting.

▲ 10. Next, remove the mold with tongs, and turn it over so that the molten metal flows to the cavity in the mold. Hold it in this position for a few moments until the metal starts to cool, and then set it aside to cool thoroughly.

▼ 12. Here is the final product, after the metal has been darkened with silver oxide and the surface has been polished. Brooch by Artur Puig Walz.

51

Alternative Casting Techniques

Cuttlebone

Casting with cuttlebone is a simple and economical method that produces a metal copy from an original model made of other metal, wood, plastic, or any other material that's hard enough to be pressed into the cuttlebone. With this technique, however, it's possible to make only one precise copy; successive castings lack the same definition, so it's advisable to make just one casting in each cuttlebone mold. It's no problem to make more copies, though, given the ease and rapidity with which a mold is made. Don't overlook how economical this process is, for you may even be able to get cuttlebones for free at a fish market, where they are merely waste.

Cuttlebone has a hard exterior, yet has an interior with a texture that's similar to plaster and that gives off a very fine dust. The inside can easily be sculpted with a dental tool, a spatula, a motorized rotary tool, or a pendant drill. Once the model is removed, molten metal can be poured directly into the cavity to produce a metal casting.

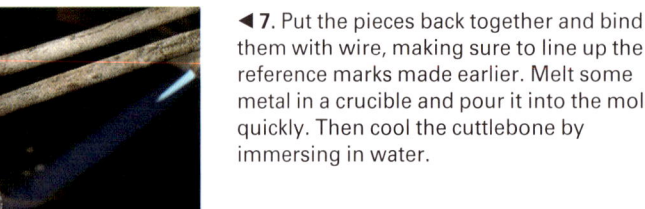

◄ **1.** Cuttlebone is the skeleton of the cuttlefish. It's cheap and easy to find, commonly used as a beak-sharpening medium in birdcages. It's soft and easy to sculpt, and you can press objects into it to make reproductions. To use this method successfully, you need a large cuttlebone of good quality.

▲ **2.** First, cut the cuttlebone lengthwise into two halves. You will need a smooth border around the piece (or the cavity) of at least 1 cm to mate with the other half of the mold.

► **3.** Next, smooth off both inner faces; sand with abrasive paper or rub the two pieces together to create a smooth mating surface.

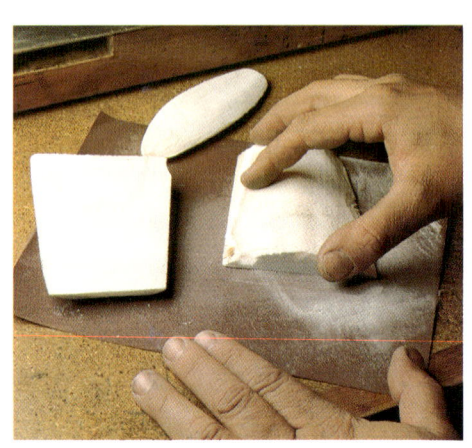

▲ **4.** Place the piece to be duplicated in the middle of one half of the mold; stick in a few metal locater pins to align with the other half of the mold.

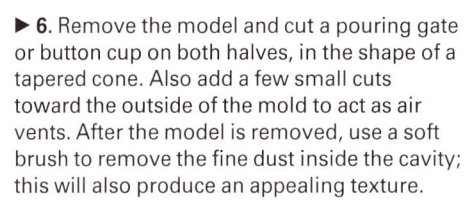

◄ **5.** Squeeze the two halves together until they close tightly. Then use a saw to make a shallow cut across the edge of both halves to serve as a reference mark for aligning the mold blocks after removing the metal model.

► **6.** Remove the model and cut a pouring gate or button cup on both halves, in the shape of a tapered cone. Also add a few small cuts toward the outside of the mold to act as air vents. After the model is removed, use a soft brush to remove the fine dust inside the cavity; this will also produce an appealing texture.

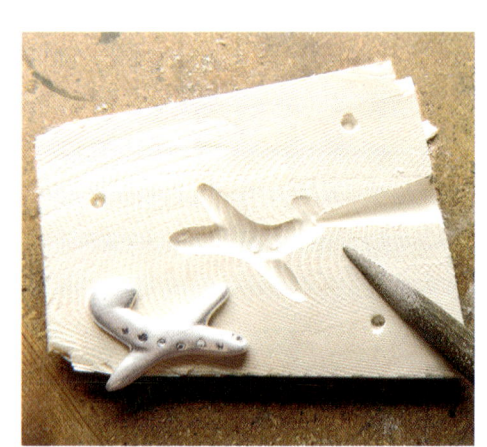

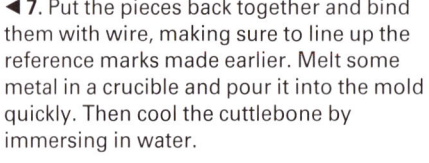

◄ **7.** Put the pieces back together and bind them with wire, making sure to line up the reference marks made earlier. Melt some metal in a crucible and pour it into the mold quickly. Then cool the cuttlebone by immersing in water.

► Forged ring that was subsequently cast in a cuttlebone mold. Work by Jaime Díaz.

Delft Sand Casting

Sand casting is a return to the origins of casting, and it remains useful in casting some large pieces of sculpture. For casting in a small format, as demonstrated here, you need a few sturdy frames that fit together and special sand that's been carefully sifted to a homogenous consistency that will hold a shape.

Here is an adaptation of this process for making small pieces of jewelry. This is a quick method of casting small rings and other objects made of any material that can be pressed into the sand. The mold has to open easily to remove the piece before casting molten metal into the cavity.

▲ 1. The sand and mold are available from regular jewelry suppliers; the mold consists of two aluminum frames of different heights that fit together; each part has a reference mark on the outside for alignment.

▲ 2. Take the shorter mold and place it onto a flat surface. Fill it with sand and compress it tightly with a mallet or a flat hammer.

▲ 3. Since the surface has to be completely smooth, scrape off the top of the mold with a knife or a straightedge.

◄ 5. Now put the other mold in place on top of the lower mold, so that the two reference marks are perfectly aligned. Fill it with sand and compress it with a mallet.

► 4. Insert the piece you intend to reproduce into this part of the mold. Push it in up to the middle so that once the piece is cast, the parting marks or seams are located at the middle. Next, dust the surface with jeweler's talc and spread it evenly with a soft artist's brush.

◄ 6. Carefully open the mold and remove the model.

◄ 7. Now, cut a vertical channel or feeder for the molten metal. Do this in the smaller mold, first with a needle and then with the handle of a file, to create the right diameter for the passage of the molten metal.

◄ 8. Open up the other end of the channel with the point of a knife to create a cone shape or pouring gate to pour the metal. It's a good idea to compress the sand in this area to avoid any loose material that could obstruct the channel when the hot metal is poured in. It's often necessary to make small air holes using a fine needle.

► 9. Put the two halves of the mold back together very carefully so the reference marks line up. Melt the metal in a crucible and pour it in through the pouring gate.

► 10. Here is the result after the silver has been cast and pickled. The sand produces a very interesting textured surface, especially if it has not been overly compressed. This texture can be removed with a file and abrasive paper, or it can be retained as part of the final finish.

Alternative Casting Techniques

Casting on Natural Stone

Incredible though it may seem, it is possible to cast some metals inside rocks, specifically, in certain types of oily stone that have low quartz content. In the following section, jeweler Maike Barteldres shows how to cast metal directly into stone. This involves applying new concepts to two techniques that are ancient. The first is one of the earliest types of casting used by humankind, and the second, using slate as a mold for casting, was used for making metal objects in southern England as early as the Roman times.

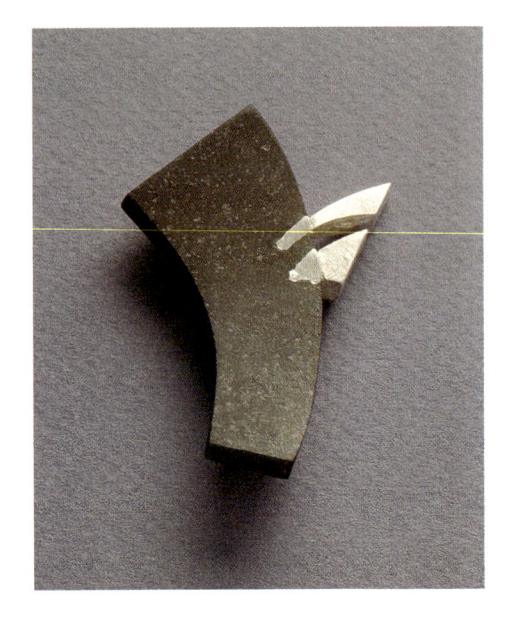

▲ Maike Barteldres, *Dolorite Brooch*. Silver cast directly into sculpted dolomite.

▲ **1.** Begin by sawing out a piece of slate in the desired shape. This type of stone is easy to cut; in this photo, Maike Barteldres is using a simple coping saw.

▲ **2.** Use old files to shape the surface of the stone as desired.

▲ **3.** Make a pattern out of any type of material that can withstand being compressed into the sand. Here, Maike Barteldres uses various cutting burs to make a spiral shape out of green modeling wax. Eventually, this piece will be set into the slate. It's essential to make a hole through the slate, as shown in the photo, to allow the molten metal to flow through the stone into the space now occupied by the wax pattern.

▲ **4.** Make two identical wood frames tailored to the size of the piece. Place the casting sand into one of the halves, compress with a mallet, and smooth off with a straight edge. Next, press the wax piece halfway into the sand, and sprinkle the surface with jeweler's talc.

◄ **5.** Screw the second frame down over the first to create a perfect match; put casting sand over the model and compress inside the frame.

► **6.** Unscrew the frame carefully; after the mold is open, remove the model and the stone.

Casting and Stamping

▶ 7. Use a needle to open up a vertical feeder about 4 to 5 mm in diameter that extends from the exterior of the frame to the main orifice in the stone. The molten metal will go through this channel in the stone. Form a pouring gate at the opposite end to allow pouring the metal. A very fine needle is also used to poke a small, parallel air hole in the area that the metal will occupy.

▶ 8. Now, place the stone in its original position inside the mold and then put the two halves of the frame together. Turn the assembly over so that the pouring gate is on top. It's a good idea to pack the upper walls of the pouring gate with your fingers to keep any sand from flaking off when the molten metal is poured.

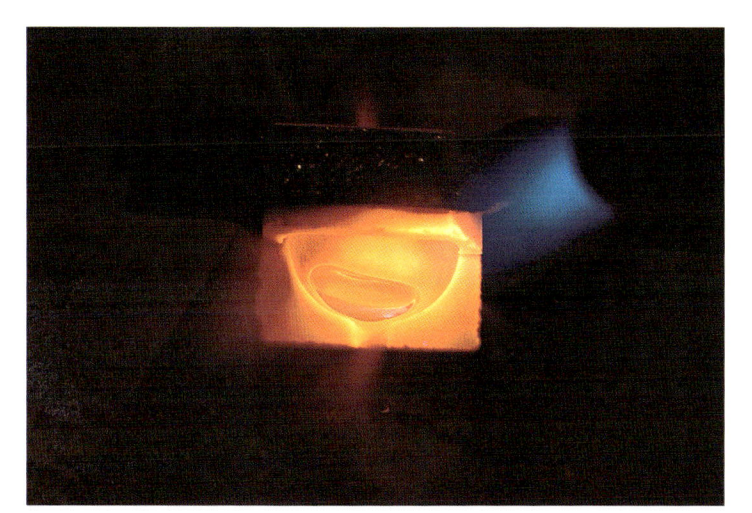

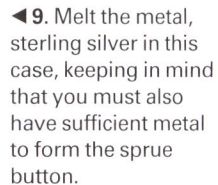

◀ 9. Melt the metal, sterling silver in this case, keeping in mind that you must also have sufficient metal to form the sprue button.

▶ 10. Pour the metal quickly and continuously into the pouring gate and wait for it to cool naturally; a quick quenching is not recommended.

◀ 11. After casting, some parts of the sand will have darkened in color and should not be used again. However, the sand that was not burned can be reused.

◀ 12. Here is the piece after the sand has been removed. The photo shows how the silver has filled the space as a sprue button; it has flowed through the slate and filled the space created by the model. To complete the process, trim the sprue button off and finish the metal in the conventional way.

▶ Pendant of cast silver in dolomite (calcium carbonate and magnesium). Work by Maike Barteldres.

Alternative Casting Techniques

Ceramic Shell Casting

The following process has origins in a casting method that was used to make armaments during the sixties. It's been adapted and technically perfected to assure successful casting with intricate projects in metal. This technique makes it possible to create very precise and beautiful objects, and it's been adapted in an interdisciplinary approach to artistic jewelry making.

This is a very interesting process, since it creates a great variety of high quality pieces at a reasonable price. But it's even more interesting to see how Pilar Cotter carries out this process in the following pages using simple, elementary materials, as she makes the crucible and the casting wax herself; she also constructs a furnace from an old paint can and a torch. With these items, it is possible to exceed a temperature of 1000° C and cast up to two kg of bronze with perfect precision and safety. This demonstration further explains the basic lost wax casting process.

Materials

As with any method using lost wax, begin by preparing a type of soft wax that's easy to model by hand and that can also be burned out easily in the step before making the pour. The compound used here is 10 percent rosin; 20 percent paraffin; and 70 percent microcrystalline wax. To make the wax compound, first melt the rosin in a clean can. Then, add the appropriate amount of paraffin, and finally melt the microcrystalline wax to create a uniform paste. Pour the wax onto a slightly dampened, smooth, clean surface, such as a metal plate. Once the wax is dry, it can be used to model different objects for casting; the unused portion can be set aside for subsequent use inside the plaster mold, and for making the Molochite mold.

To make the melting pot, first build a plaster mold in two halves that fit together in the middle. This is very easy to construct: make a shape of modeling clay and cover the surface with 2 to 3 cm of plaster. You also need colloidal silica, gum lacquer, a little graphite, and Molochite in three granulations: fine, medium, and coarse.

To figure out how much metal to put into the melting pot for casting the prepared wax pieces, weigh the pieces. Then multiply their weight by a hundred and double the product. It's very important to double the weight, since this extra amount adds the metal that's required to fill the mold cavity created by removing the pieces of wax. See Figure 1 for the calculatons to determine the amount of metal needed for 50 g of wax pieces.

▼ Figure 1. Metal formula

50 g x 100 = 5000 g x 2 = 10,000 g

◀ Ceramic shell casting adapted by Pilar Cotter; it's possible to achieve very sculptural results with this technique, as in this end table.

▲ 1. Bind the two halves of the plaster mold together and pour in the wax; move the mold around so that the liquid wax spreads out evenly on the inner walls. Once there is cooled wax on the walls, pour the remainder into the can.

▲ 2. Repeat this action two or three times to create the desired thickness. It's important that the wax be clean and melted properly, free of any air bubbles that might cause subsequent imperfections.

▼ 3. Open up the mold and take out the wax form; use a knife to cut away the casting fins.

Casting and Stamping

▲ 4. Model the desired pieces and attach them to the top end of the wax form using various pouring gates made of round wax wire, sized to each piece. These wax wires have to be as straight and short as possible, without unnecessary or acute angles.

◄ 5. Here, the wax form is ready for the stucco phase. (Design by Juan Carlos Alvadalejo, department chairman at Laguna University in Tenerife, Spain.)

► 6. Apply a thin coat of gum lacquer diluted with alcohol; allow to dry.

◄ 7. Now, prepare the paste by mixing the fine-mesh Molochite with the colloidal silica to create a yogurt consistency; then add a small percentage of graphite (about 10 percent of the entire blend) to the mixture to make it easier to remove the bronze piece from the mold after casting. Pour it over the wax form to create a crucible.

► 8. Sprinkle on medium-mesh Molochite to cover the surface and then allow to dry. Prepare a second paste without graphite; coat the surface with it and apply a slurry consisting of a mixture of medium- and coarse-mesh Molochite. Once that's dry, apply a third layer using the second paste and cover it with coarse Molochite. Allow between five and eight hours of drying time between layers.

Wax Removal and Casting

Once the three layers of slurry and Molochite have dried, remove the wax from the interior of the crucible using a powerful propane torch. To remove the wax, heat the inside of the furnace (without the crucible) to a temperature of around 600° C; then raise the hood and insert the crucible. Leave it there until the wax burns out and the shell changes from dark (caused by soot) to a clear white. Introduce the flame from the torch through the open bottom of the hood held up by the grate, and train it directly onto the crucible. Once the flame is removed, let the crucible cool off and apply two final coats of graphite-free, medium-mesh Molochite slurry to the surface.

After the wax has been removed, fill any cracks in the crucible with a little ceramic insulation soaked in a thin slurry containing no graphite. Apply it, and plaster over it with a slurry of mixed Molochite granules; then apply heat from the torch until it has hardened entirely.

Now, prepare the same furnace for casting. Cover the metallic grate, which will be the base for the hood, with several refractory bricks. Place a strip of ceramic insulation on top, and then sprinkle a layer of coarse Molochite over it to assure that the lid fits properly on the base of the casting platform. Insert the nozzle of the torch through a port in the side of the hood designed for that purpose. Next, heat up the furnace, with the Molochite crucible and the metal inside. When the metal is molten, lift the crucible with tongs and tip it toward the end where the pieces are located until the metal entirely fills the mold; hold it in this position for several minutes, until the metal cools.

► 1. In order to cast conveniently and safely, you have to construct a furnace and a steel structure for a support. This photo shows Pilar Cotter, Jaime Díaz, and Carles Codina preparing to construct such a furnace near the latter's studio.

Alternative Casting Techniques

▲ 2. To facilitate the burnout procedure and casting, Pilar Cotter is constructing a device to support the furnace. This entire structure was fashioned from iron pipe and various discarded materials.

▲ 3. For greater convenience, two extendable legs have been included so the structure's height can be adjusted. These are constructed using one piece of square tubing that telescopes inside a larger one; they are secured by a threaded lock nut. The two legs have to be perfectly parallel and of the same length. In the photo, Joan Soto is helping with the construction.

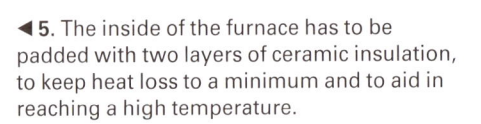

▶ 4. The furnace is made from an old paint can whose bottom has been removed with a radial saw.

◀ 5. The inside of the furnace has to be padded with two layers of ceramic insulation, to keep heat loss to a minimum and to aid in reaching a high temperature.

▶ 6. There's a set of pulleys on top of the furnace with a counterweight that makes it easy to raise the structure and insert the crucible.

▶ 7. During the burnout procedure, the flame is introduced directly through the base of the furnace to heat it before placing the crucible inside.

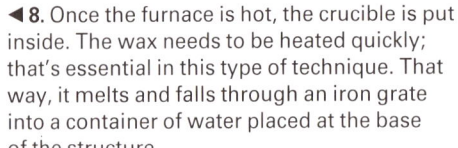

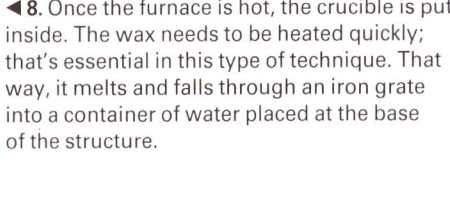

◀ 8. Once the furnace is hot, the crucible is put inside. The wax needs to be heated quickly; that's essential in this type of technique. That way, it melts and falls through an iron grate into a container of water placed at the base of the structure.

▶ 9. Bronze with a melting point of 1050° C— an appropriate alloy for casting—has been selected for the subsequent melt. The metal is placed inside, and everything is ready for melting. Before beginning, all traces of Molochite must be eliminated, since it could obstruct the flow of the metal inside the mold.

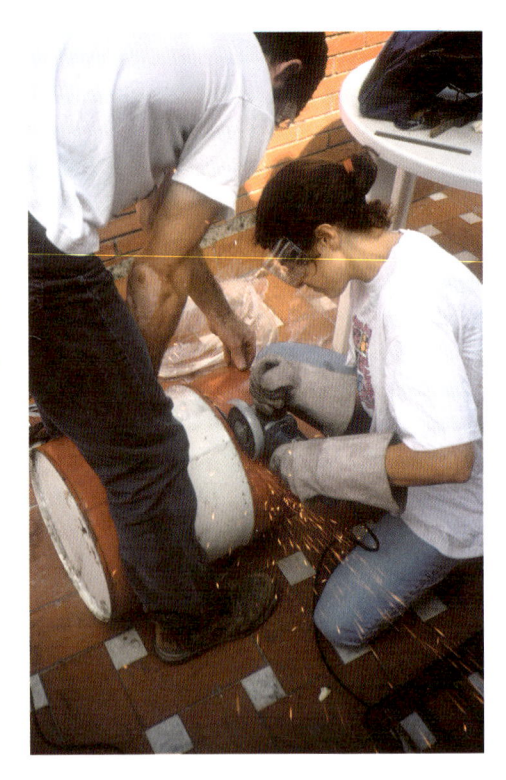

Casting and Stamping

▲ 10. The crucible containing the metal is placed onto a bed of a refractory brick, covered with both thermal insulation and Molochite that remains from making the crucible.

▲ 11. When the furnace was made, it was designed with a port or flue at the top for venting gases, as well as an opening in the side for introducing the torch and heating the furnace with a minimum of heat loss.

▲ 12. To keep the heat from escaping at the bottom, the furnace should rest on top of the base comprised of refractory brick and Molochite.

▼ 13. The flame is applied to the back of the crucible, where the most metal is located. The metal must be completely melted before the crucible is tipped.

▶ 14. When the metal melts, the crucible is tipped forward into a vertical position to allow the metal to flow into and flood the cavity left by the wax, so the level of the metal is higher than the pieces.

▶ 15. The crucible stays in this position until the metal cools.

◀ 16. After the metal has cooled, the bronze is struck gently with a mallet to avoid damaging the casting; small pieces of shell are removed by knocking them off with a chisel. Once the casting is cleaned of refractory material, it is pickled in a solution of sulfuric acid and water. A stronger pickling solution, a solution of nitric acid and water, should be used if you intend to apply a patina to the piece.

▶ One of the hanging objects cast using the ceramic shell technique. Work by Pilar Cotter.

Making Casting Patterns

▲ Bronze bracelet from Burkina Faso

Every casting technique is based on the reproduction of a previously prepared pattern. To reproduce objects using modern casting techniques, a specific type of metal pattern and a vulcanized mold are typically used. Usually these molds are made of silicon or rubber, and a certain type of wax is injected into them as a pattern for subsequent casting in metal. Sometimes, due to the nature of the work, or to save time, this pattern is made directly of wax, using various tools or lathes. Sometimes, it's not possible to vulcanize certain materials, such as some woods, plaster, and so forth, so you have to use materials that vulcanize at room temperature. It's even more difficult to make reproductions of natural, fragile elements for which there is no mold. This is the case with soft leaves and insects; in such instances you have to prepare the pattern properly and cast it in a tree—an interesting technique that requires careful and precise preparation.

Shapers for Modeling Wax

Now, it's possible to create high-quality hard wax patterns. Given proper casting techniques, they allow an infinite variety of patterns that can't be made from metal; previously, these wouldn't have been worth the time and expense to make.

There are carvers and tools for making wax patterns or models; these tools create basic shapes that can be used in a variety of ways. These patterns, once cast in gold or silver and finished properly, are converted to pieces of jewelry or to masters that are vulcanized and subsequently reproduced through investment casting processes. The advantage of working with a shaper is the rapidity and precision in creating uniform thickness and dimensions in wax, which is very difficult to achieve by hand.

There are various models of wax carvers and shapers available in the marketplace; they come with different features and vary in quality. In choosing a wax-carving tool, it's important to consider the quality of the materials from which it's made, its versatility, and its precision.

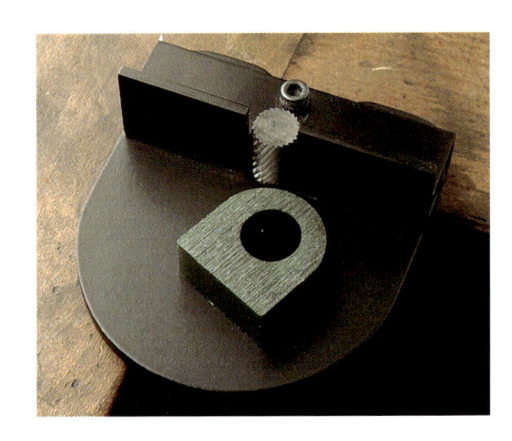

Baguette Ring

This example—a wedding ring with a baguette profile—explains the basic operations that can be done with a manual trimmer. Begin by cutting the inside of the wax tube in a concentric shape with a straight inside blade; next, turn the exterior using a metal trimmer in the desired configuration, moving it manually around the wax tube. The ring is made in green wax, a slightly harder type of wax than the blue, but equally easy to work if you use the right files and cutters.

▶ 1. Begin by turning the inside with a straight cutter, but first set the desired diameter and depth. Once the blade is set up, turn it manually while you press it into the wax tube.

◀ Rings initially modeled in wax and subsequently cast. Work by Bruna Havert.

▲ Type of shaper with a rigid table that can be used for milling any shape from a sheet of wax. Draw the shape of a model and cut it out from sheets of hard wax.

▼ This is another variety of the preceding type of shaper, attached to a pendant or flexible shaft drill underneath the table.

Casting and Stamping

◀ 3. Here is a simple wedding ring that could be used as the basis for any other project.

This ring is made initially in green wax. It is turned in the shape of a baguette, then the inside is scooped out with wax carvers. Cut the hollow for the gem in a size smaller than needed, since it's always better to adjust metal with metal once the wax has been cast in gold. Shown at the right is the cast ring with the setting soldered in place, the inside lined and ready for mounting.

◀ 2. Next, turn the outside, using the proper baguette or half-round cutting tool.

A Grooved Wedding Ring Modeled in Wax

The next project demonstrates how to make a sized wedding ring based upon a desired number of stones. The procedure is done on the manual wax trimmer, which works as the cutting tool moves around the wax bar; this tool probably is more versatile than any others demonstrated in this section. For example, it can be used for *lapidary* work and even *transverse milling*, which allows you to create a multitude of different patterns.

With a design like this one, there are two essential factors that have to be considered. The first is the size of the finger that the ring has to fit; and the second is the available budget. Since the size of the finger is a fixed quantity, you should first figure out the amount of money available for the gems and settle on a weight that is suitable. To do this, subtract the cost of the metal, the labor, and the desired profit from the final budget. Then, divide the entire amount of money for the precious stones by the number of stones that you figure the ring will need based on ring size, as well as the quality and price of the gems, in order to determine the diameter of the diamonds. To figure out the number of holes required in a wedding band, the formula in Figure 1 may be helpful.

◀ 1. Determine the inside measurement of the ring based on the desired size, and take a bar of blue wax, attach the wax trimmer with a flat inside cutter, and cut the inside of the bar in a perfectly concentric, flat shape to precisely the right size.

▶ 2. Trim the outside of the bar to the desired dimensions, based on the number of gems. Cut by turning the right hand, while the holding the wax bar firmly with the left.

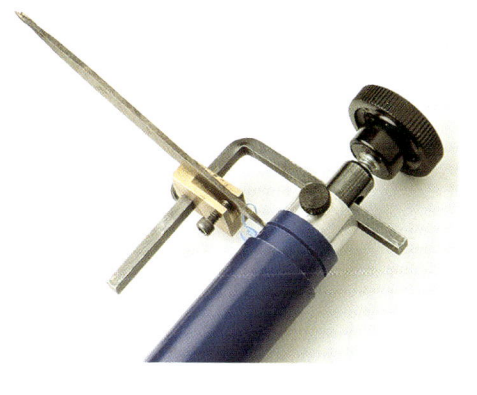

▲ 3. Next, cut an inner groove a little deeper than the diameter of the stones. Since the stones will be mounted inside the metal rails, they need a little clearance all the way around for the setting.

▲ 4. Cut the wedding ring from the end of the bar, deepening the cut until it's complete and the outer rails are clearly defined.

▼ Figure 1. Ring formula

$$\text{Number of holes} = \frac{\pi \text{ diameter of the ring inside the groove}}{\text{the diameter of the stones}}$$

Making Casting Patterns

▲ 5. On the other end of the wax bar, use a divider tool with a toothed wheel for marking the number of holes that the wedding ring will have. Since there is an assortment of toothed wheels, choose the one that corresponds to the desired number of holes.

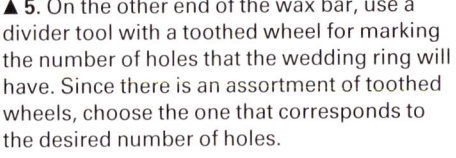

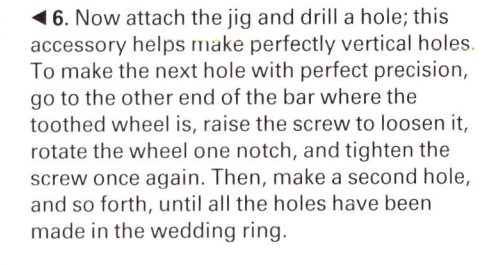

◀ 6. Now attach the jig and drill a hole; this accessory helps make perfectly vertical holes. To make the next hole with perfect precision, go to the other end of the bar where the toothed wheel is, raise the screw to loosen it, rotate the wheel one notch, and tighten the screw once again. Then, make a second hole, and so forth, until all the holes have been made in the wedding ring.

▶ 7. Once all the holes are in place, they should be perfectly centered and aligned; if necessary, go over them a little with a ball bur to get rid of any small burrs.

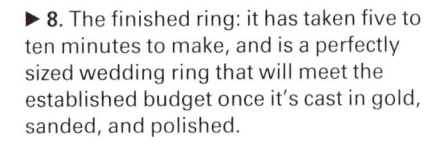

▶ 8. The finished ring: it has taken five to ten minutes to make, and is a perfectly sized wedding ring that will meet the established budget once it's cast in gold, sanded, and polished.

A Room Temperature Vulcanizing (RTV) Mold

Sometimes, it's necessary to make copies of objects for which vulcanized molds can't be used, since the heat would damage the objects. This is the case with organic materials such as wood, as well as certain types of plastics. It's very easy to make a room temperature mold of the object by using any of the liquid silicones that are available on the market.

Silicones come with an activator and a technical sheet that indicates the time requirements and the correct proportions for the catalyst; this is mixed with the silicone to harden, which then allows you to extract the pattern and copy the inner shape in wax.

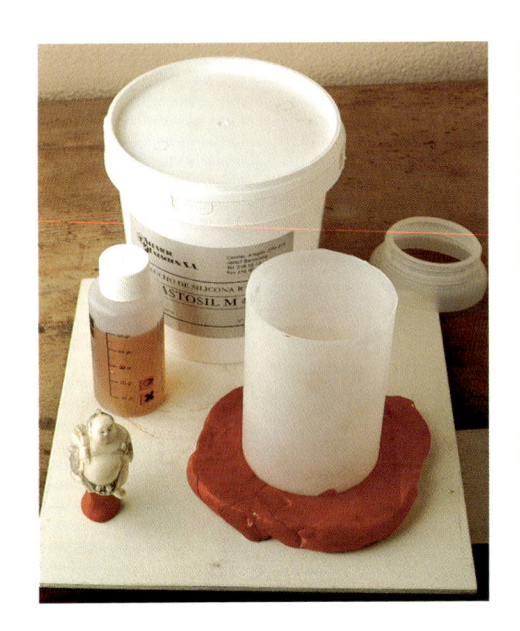

▲ 1. In this demonstration, a model has been set upright on a base of modeling clay.

▲ 2. The bottom and neck have been cut out of a plastic jug to serve as a shell for the silicone; it is placed on the base of modeling clay. Set the object to be copied in the center of the base, and mix the silicone with the activator to create a homogenous mixture. The catalyst should be mixed in slowly, in the proportion indicated by the technical sheet.

◀ 3. Slowly pour the mix into the mold, avoiding any agitation that could cause unnecessary bubbles, and let it harden.

◀ 4. Once it's hard, remove the model and inject a little hot wax into the mold. Wait a few moments until the wax shell cools as it comes in contact with the walls of the silicone mold, and then turn the mold over once or twice to distribute it evenly. Then pour in the rest of the hot wax.

◀ 5. Once you have created the wax casting, take it to a shop that specializes in investment casting and have it cast, or use one of the methods presented earlier in this chapter.

Preparing Natural Models

There are many materials that can be cast directly, if they are placed in a cylindrical mold and then subjected to a complete heat curve in a burnout oven. Some plastics, cardboard, leaves, pasta shells, and so forth, can be incorporated into a casting tree as if they were made of injection wax; problems arise when you want to cast delicate objects, such as small leaves or insects, directly in the casting cylinder. Since the silicone contains a lot of water, the texture, moisture, and thick mass in the surrounding mold distort the pieces completely when they are pressed into it. As a result, the pattern crumples or simply collapses before the mold sets. To compensate for this problem, the pattern must be made rigid to build up sufficient thickness for the molten metal to penetrate to the interior of the pattern.

Preparing Leaves and Natural Patterns

There are several ways to prepare natural models. To use an insect, euthanize the specimen with chloroform and freeze it. Then, set up a sprue base or tree and use a wax pen to attach the specimens. Next, pour in the investment for the mold. Delicate leaves, such as those from the geranium, have to be prepared properly so that they look natural once they are cast in gold. Begin this process immediately after the leaves are picked and cleaned. To do this, treat the leaf with spray lacquer and coat the underside with inlay wax. This procedure will increase the size and rigidity of the leaves so that the metal will have enough space to flow into the mold after the leaf is burned out.

▲ Gold and silver rings made using straw; work by Kay Eppi Nölke

▲ These earrings by Carles Codina were made from the skin of fresh litchis. Since this is a fragile material, the obverse has been prepared by reinforcing the structure with successive coats of inlay wax.

▲ 1. As stated before, natural leaves like these can't be placed directly into the casting cylinder; prepare them with lacquers and waxes to impart the necessary rigidity so they can withstand the setting of the investment without crumbling or distorting.

▲ 2. One way to prepare these specimens is to spray or brush on successive layers of varnish. The varnish or lacquer has to be insoluble in water and easy to burn out.

◀ 3. The aerosol application in step 2 seals the pores and adds a certain amount of rigidity to the leaf; still, it needs to be made thicker. Use a wax tool to apply a thin layer of inlay wax to the back of the leaf.

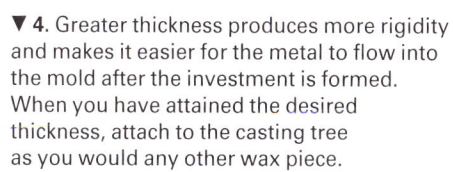

▼ 4. Greater thickness produces more rigidity and makes it easier for the metal to flow into the mold after the investment is formed. When you have attained the desired thickness, attach to the casting tree as you would any other wax piece.

Making Casting Patterns

▲ 5. The heat curve in a burnout oven can be modified by increasing the maximum temperature and the time spent at the highest point on the heat curve. To do this, pay attention to the technical specifications for the type of investment used. The photo shows the leaves that were cast in gold and subsequently used in making the bracelet that appears in Step by Step on page 142.

▶ Some plants can be added directly to the casting tree with scarcely any preparation; you merely need to apply several coats of sealing lacquer to the entire casting tree and plunge it quickly into the investment, taking advantage of the plant's natural stiffness.

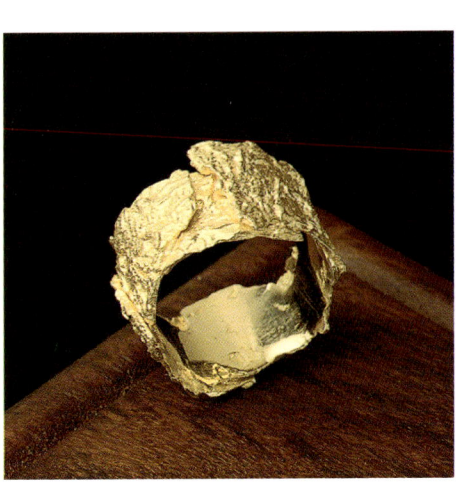

▲ Close-up of a creation by Carles Codina

▼ The ring pictured here was made from a direct casting of the leaves already shown. Work by Carles Codina.

◀ This ring by Carles Codina was fairly easy to make, since the oak bark is quite sturdy and can hold up for the ten minutes it takes for the investment to harden.

64

Metal Stamping

In ancient times, artisans realized that cast tools and arms became tougher and more durable when they were forged or beaten; these cold forging and stamping processes are very old. The minting of coins as valuable objects originated with stamping, which was also frequently used as an ornamental technique as early as the second century B.C. Normally, these decorations were made with hard metal stamps on softer metals; bronze stamps were used in ancient Egypt, and wooden or horn stamps were used by the Greeks in the sixth century B.C.

In essence, stamping consists of imprinting and shaping metal by exerting pressure with a harder and more resistant tool. It's a commonly used manufacturing process, since most of our daily objects are made using some production process based on stamping and die stamping. Contemporary stamping with complex dies has evolved tremendously; now it's a technique that's associated more closely with industrial engineering than with handicrafts. This chapter will examine the concept of steel stamping, as well as other very simple types of stamping that easily produce attractive, interesting shapes and decorative features at a very reasonable cost. This involves using older production methods, yet still taking advantage of the resources and products that are available and affordable in today's market.

▲ Stamping led to the minting of coins as objects of value and beauty. The first minted gold and silver disks were struck by the Lydians in Asia Minor in the seventh century B.C.; the practice then spread throughout the Near East as far as Greece. The photo shows gold coins from the Spanish galleon *Nuestra Señora de las Maravillas*, which sank in 1656.

▶ Brooch made from various stampings in silver. Work by Itxaso Mezzacasa.

▼ Stamping is commonly used, especially in mass production of jewelry, since this process produces a very fine thickness of metal that is also very strong and durable. Given the great number of pieces that can be made, the result is a vast savings in production costs. Shown here are the different stamped pieces that were used in making a brooch created by T&J Bragg, 1875, Birmingham, England.

▲ Earrings stamped in fine sheet gold by Carles Codina

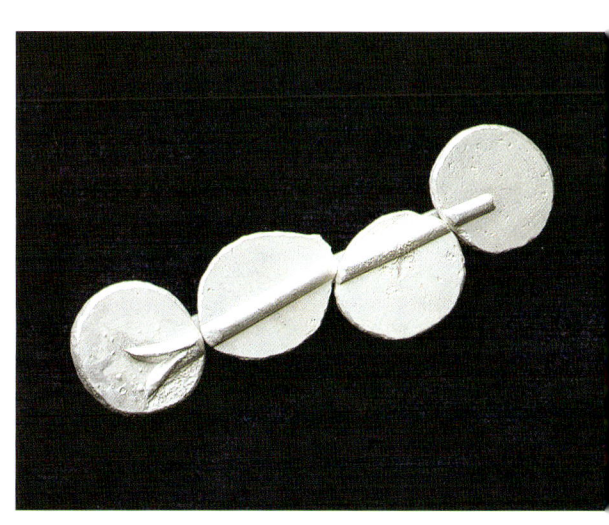

Steel Die Stamping

Making a steel punch and die is the most common method used in the industry, since it offers greater durability and precision. Just the same, it's the most costly procedure, requiring quite a large punch press, and thus it requires extensive production to pay for itself. A preliminary evaluation of the production goals and costs is recommended before utilizing this method. A properly tempered steel punch has unmatched durability, though, and the quality of the pieces produced is comparable to the original.

Begin with a block of steel appropriate to the type of relief the punch is intended to produce. Once this steel is annealed and rendered ductile, shape it with milling cutters, files, and gravers. It has to be as smooth and polished as possible—as if it were a piece of jewelry—so that a metal piece stamped in the mold is easily released.

Metal Stamping

Next, the soft steel is tempered; this is a process that has to be done in specialized shops, since it's more involved than merely tempering a chisel. Tempering is a heat treatment that gives steel the adequate hardness and flexibility for hammering the punch into another piece of soft steel that actually serves as the die. To do this, the punch is heated to about 900° C and quenched in water or oil; since it's now excessively hard and subject to breakage, it has to be tempered. This involves heating it to a lower temperature for a certain amount of time to achieve the right balance between hardness and flexibility.

Once the punch is tempered, it's struck into another piece of annealed steel, which will serve as the die; it must be polished as required, and tempered properly. The shaped die is used to fabricate the pieces. The press lowers the die onto the sheet of metal placed on (or against) another punch made of softer metal that has a certain amount of tolerance or play.

The steel punch is used only to make the original model; it has to be stored carefully, for if the die is damaged in stamping, the punch will have to be struck into the die again.

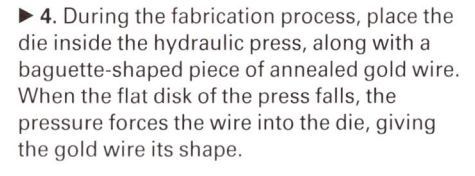

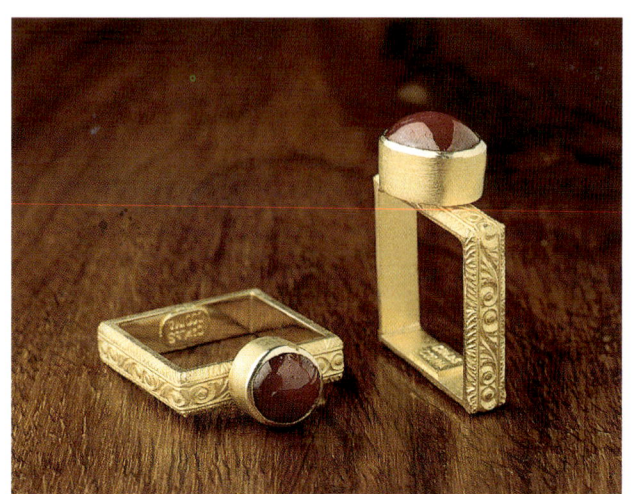

▲ **1.** Start with a block of annealed steel; various milling machine cutters and files are used to turn it into a punch. This piece has to be a bit larger than the model created on it.

▲ **2.** File, mill, and engrave the steel with various gravers to create the desired design; keep in mind that the punch will be struck into the die, and the model will end up being the mirror image of the initial design.

▶ **3.** Drive the punch into a soft piece of steel with the aid of a powerful press; once the die is tempered, it will be used to fabricate the pieces. The die must be tempered before use to give it the hardness needed for stamping out the different pieces of metal.

▶ **4.** During the fabrication process, place the die inside the hydraulic press, along with a baguette-shaped piece of annealed gold wire. When the flat disk of the press falls, the pressure forces the wire into the die, giving the gold wire its shape.

◀ Gold rings stamped by Carles Codina

▲ **5.** The process can be carried out by a friction press, or, as shown in this photo, a hydraulic press that produces 150 tons of pressure.

Characteristics of Types of Steel

Steels designated B-2, U-3, and K-455 are appropriate for relief dies, since they are fairly soft and durable, and they allow the inclusion of detail. Steels designated K-100 and K-720 are more brittle and hard, and therefore less resilient than the preceding ones; they can withstand lots of pressure, and they are good choices for large production runs. (Note that each manufacturer may have a different numbering system for its steel.)

Stamping Process for a Silver Necklace

When producing many pieces of the same shape and size, you have to prepare a shearing die that makes it possible to produce a large quantity of the items quickly and precisely. In this segment, Estela Guitart uses a mechanical process that involves a steel shearing die, specifically, a two-part circular disk shearer, and subsequently, a mechanical press. This method allows her to make a large quantity of jewelry and cut down the time and cost of production.

▶ **2.** After the disks are cut out, she presses them in a stamping die like the one shown in the photo; this shapes the disks into hemispherical shapes with a single blow.

◀ **1.** First, she installs the punch in the top of the shearing die and centers the base of the die. When she inserts a strip of silver in the channel in the base, the punch can be used to cut out any number of silver disks quickly and precisely.

◀ **3.** To finish the necklace, she bends the disks and pierces them with a small drill bit to accommodate the strong wire that will hold the piece together.

▶ Silver necklace by Estela Guitart

Punches

Stamping out shapes with punches should not be confused with chasing or repoussé. Steel chasing tools are used in repoussé to create shapes in sheet metal by working it on one side, then the other. But die stamping creates low relief and designs that embellish the surface of the metal only, as this section explains.

The punch or stamp, which is normally made of steel, is struck onto a gold or silver sheet or wire that has been annealed; the metal has to be placed onto a smooth surface, such as a steel anvil. The pressure from a hammer blow on the punch or stamp leaves an impression in the soft metal only on the side that was struck. Punches can be made of any material, as long as they are harder and more resistant than the metal on which they are used. For example, they can be made quickly from brass or bronze rods and used on thin sheets of silver or softer metals, but this method has disadvantages: it can't be tempered; it loses its shape very quickly when it's struck; and it can't be used repeatedly.

Preparation

Steel is the best material for making punches. A tool steel or B-2 steel is appropriate, but the choice of steel is a personal matter. The process is practically the same as the one used in making a chasing tool for repoussé; the difference is in the type of steel and the dimensions. The stamp shouldn't be too long; otherwise, it could bend in use. It needs to be only about 8 cm long and at least 9 mm in diameter.

The first step in making a steel punch is to anneal the steel; then create a design in one end using files and gravers. Then, temper it again to restore the hardness; heat the punch to a cherry red, then plunge it quickly into water or oil. Oil is the best choice, especially if a B-2 type of steel is used, since it provides a gentler quench than water does. Once the punch is hardened, it's excessively brittle and the temper needs to be adjusted to the right degree.

Use the torch to adjust the temper. Start by heating the punch at the end that will receive the hammer blows. Heat it with the torch to a black color, then to a light straw color. Use the torch to advance the color until it reaches a darker yellow shade; at that point, plunge it into oil once again. After adjusting the temper, the surface has to be polished with fine abrasive paper. If you make a mistake, harden and polish the punch once again before making a second attempt.

Metal Stamping

◀ This photo shows various steel punches that have been engraved, hardened, and tempered.

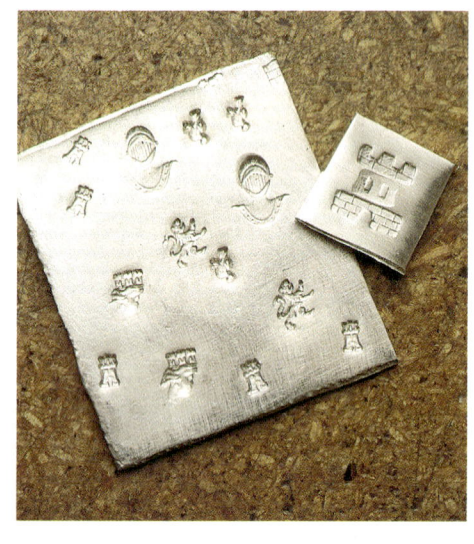

◀ To create these designs, place the sheet of metal on an anvil, hold the punches vertically and strike with a hammer.

▶ Gold and silver medallions with stamped designs by Carmen Amador

Stamping on Lead

To begin, prepare a block made out of soft lead for punching the metal. Take an old pot or pan and put in some clean leftover lead scraps and heat the bottom of the pan with an indirect flame. Once the metal is melted, use a piece of cardboard or wood to skim off the impurities that float to the top. After it has cooled, you have a lead block that will be useful not just for stamping with punches, but also for shaping all kinds of gold- and silversmithing projects. This process has to be done in a well-ventilated area; wear a respirator to protect yourself from the vapors given off by the molten lead.

Steel punches can be made as already described, starting with a round rod of tool steel; if you don't intend to make many pieces, the steel doesn't even need to be hardened and tempered. In fact, if the piece is small and the sheet metal thin, you can stamp on lead using punches made of materials softer than steel.

First, strike the punch repeatedly into the lead to create an impression; then prepare various fine, annealed sheets of gold or silver. The right thickness is about .5 mm, and the sheets need be a little larger than the diameter you wish to stamp. Next, place a piece of thin, tough paper between the lead and the piece of gold or silver, and strike the metal with a mallet or heavy hammer, driving it into the lead. It's important to keep the lead from coming in contact with the gold or silver, since a tiny fragment of lead can contaminate a large quantity of these metals. That's why it's imperative to place a thin piece of paper between the lead and the metal. Be sure to clean the metal thoroughly with a bronze brush to get rid of any traces of lead before annealing the piece again.

▲ 1. Cut out several metal disks using the disk-shearing die; then, anneal and pickle the disks.

▶ 2. Strike the disks with the punch and drive them into the lead to give them shape.

Simple Dies Made from Resins

In earlier days, dies were made by engraving stone and pressing the metal into or around the form. Later on, the dies were made of bronze and other materials. Today, it's possible to make dies out of all kinds of materials, such as nylon, steel, methacrylate, and various types of resins. In fact, resin doesn't have the strength of a bronze or steel mold, but it works perfectly for making a series of small pieces in a workshop and creates some very interesting results.

▲ Stamped gold rings made by Carles Codina

▲ This type of resin die is made by hollowing out a prepared plastic in a set of brass cylinders. These dies can be used to make quite a number of high-quality pieces, and that greatly reduces production costs.

Resin Dies

Resin molds are generally made by mixing polyester resin with a catalyst supplied by the manufacturer; these ingredients have to be mixed properly. The catalyst hardens the mixture after a couple of hours. This type of mold can be used several times, but its durability is limited. It is possible, though, to repair it using another type of prepared resin that is mixed with powdered metal, since this type of resin is much stronger and can be used for many more impressions without distortion. This very simple method uses a type of plastic steel that's easy to find at any specialized supplier; the resulting mold can be stamped in a press, or pressed using a bench vise.

▲ 1. Start with a frame about 2 cm deep; the dimensions will depend on the size of the piece to be created. The aluminum frame shown in this photo is commonly used for making rubber molds, with a sheet of steel as a support or base. The design to be reproduced is a solid silver cross, first done in wax and then cast in silver.
 Place the sheet of steel underneath the frame, center the design on it, and glue it in place.

▲ 2. Prepare a thick mixture of plastic steel that creates a homogenous mass, yet is still liquid enough to fill all the corners of the mold. Then, pour it in and cover the design; tap the frame lightly to settle the plastic steel.

▶ 3. Set it aside until the mass is dry; then, prepare the mold model and clean up any imperfections in the cavity, especially around the edges.

▶ 4. To complete this process, layer the materials as follows: a sheet of thick steel on the bottom; the plastic steel die; the sheet of annealed silver; a filler and countermold layer of soft material such as paper, neoprene, or hard foam; and a second sheet of thick steel on top. If you don't have a hydraulic press, squeeze it tightly in a bench vise, but the result won't have the definition that you can get with a press.

Metal Stamping

▲ 5. Although a commercial press is shown here, it's easy to make a simple press using a hydraulic jack for vehicles. The pressure shouldn't be excessive, since this type of mold doesn't have a supporting frame to prevent breakage.

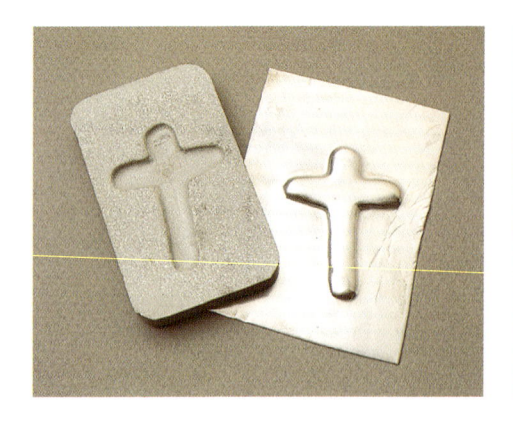

▲ 6. Here's the sheet of silver after stamping. Now it has to be sawn out; the base has to be leveled with a file; and it has to be soldered to another flat sheet of silver. When that's done, saw off the extra sheet, file the edges, polish the cross with abrasive paper, and finish by buffing the surface.

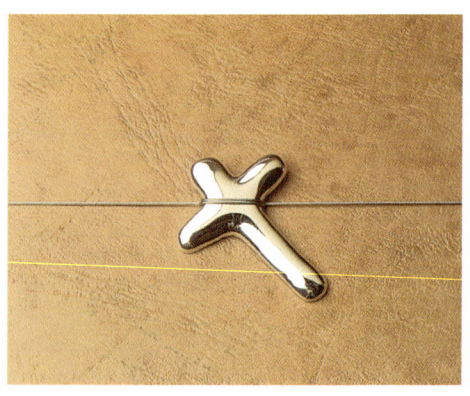

▲ 7. Here is the finished hollow cross, after polishing.

Rigid Plastic or Embossing Dies

It's possible to create some intriguing projects with very simple stamping processes. This method involves using various burs to carve sheets of hard plastic, such as methacrylate. Place thin sheets of annealed metal into the press and squeeze them, along with a soft material such as polyurethane foam or even paper towels; this stamps the metal into the plastic and produces some interesting and varied shapes.

▲ 1. This photo shows designs that Silvia Walz has carved into various sheets of methacrylate using several common rotary tool accessories.

▲ 2. After she creates the design in the methacrylate, she places a thin sheet of annealed metal covered with a piece of foam into the press and squeezes it all together.

▼ 3. Here's the final product from the methacrylate die, once the metal has been patinated. Brooch by Silvia Walz.

▼ Brooch stamped in methacrylate by Silvia Walz

70

Casting and Stamping

Creating a Symmetrical Shape

This next method is very simple; it makes slightly convex shapes that are very useful in enamel applications, or in making series or sets of pieces from thin gold or silver sheet. The advantage of this process is that it creates perfectly symmetrical halves for earrings, jointed bracelets, and hollow pieces.

▲ **1.** Cut a thick piece of fiberboard, and screw a piece of methacrylate or other hard plastic to each side. Once the pieces are joined, follow the profile or contour of the design with a jeweler's or piercing saw; then go over the entire piece and make sure that the top edge of the plastic is smooth.
  When that's done, attach a sheet of annealed silver to each side of the assembly.

◀ **3.** You can also create the shape by using various punches made from nylon bar stock. Begin administering blows at the edges of the hole in the die and apply them around the circumference, working toward the center in a spiral pattern.

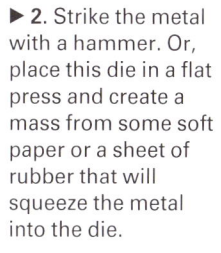

▶ **4.** Then, saw out the pieces and assemble them.

▶ **2.** Strike the metal with a hammer. Or, place this die in a flat press and create a mass from some soft paper or a sheet of rubber that will squeeze the metal into the die.

Surface Textures Using Hard Metals

With just a simple bench-top rolling mill and a little imagination, you can produce sheets and wires with innovative and fascinating textures that will give your creations greater expression. The hardness of the metals used, as well as the pressure to which they are subjected, are factors in creating textures.
  Under the pressure exerted by the rolling mill, the softer metals—gold and silver in this case—are pressed into the cavity sawn in the harder steel sheet; this process can also be done with nickel (German) silver or any other material that's harder than gold.

▶ **3.** Place the entire assembly into the rolling mill, adjust the pressure, and roll it through.

▶ **4.** Here are the results, on sheets of gold and silver. Remember that the pattern from the sheet may look a little distorted on one side.

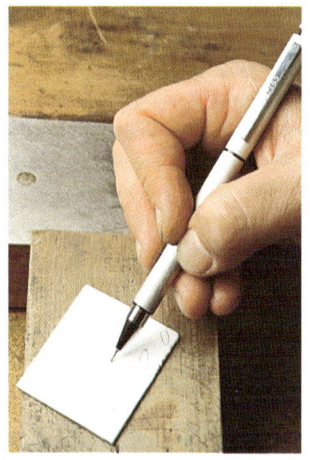

◀ **1.** Prepare a sheet of steel or other hard metal; paint it with plastic paint and let it dry.

▶ **2.** The sheet mustn't come into contact with the steel rollers of the rolling mill, since it would damage them. To avoid that, sandwich the steel die between a piece of copper on the bottom and the sheet to be textured.

71

History will attest that humankind has always treasured objects of beauty. Precious stones have been attributed with magic and curative powers, their possession has been envied, and they have been a symbol of power in many cultures due to their rarity and expense.

To observe and identify these precious gems professionally, a broad background in gemology is required, along with very precise instruments.

This is a captivating field. In the following chapter, jewelers and aficionados will find some background information for studying and identifying precious stones. You will learn that a simple glance in a 10x loupe can help you recognize some of the characteristics that are important in evaluating and identifying gems, and let you delve into this specialized—yet fascinating—world.

Gems

Precious Stones

Nature offers an endless array of organic and mineral substances, some with individual characteristics that distinguish them from more ordinary materials—qualities that determine their classification as gems or precious stones. Of course, this designation is influenced by many factors, some cultural and some symbolic. In any case, people have always been tremendously attracted to gems, and their unique qualities, such as transparency, hardness, color, and shine, remain every bit as seductive today.

Origins and Special Considerations

Minerals formed inside the earth have specific chemical compositions and atomic classifications; crystals have very specific physical and visual qualities. In general, for a mineral to be considered precious, it has to possess certain optical qualities—essentially, good color, extreme hardness, resistance to wear and scratching, and finally, rarity and uniqueness. These factors account for a stone's elevated price in the marketplace. However, the attributes of good color, hardness, and rarity are not always entirely evident; there are also remarkable minerals that are considered to be gems because of their *inclusions*, their geological rarity, or their shape. Furthermore, there are also many types of gems with unusual colors and shades that are considered very valuable. And there is yet another decisive characteristic of a precious gem: the cut, a human element that imparts its distinctive appearance and allows the beauty of the stone to blossom forth.

Crystalline gems are atomic formations that acquired a particular solid form as the result of the pressure and high temperatures they were submitted to billions of years ago. There are crystals that have a rhombohedral structure, such as sapphire; a hexagonal structure, in the case of beryl; or a cubic structure, as in a diamond. Crystals have planes or external faces that are determined by this internal atomic structure, which is rarely perfect; the arrangement follows a specific pattern, called a *polyhedron of coordination*. There are seven different classes of symmetry that are defined as crystalline systems: *cubic, tetragonal, hexagonal, trigonal, orthorhombic, monoclinic, and triclinic.*

Although most precious stones, such as diamonds, emeralds, and rubies, are mineral in origin, there are also precious stones that are animal or vegetable in origin. Pearls are formed inside an oyster shell, for instance, and others come from different substances: amber from a fossilized resin; coral from fossilized animals; and jet from fossilized wood, among others.

▼ Some minerals are plentiful and easy to mine, but others are very scarce, and it may be very difficult and costly to extract them. It's rare to encounter materials with identical characteristics. Not all minerals extracted have the gem quality necessary for cutting, and that's why rarity becomes an essential factor in making a gem precious—a quality that has a direct bearing on its ultimate price.

◄ Carles Codina, *Ring with Precious Stone, Year 2000.* Permanent collection of the Museum of Decorative Arts in Barcelona, Spain.

Precious stones transcend social and symbolic considerations, since each person and society is free to bestow its own value, based on cultural factors or other considerations.

▲ Precious stones originated billions of years ago in the depths of the earth's crust; they are the products of enormous pressures and temperatures caused by continental drift. The outward appearance of a crystal, with its facets and angles, is a faithful reflection of its internal atomic structure. The photo shows hexagonal amethyst crystals from Mexico.

◄ After the gems have been studied and cut, they achieve their maximum brilliance and splendor. Here are a few gems cut by Tom Munsteiner.

▼ Amber is a petrified natural resin; despite its softness, it can attain considerable value in the marketplace if it contains an insect inclusion. One way to identify real amber with an inclusion is to check for evidence of the insect's struggle to escape the original resin in which it was caught.

74

Extraction

Minerals, and consequently gems, are composed of common elements in nature that experienced specific conditions of temperature and pressure at some point in their evolution. The more or less perfect crystals were formed in these conditions. As a result of movements in the earth, eruptions, and erosion, these crystals were brought to the surface in places that were accessible to people, such as volcanic chimneys and rivers.

Extracting Precious Stones from the Ayoreita Mine

Ametrine is a rare variety of quartz that contains the colors of amethyst and citrine in the same crystal. The following photos from the Ayoreita mine show the extraction of amethyst with coloration indicative of ametrine; this site is one of the few sources of this material in the world. The mine is located about 33 miles (55 km) from "Tiger's Corner" in the center of the Bolivian jungle. Getting a simple four-wheel drive vehicle or an excavator to this point involves 15 days of hard travel on the Amazon River and 12 days of travel through the jungle. Any breakdown, accident, or need for supplies requires tremendous effort and could doom the trip. The work conditions—60 feet (18 meters) underground in a 265-foot (80 m) horizontal gallery—are extremely difficult, as is life in the Amazon jungle; these circumstances are not for just anyone.

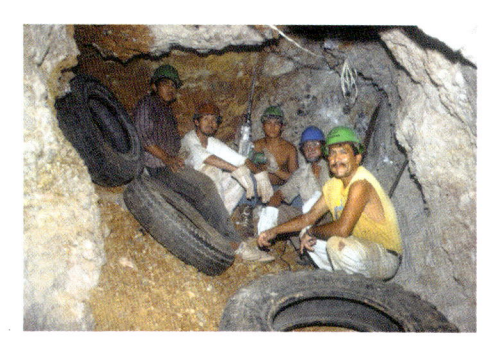

▲ Work area inside the Ayoreita mine, 60 feet (18 m) down in a 265-foot (80 m) horizontal gallery. Pneumatic tools are used to avoid breaking the material that's removed from the ceiling and walls.

▲ Medina, the "point man," drills at the front of the main deposit.

▼ Various ametrine crystals that have been selected prior to cleaning and classification

▲ Group of miners from the Ayoreita mine after hauling the crystals to the surface. These experienced men work in small mines like Ayoreita; without them, it would be impossible to obtain such precious materials.

▼ Sometimes, nature produces surprises with excellent formations. Marcelino and Chunco, two highly skilled miners, are pictured here next to a wonderful crystalline formation they extracted from Ayoreita.

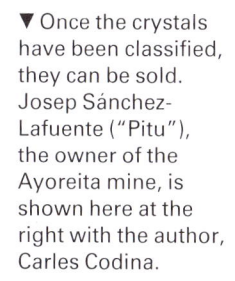

▼ Once the crystals have been classified, they can be sold. Josep Sánchez-Lafuente ("Pitu"), the owner of the Ayoreita mine, is shown here at the right with the author, Carles Codina.

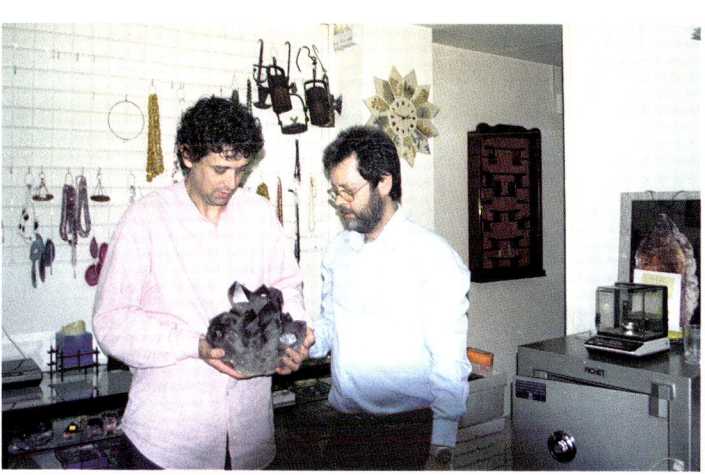

▶ Ametrine crystals like the one in the photo come from the depths of the earth in the Ayoreita mine. These crystals have excellent shape and are ready for the cutting process.

Color

The color of a gem is determined by the way it absorbs white light. When the human eye sees a gem, some colors in the spectrum are absorbed, and the ones that are not absorbed are reflected; these combine to give the gem its characteristic color. If none of the spectrum is absorbed, the gem or crystal will appear transparent. Chemical elements in the gem, such as chromium, iron, copper, manganese, or titanium, as well as irregularities in the crystalline structure, cause absorption.

The sparkle of color in a gem is caused by the decomposition of light into the seven colors of the spectrum visible to the human eye. This phenomenon is called dispersion; the play of color increases with greater light dispersion.

Materials can be transparent, translucent, or opaque.

▲ In reality, the human eye sees only certain colors in gems; it distinguishes just seven colors in the wavelengths between 4000 and 7000 angstroms, the visible spectrum. When light passes through a gem it breaks down, and the gem's internal structure absorbs certain colors. The tones that are not absorbed combine to produce the different colors that the eye perceives.

▶ Emerald is a variety of beryl, which is crystallized prismatic hexagons; its green color is due to traces of chromium and iron. Real emeralds are red when they are examined through a Chelsea color filter; false emeralds appear green, because this filter eliminates all the colors of the spectrum except for red and green. The photo shows a high-quality emerald crystal.

▼ Small molecules of silicon dioxide contained in this opal form a network of diffraction. This property can make it appear flat, or to change color from red to violet, green, and blue, depending on its orientation, the angle of the light, and the size of the spheres.

◀ Spectrolite is the gem variety of labradorite. In the example shown here, dispersion is caused by different growth planes.

Refraction and Reflection

In evaluating a gem, it's necessary to study its refraction. When light enters the gem, its velocity decreases, and it changes direction. This directional change can be measured with a device known as a *refractometer*, which provides a refraction index or numerical indication of the curvature of the light entering the crystal. It's easy to understand this phenomenon by observing the visual distortion of a spoon placed in a glass of water; the spoon seems to be bent. By way of analogy, you could say that the bend is the refraction, and this effect becomes more pronounced as the depth of the water increases. Refraction really depends on the internal structure of each mineral, and it is a decisive factor in identifying a gem, since every mineral has a specific refraction. For example, when examining a gem, it will exhibit simple or double refraction; double refraction is referred to as *birefringence*. This quality is basic to the proper identification and subsequent determination of a stone's value; for example, tourmaline is birefringent.

Many other gems exhibit birefringence, for when the light enters the crystal, it is refracted and separated into two rays of different speeds and trajectories. Gems that are not characterized by a cubic structure exhibit birefringence; it is seen as a visual doubling of the rear facets when observed from the *table*.

▶ Double refraction occurs when a ray of light passes through a crystal and divides into two rays that continue in different directions at different speeds. This phenomenon occurs in all crystals except ones that have a cubic structure.

REFLECTION

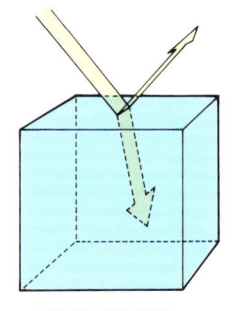

REFRACTION

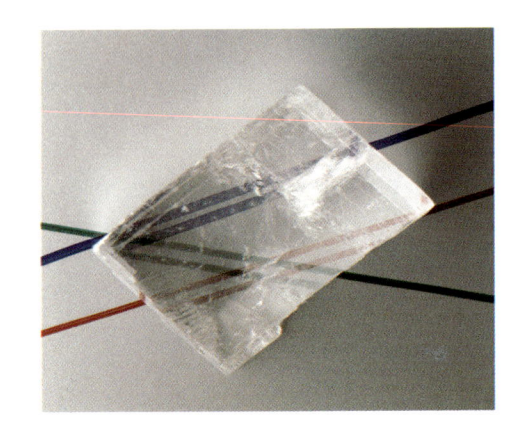

Brilliance and Transparency

For a mineral or a stone to be considered a gem, it has to have good color, and its brilliance and transparency are also important factors in this designation.

Brilliance refers to the surface appearance and the quantity of light reflected by the surface; every gem is different in this regard. Brilliance is classified using different adjectives such as *cereous*, *oily*, *adamantine*, and so forth.

Transparency, on the other hand, involves the path of the light inside the crystal and the ease with which it passes through the gem, given that part of the light is reflected and part of the light enters the gem in varying intensity. That's why gems are classified as *transparent*, such as quartz, topaz, and beryl; *translucent*, such as opal, jade, and chalcedony; and *opaque*, such as hematite and malachite.

▲ The final shape of a gem or precious stone defines its ultimate weight, and its color and shine should be improved by the cut; as a result, the asking price rises. Here are some gems cut by Tom Munsteiner.

Specific Properties of Gems

A crystal grows as a function of its surroundings. As the atoms are arranged, they pick up various chemical elements from their surroundings, such as chromium, titanium, and manganese—a whole series of atoms that are assimilated to form larger structures.

In summary, a crystal develops because of pressure and temperature, combined with the chemical elements that it absorbs from its surroundings; as a result, it's often difficult to find completely pure gems, and any that are found are very costly. In many cases, the special characteristics that were produced during the formation of a gem increase its worth, for people also value gems for their inclusions and often assign them a special value beyond the market price. One example is *demantoid* garnets; they are appreciated for their typical inclusions of "horsetail," a green garnet that's found only in some mines in the Ural Mountains in Russia and in Valmalenco, Italy; these can have a very high market value.

In certain instances, inclusions are considered defects that reduce the value of a gem, but for many *gemologists* and *lapidaries*, an inclusion can reveal a gem's identity, its formation, and its origin, especially in view of the quality and quantity of some synthetic or imitation gems.

▶ This star effect is produced by rutilated crystals that grow next to one another in a crystalline corundum network during their formation. The cutting has to be oriented correctly to produce this effect—in the same direction as the optical axis. The six points of light on the star reflect its internal structure.

▼ A gem that is subjected to constant friction and rubbing has to have a hardness equal to or greater than that of quartz if it is to remain polished and durable. Here are several pieces of quartz that contain interesting and varied inclusions.

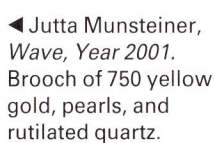

◀ Jutta Munsteiner, *Wave, Year 2001*. Brooch of 750 yellow gold, pearls, and rutilated quartz.

Quartz is a very common material that contains numerous inclusions such as tourmaline crystals, or, as in this piece, subtle rutile inclusions.

Hardness and Durability

Hardness is a gem's resistance to scratching; it's a quality determined by the gem's atomic structure. Hardness is an important factor in appraising a gem, since it has a decisive influence on its *durability*. Durability is evaluated with respect to quartz, since this is the most abundant mineral in nature; the environment in which we live, the dust that we clean up every day, is filled with quartz particles. Quartz has a hardness of 7, and every mineral that has a higher number than this is considered to be everlasting. There is a simple method for determining hardness that analyzes gems based on their resistance to scratching, according to a scale devised by Friedrich Mohs. This scale is based on ten minerals, arranged in order of increasing hardness; thus, a mineral can only scratch the ones below it on the scale. This test generally is not performed on stones that have already been cut and polished, as it's an aggressive method that scratches the gems.

Any thorough study of hardness involves an analysis of the internal structure of the mineral, since hardness varies as a function of the mineral's atomic structure—basically, how the carbon atoms are interlaced with one another. Since hardness is directly related to this atomic structure, a gem can be simultaneously hard yet fragile. The hardest gem in existence, the diamond, is easy to cleave by hitting it precisely where its atomic links are weakest, in other words, in the structural *exfoliation* planes. Hardness is not uniform, and its index varies slightly depending on direction; as a result, a diamond can be cut using another diamond, depending on the direction of the cut.

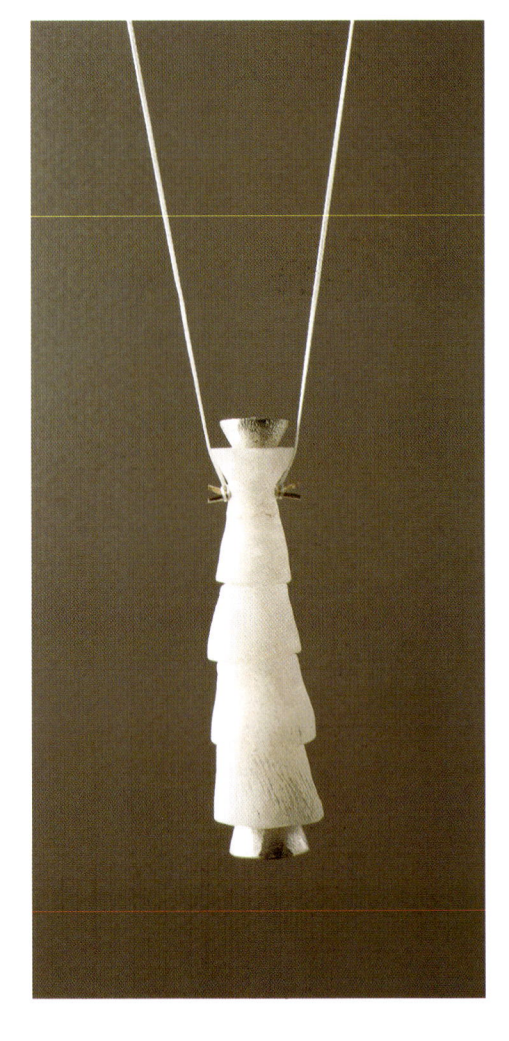

▶ Alabaster is a sedimentary rock of low hardness, a compacted form of gypsum that's easy to cut and shape with a simple file. Even though it's delicate, it has an interesting transparency and can be used for pendants and other jewelry that is not subjected to friction and wear. Pendant made of silver and alabaster by Jimena Bello.

◀ Diamonds and graphite are pure crystallized carbon, though the latter is much softer; both minerals possess the same chemical composition, but with different physical and optical properties. The latter became crystallized in the hexagonal system, because of lower pressure experienced during the formation of the material billions of years ago. Diamonds, on the other hand, crystallized in the cubic system because of temperature and pressure conditions; this accounts for the difference between the two minerals.

Cut and Weight

Gems don't exhibit much beauty in their raw state; color and brilliance appear in their greatest splendor only when the gems are cut, and so the quality of the cut has a direct influence on their monetary value. Cutting is increasingly important; it depends on human skill and creativity. Good material in the hands of an expert cutter will yield the utmost beauty and brilliance in the piece, and it will also have the appropriate weight. In most instances, the commercial value of a gem is determined not only by color quality, purity, and size, but also its weight in *carats*.

▶ Most precious stones are cut to be set into various pieces of jewelry. Ring by Carles Codina in yellow gold, with amethyst cut by Tom Munsteiner.

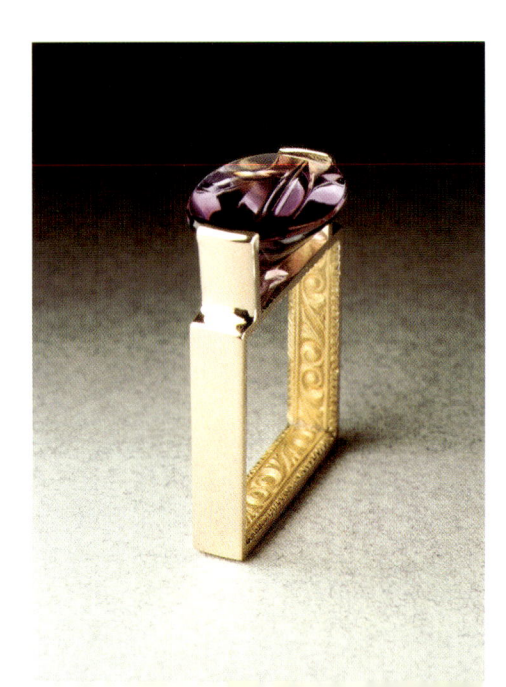

▶ Tom Munsteiner, *Inside Selecting*. Pendant with fire opal weighing 104.34 carats.

▲ The cabochon is one type of cut that's used very frequently with stones that are fairly opaque, such as turquoise and malachite; it's also used a lot with gems that contain many inclusions. The delicate nature of some gems, such as opals, suggest this type of cut. Earrings with ruby cabochons by Carles Codina.

Synthetic and Imitation Gems

Synthetic gems are commonly considered to be false stones of low value; however, they have the same chemical composition as the naturally occurring ones, with nearly identical physical and optical properties. Even though they are produced in a laboratory, they can occasionally reach high prices, even higher than their natural counterparts can.

Current technology makes it possible to imitate nature by accelerating the process of crystal formation. By taking chromium, iron, and other minerals and subjecting them to the proper pressure and temperature in laboratory ovens, it's even possible to produce a crystal that contains inclusions. When materials such as pyrite and mica are introduced in advance and become crystallized, it's hard to detect the difference between an artificial and a natural crystal.

Imitation or fake stones are another matter; they may be made of glass or plastic, and sometimes the base of the stone is covered with a metallic paper that artificially enhances its low brilliance. These imitation stones may be composed of various materials, but in general, they're easy to detect, since they have superficial scratches and small bubbles inside them. They can also be identified by the simple refraction of their glass composition, as opposed to the double refraction of most real gems.

Identification

Since synthetic and natural gems have very similar physical properties, they can't simply be identified by visual inspection. In many cases, the use of a microscope is required. Generally, synthetic gems don't display irregularities, and commonly, they are very clean on the inside. Inclusions found in natural gems are in small fractures, even though it's also possible to reproduce them in synthetic and imitation gems. To positively identify a gem, it's necessary to use various laboratory tools. One is the refractometer, which measures light refraction; another is the polariscope, which checks whether materials are singly refracting (diamonds, spinel rubies, garnets, and glass) or doubly refracting (emeralds, amethysts, and natural and synthetic rubies and sapphires). A spectroscope is also used to determine the spectrum of absorption. Other tools include a microscope, a dark field illuminator, and the binocular loupe, especially for colored, transparent, and translucent stones.

Gems can also be identified by their density or specific gravity. This test involves a series of approximations based on liquids of known density. That way, if a stone floats in a liquid with a relative density of 4 and sinks in another with a density of 3, its density will lie between those limits and be around 3.5.

▲ These synthetic gems have the same internal structure as a natural crystal, and possess visual qualities that are very close to those of a fine gem. They can be distinguished by their lack of inclusions and growth curves. The first cut on these bottle-shaped boules is usually longitudinal.

▼ Synthetic zirconite, in raw and cut form

Diamonds

Diamonds have very special internal qualities. In addition to being the hardest stones known, they have specific colors, and they can be cut only in certain ways.

While they were being formed, diamonds were subjected to great pressure and temperature. The external conditions in their surroundings, specifically, *kimberlite* or diamond rock, which grew on a geological scale and assimilated pure carbon from the surroundings, also contributed to their development. A diamond begins in an atom of pure carbon; it coordinates tetrahedrically with its four neighbors, forming what's known as a polyhedron of coordination. This is an atomic formation in cubes that grows in a consistent way, so that the outer appearance is a reflection of the interior. By way of analogy, it's like piling up ice cubes to produce a larger cube; it would be difficult make a cube if the individual parts were not cubes.

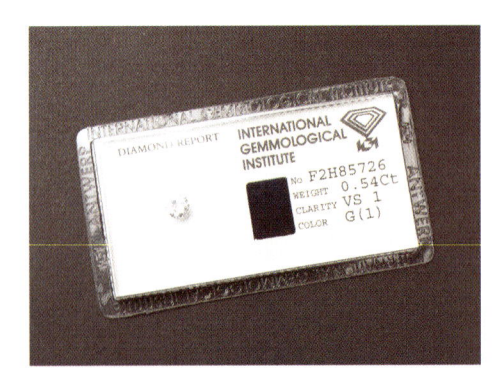

◀ Each diamond is unique and possesses an identifying set of characteristics. After the stones are cut, gemologists who specialize in diamonds examine and rank them according to an internationally accepted classification.

◀ Diamonds are 100 percent cubically crystallized; this is an essential, definitive factor in their exfoliation and subsequent cutting.

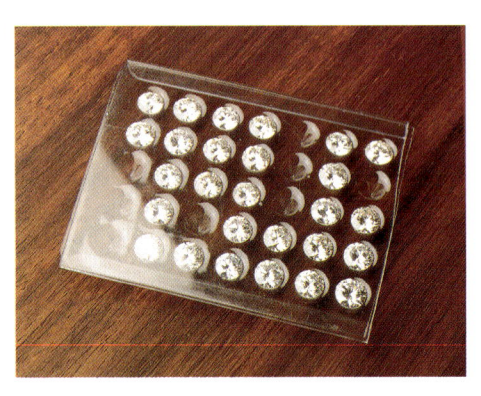

◀ The color in diamonds is due to nitrogen; in fact, diamonds are classified as *group A* when they have no nitrogen atoms or molecules and are therefore very white; *group B* is for diamonds that contain nitrogen, and therefore exhibit color.

DIAMOND COLOR SCALES

GIA	CIBJO / HRD	SCANDINAVIAN
D	Exceptional white +	River
E	Exceptional white	River
F	Rare white +	Top Wesselton
G	Rare white	Top Wesselton
H	White	Wesselton
I	Slightly tinted white	Top Crystal
J	Slightly tinted white	Crystal
K	Tinted white	Top Cape
L	Tinted white	Top Cape
M	Color 1	Cape
N	Color 1	Cape
O	Color 2	Cape
P	Color 2	Cape
Q	Color 3	Light Yellow
R	Color 3	Light Yellow
S	Color	Light Yellow
T	Color	Light Yellow
U	Color	Light Yellow
V	Color 4	Yellow
X	Color 4	Yellow
Y	Color 4	Yellow
Z	Color 4	Yellow

Four Characteristics that Determine the Quality of a Diamond

◆ **Color**

In diamonds, the most sought-after color is white, or the absence of color. The color scale goes from pronounced white to yellow, according to the internationally accepted classification that's used for evaluation; this classification is performed by a specialized gemologist. In order to determine the color gradient, a specific quality is assigned by comparing the stone to samples. Various color scales are used in the diamond industry; the ones most commonly encountered are *GIA*, *CIBJO*, and *Scandinavian*.

◆ **Purity**

Diamonds contain tiny impurities and inclusions; their number, color, size, and location determine a stone's quality, and therefore its price on the market. Impurities also affect the stone's brilliance. Diamonds can be classified by a gemologist using a 10x loupe.

◀ Clean diamonds that have no inclusions are rare. It's estimated that, of this number, around 70 percent of them are not usable for jewelry. And on average, a stone cut in the shape of a diamond weighs just a little more than 40 percent of its original weight. This photo shows a brilliant cut diamond of exceptional purity and color.

SCANDINAVIAN	GIA	CIBJO
FL-IF	FL-IF	Flawless under a 10x loupe
VVS-1	VVS-1	VVS-1
VVS-2	VVS-2	VVS-2
VS-1	VS-1	VS-1
VS-2	VS-2	VS-2
SI-1	SI-1	SI-1
SI-2	SI-2	SI-2
*		
P-1	I-1	P-1
P-2	I-2	P-2
P-3	I-3	P-3

▲ FL: *Flawless* (no inclusions)
 IF: *Internally flawless* (no internal inclusions)
 VVS: *Very, very small inclusions*
 VS: *Very small inclusions*
 SI: *Small inclusions*
 P: *Piqué* (large or significant inclusions)
 I: *Imperfect*

* *Recently there has been a tendency to use a new grade, S13, a commercial classification that permits setting a price between SI and Piqué.*

▶ The professional way to buy a diamond: weigh the diamond on a balance or carat scale, and multiply its weight by the reference price per carat.

◆ **Weight**

Formerly, the weight of a gem was compared to that of a carob seed; since four of these seeds weighed about 200 mg, the weight of the carat unit was set at 200 mg. Now, a carat is the standard unit of weight measurement for gems, and the combination of the weight and the quality of the stone determines the diamond's final price.

A carat is divided into 100 points, expressed to two decimal places. Thus, a half-carat diamond is expressed as 0.50 ct.

▼ Weight, color, purity, and cut are the characteristics that determine the value of a diamond. An expert gemologist evaluates these factors with a little equipment: a 10x loupe, a precision scale, a sieve, and some tweezers. The diamond is examined against a background (preferably white), using a cold fluorescent light.

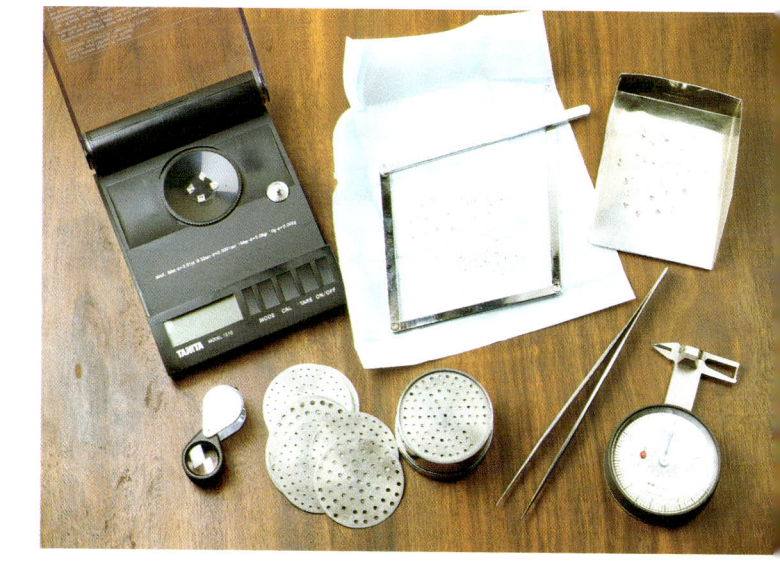

◆ **Cut**

Diamonds are normally cut to specific dimensions that will produce the greatest possible brilliance and reflection. The most common cut for diamonds is the brilliant cut. The quality of the cut is crucial in evaluating a diamond, and thus it is a decisive factor in the ultimate price of the stone. The proportion, shape, symmetry, and finish are important considerations.

Identifying Diamonds

So far, *zirconite* and *moissanite* are the most perfect imitations of a genuine diamond. Zirconite, with a refraction and dispersion index close to diamonds, is a very good imitation. Just the same, it's easy to identify with a 10x loupe, or, with a little experience, the naked eye. In recent years, new materials such as moissanite have appeared; some are very nearly perfect and difficult to identify.

In reality, the identifying characteristics of a diamond are its physical properties. Diamonds convey heat quickly, and thus can be identified with a *conductimeter*, which

◀ The most common way to cut a diamond is a round brilliant. But diamonds are also cut in an oval or tear-drop shape, using the same number of facets as in the brilliant cut; thus, these cuts are referred to as oval brilliant, teardrop brilliant, and marquise or pear brilliant. There are other possibilities, with different numbers and shapes of facets, such as the emerald or rectangular cut; faceted girdles can also be created.

measures the speed at which heat is transmitted through the gem. The conductimeter makes it possible to distinguish zirconite from diamond; however, this device doesn't work with moissanite, although there are some new testers that can identify this material. Conductivity can also be detected without the instruments. If you breathe on a diamond, the vapor disappears quickly; but if you repeat the process with a zirconite or other diamond-like material, the vapor takes longer to evaporate. A little practice with this technique can help identify a diamond without using any equipment. Another way to identify a diamond without the aid of technology is to place a droplet of water from a syringe onto the top facet or table; the droplet doesn't spread out, but remains in a hemispherical shape because of the *lipophilic* property of diamonds; in other words, diamonds have an oily quality. This property is also useful when separating diamonds from the rest of the material as they are extracted from the mines. Another test involves putting the stones into *methylene iodide* diluted to 3.32; moissanite will float, and diamonds and zirconite will sink.

With the 10x loupe, it's possible to see any irregularities that help identify a diamond; these can include a speck of carbon, a defective facet, or an extra facet on the diamond's pavilion. Any imperfection can serve as an indication that the stone is indeed a diamond. The girdle is often slightly matte in diamonds; that's not the case with zirconite, however, which tends to be uniformly brilliant, even though it may sometimes appear to have a thick, pronounced stripe. In some diamonds, the girdle is cut with up to 100 extra facets, and some stones even have a faceted and polished culet.

Moissanite and Zirconite

Currently, moissanite is the material that's most similar to diamonds. Its hardness, brilliance, and transparency are very close to that of a diamond; its high refraction produces gems with great luster, and it looks practically the same as a diamond. It's possible to distinguish the difference with a 10x loupe, but it's not easy; the girdle is commonly polished the same way as a diamond, but through the loupe it looks a bit satiny, with brighter edges than zirconite. Its fluorescence is variable, of a very weak orange-mustard color; also, it shows much more color play or *scintillation* than a diamond, since it has better dispersion and produces scintillations in all colors of the rainbow. Moissanite has double refraction that is visible in its double facets, since its structure is hexagonal, rather than cubical, as with diamonds. This birefringence can be seen with a 10x loupe by looking at the facets of the culet through its table.

Even though zirconite is artificial, it's crystallized in the cubic system, and consequently it doesn't exhibit the phenomenon of birefringence. Moissanite also may present small inclusions in the form of tiny, white tubes parallel to the optical axis. Zirconite is distinguished from diamonds because its edges are more blunt, and it may show tiny fractures in the girdle; the edges exhibit a mustard-yellow fluorescence that gives a false reading on a conductimeter.

Another good imitation of diamonds is *strontium titanate*, which is not as hard and can be scratched by a diamond. It also has spectacular color play, which is one way to identify it. Other imitations include white sapphire, rock crystal, clear quartz, and the chemical imitations GGG (*gadolinium gallium garnet*), YAG (*yttrium aluminum garnet*), and *lithium niobate*.

▼ A 10x loupe is essential in jewelry making; for grading diamonds, it must be a dichroic lens composed of three pieces of glass, joined together to form one compound lens. The loupe must be corrected so it has no chromatic aberration or sphericity.

REFERENCE TABLE				
	Refraction Index	Dispersion	Density	Hardness
Moissanite	2.65-2.69	0.104	3.21	9.25
Diamond	2.42	0.044	3.51	10
Zirconite	2.19	0.060	5.65	8-8.25

Pearls

In contrast to precious stones, pearls are an organic material formed inside a mollusk (either an oyster or a mussel). They are produced as a natural reaction to the presence of a foreign body, such as a grain of sand (introduced naturally) or a piece of natural shell (introduced artificially by humans). With the presence of this foreign body and proper conditions, the oyster produces successive, concentric layers of *nacre* as a defense mechanism, covering the irritant and producing a pearl.

Nacre is composed of microscopic crystals of *aragonite* (a form of calcium carbonate) combined with *conchiolin*; its quality and thickness endow the pearl with its ultimate beauty and its value.

◀ Piero della Francesca, detail from *Portrait of Battista Sforza and Federico de Montefeltro,* 1450-1466. Florence, Italy.
Pearls are one of the most commonly used classical elements in jewelry. Because of their organic nature, they seem designed to be worn and exhibited.

Cultured Pearls

In a desire to produce more pearls of a better quality, man learned to insert a small foreign body into the oyster. Commonly, this object is a small piece of polished shell, which is converted into a pearl after a couple of years of very delicate care. These are cultured pearls.

Nowadays, research and technical advances have increased pearl production and created better quality gems; breeds of oysters have been isolated that produce pearls of very fine luster and exceptional quality. No matter how many pearls are produced, no two are identical; in order to produce a piece of jewelry such as a necklace, you must carefully select pearls with comparable luster and color, and that takes a lot of experience in the field.

Culture

The first step in producing cultured pearls involves implanting a small bit of polished shell and a piece of mantle tissue inside the oyster, so that the oyster begins to secrete successive layers of nacre. After the oysters have been implanted, they are given optimum conditions to develop. As they grow, the oysters are suspended in pools, where specialists continually monitor the temperature and feeding conditions to assure ideal development. Oysters will be cleaned, freed of parasites and algae, and even medicated, in some instances.

It's very complicated to culture a quality pearl. It's estimated that only five percent of all implanted oysters produce a pearl of extraordinary quality; the vast majority of oysters don't live through the implantation phase, and the rest don't survive changes of temperature and salinity. Invasions of plankton, such as the red tide, can deplete the oxygen supply and suffocate the oysters.

▶ *Swiss Soldier*, 1680. Museo degli Argenti, Florence, Italy. Enameled gold, pearls, and pink diamonds.

Types of Pearls

Pearls cultured in Japan and China have excellent luster, especially the Japanese ones, from the Akoya oyster. There is also the pearl of the southern seas (Australia, Myanmar, and Indonesia), which commonly is larger. There are also black pearls that come from French Polynesia; these are continually gaining in acceptance. The river or freshwater pearl, which comes primarily from Japan, China, and the United States, is cultivated in mussels that live in fresh water and has lower luster and is less valuable.

How to Choose a Quality Pearl

There are five basic characteristics for choosing a quality pearl.

The **luster** of a good pearl should be brilliant, not opaque; you should be able to see your own reflection on the surface. As light is reflected in the successive layers of nacre, it produces an iridescent sheen that's known as the *orient of the pearl*; this is one of the prime characteristics of a good pearl. Disregard opaque pearls that look like plaster.

The **surface** must be clean and free of bulges and hollows; the smoother the surface, the higher the value of the pearl.

The **shape** of the pearl should be as spherical as possible. The more perfect the sphere, the greater the value.

The **color** can range from white to pink, but brown and black are also acceptable, depending on the area and the type of mollusk used in culturing.

The **size** of a pearl is calculated in millimeters of diameter. Pearls can reach a diameter of 20 millimeters. The greater the size, the higher the price.

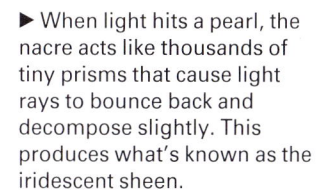

▶ When light hits a pearl, the nacre acts like thousands of tiny prisms that cause light rays to bounce back and decompose slightly. This produces what's known as the iridescent sheen.

▲ Australian pearl necklace by Carles Codina

▲ Various strands of cultured pearls classified according to their quality, diameter, and brilliance

Cutting Precious Stones

In general, gems in their raw state are not particularly beautiful. Their magnificent color and brilliance reach maximum splendor only after being cut. Cutting is an important factor that has a tremendous impact on the ultimate price of a precious stone; it's a feature that is continually gaining in appreciation, since it depends entirely on the skill and dexterity of the artist. During the cutting process, the artisan penetrates right to the natural shape of a crystal; this independent variable will enhance or diminish the natural characteristics inherent in the crystal.

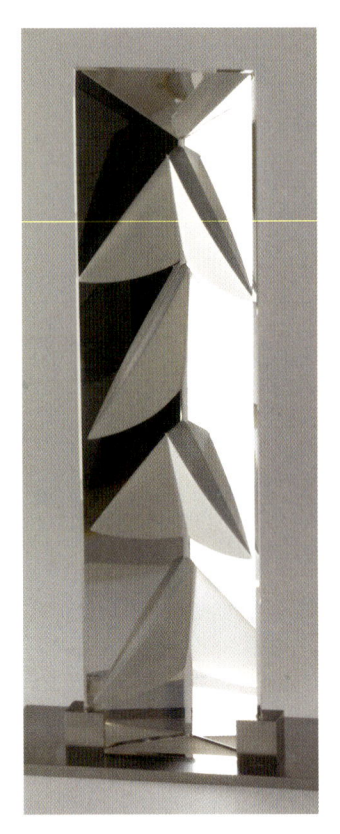

◀ Tom Munsteiner, *Magic Eye*. Piece using a 5.20-carat cut amethyst and quartz with tourmaline inclusions.

◀ Gem cutting is undergoing considerable development today, and this chapter explains that there is tremendous latitude for creativity in this endeavor. Here, Tom Munsteiner is photographed through one of his creations.

◀ In most instances, the intent of the cutting process is to produce the greatest possible reflection in the material, to highlight this quality in some piece of jewelry. But that's not always the case, as demonstrated in the innovative works of the Munsteiners. Their techniques represent a new way of understanding light refraction and reflection that is far removed from traditional concepts of cutting and closer to sculptural, artistic values. This photo presents a rock crystal sculpture by Tom Munsteiner.

◀ Cutting essentially gives shape to a crystal to highlight some of its characteristics, such as its brilliance and color, or any natural properties of the material that the lapidary wishes to preserve. The photo shows several gems cut by Bernd Munsteiner.

Crystalline Structure, Hardness, and Fracture

With the exception of the gems that are organic in origin, such as amber, pearls, and coral, gems are obtained from crystals, as discussed earlier. They are solid formations with a definite, ordered internal atomic structure; they are grouped in one of six known crystalline systems according to the specific molecular structure in which the atoms are arranged. Crystals are defined by a series of flat external surfaces known as *plane surfaces,* whose orientation defines the shape of the crystal.

The degree of hardness in a crystal does not necessarily indicate its durability, since crystals tend to fracture in definite directions as a direct consequence of the regular distribution of their atoms. In general, the hardness of a crystal, and therefore of a gem, is a function of its internal structure, and specifically of how the atoms are interconnected; in other words, hardness relates to the gem's atomic structure and the attendant chemical bonds. Some atomic layers are tightly bound together in the interior, and the forces that connect them with the layers immediately above or below are weaker. These layers are known as *planes of exfoliation*, and they are a consideration in any cutting process. As a general rule, the planes are parallel, but they may also be perpendicular or diagonal to the plane surfaces or faces of a crystal, since these surfaces relate to the atomic structure. As a result, the structure of a gem is what determines its hardness and its subsequent exfoliation or fracture. An example of this involves diamond and graphite: both have the same content of carbon atoms, but a diamond is much harder than graphite.

▲ When a mineral or a gem cleaves along a plane, it exfoliates; on the other hand, when the split doesn't follow these planes, it fractures. Sometimes these planes of exfoliation are varied and present a staircase appearance that is very difficult to polish. This gypsum mineral has several exfoliation planes that are visible in this photo.

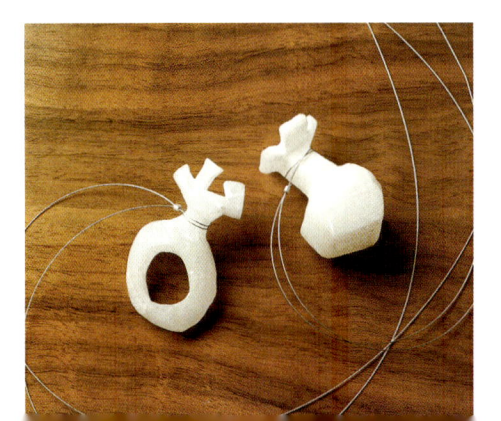

◀ Alabaster is a very soft substance that can be easily and intuitively worked with nothing more than an old file. Jimena Bello created these alabaster pendants.

General Considerations

When choosing a stone to cut, be sure that it is very hard, since this is a crucial factor in the polishing process. Without years of cutting experience, it's preferable to choose a material that's not subject to very simple exfoliation, since unwanted fissures and breaks can develop during the cutting process. These breaks might be induced by a change of temperature, or the tension in the material due to distortions in its growth. If you are a novice, it's a good idea to choose economical material that's also interesting; quartz or a natural spinel ruby might be a good choice, and later on perhaps a garnet. However, avoid gems such as kunzite or topaz, because they are prone to *basal exfoliation*.

Once you have selected the material, study its size in the raw form, as well as the location of possible inclusions and fractures in the crystal, and evaluate the optical and physical characteristics—mainly color, structure, and shape.

▼ In antiquity, gems were used in their natural form; they were simply rounded to create a cabochon using grinding wheels of increasing fineness; then they were polished on a flat disk with abrasives. Gold ring with a cabochon star ruby by Carles Codina.

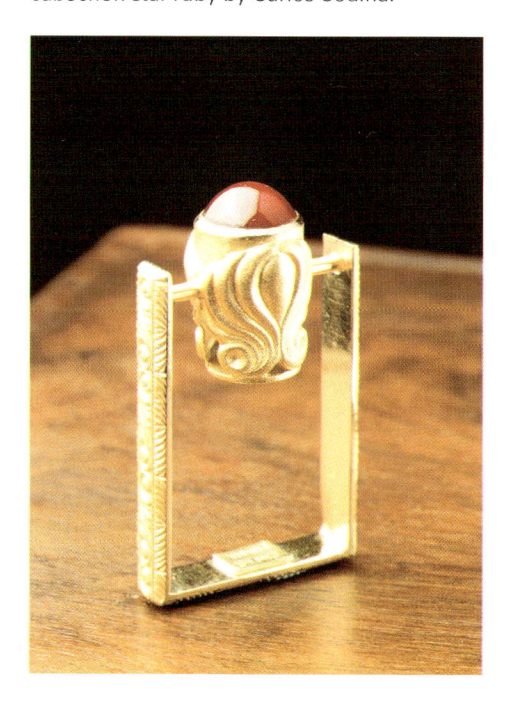

Basic Cutting Procedures for Gems

The cutting of precious stones has evolved tremendously with the advent of completely automated processes, especially with respect to smaller gems. But the procedure remains essentially the same, and today many cutters still work manually, with perhaps only partial automation. (See instructions for cutting diamonds on page 86.)

The first step involves giving the gem an approximate shape or preliminary form. This entails defining the intended shape and size, and each cutter determines this according to the final objective: maximum weight, number of gems desired, highlighting a specific inclusion, producing the right asterism, maximum brilliance, color and transparency, and so forth. These decisions are based on a series of basic procedures.

Sawing and Cleaving

Create the initial shape by sawing the mineral with various metal disks of the thinnest possible construction; these disks contain fine diamond particles and must be cooled constantly with water. These abrasive disks wear down the mineral and penetrate it through abrasion. Some gems, such as diamonds, can be cleaved by striking them, but in general it's a good deal safer and more common to use the diamond saw. In any case, a *crystallographic analysis* should be done before determining the best way to proceed.

Roughing Out

The roughing-out process generally eliminates parts of the gem that have excessive defects and defines the approximate shape of the stone. Held by hand or dopped to the end of a rod, rough out the gem on vertical *silicon carbide* or sintered diamond wheels, or on horizontal cast iron plates that act as a support for the diamond abrasive or silicon carbide powder. Silicon carbide grinders have to be cooled continually with water, as mentioned previously. Press the material against the grinding wheel to remove the excess and create the shape of the gem. Then, the gem will be ready for *faceting*. Silicon carbide wheels tend to leave a very rough surface, and sometimes it is necessary to switch to a finer abrasive. In that case, rub the gem on disks made from an alloy of lead and tin, using a finer-grit abrasive; these materials will produce a finer, matte finish, but the stone won't yet have much transparency.

▲ The cabochon is an appropriate cut for many kinds of gems, including opals. Here is a magnificent brooch using several opal cabochons created by Daniel Kruger.

Perforation

To drill a hole in a gem, first consider the type of mineral and its hardness; the harder it is, the more complicated it is to pierce. Also consider the exfoliation plane and the location for the hole, since some minerals need a certain amount of material surrounding the hole, based on their hardness or fragility. There are some very simple ways to drill a hole in a gem. One of these methods involves using a copper tube mounted like a bit in a drill; the tube helps remove the material and keeps the gem from breaking during the process. The stone and the end of the tube are submerged in a small container of water and fine abrasive, and the stone is slowly drilled. There are also various tungsten carbide drill bits and burs with embedded diamond particles that can be used in small hand drills, as well as some diamond-like composites, if required by the hardness of the material. In any case, it's essential to continually lubricate with water or light oil.

Faceting

Light penetrates the upper part of a cut gem and is reflected by the different facets cut in it, especially the ones on the bottom. These facets function as light mirrors, and they form perfect angles that vary as a function of the optical properties of each mineral, specifically, of their refraction and reflection. For that purpose, each gem requires a specific angle of cut that allows the light to reflect properly through the table.

The faceting process begins with the table or the main facet; this is usually the largest and cleanest one, and is usually opposite the color zone. This operation is done with

◀ Facets reveal the beauty and the brilliance of a gem, especially transparent stones, since the light is reflected from the upper facets after passing through the gem and bouncing off the lower facets. In general, the classic cut has a main facet or **table** on the upper part, which is larger than the rest of the facets; a **crown** that is formed by multiple facets that link the table to the waist or **girdle**; and a **culet,** the lower part that contains the conical shape.

▼ A creative cut like this aquamarine by Tom Munsteiner, with a final weight of 84.54 carats, illustrates how to deviate from the norm and give a gem a personal identity.

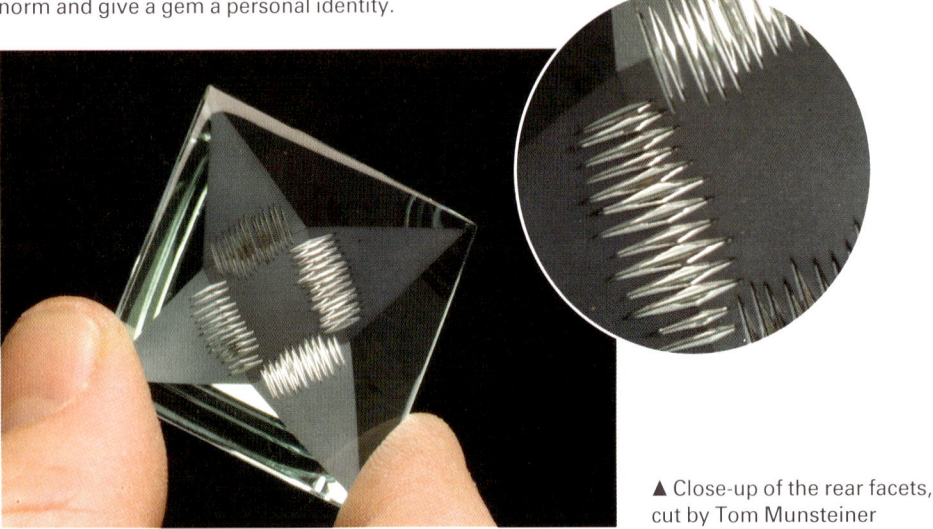

▲ Close-up of the rear facets, cut by Tom Munsteiner

Cutting Diamonds

Diamond cutting requires different conditions and follows different criteria than the methods discussed in the previous section. In general, it's desirable to keep weight loss to a minimum to achieve maximum commercial potential, since the raw material is extremely costly in the marketplace.

Just because diamonds are the hardest stones known doesn't mean that they aren't fragile; a blow in the right place can cleave them, since diamonds exfoliate in directions parallel to the faces of an octahedron (*octahedral exfoliation*). This phenomenon occurs because hardness is a property that varies with the grain direction of the crystal. Diamonds, for example, don't have a uniform hardness; instead, their hardness varies according to the direction of a cut. While cutting, there are some directions of greater hardness that would be preferable compared to others of lesser hardness. Diamonds can be cut only with other diamonds.

Before beginning any cutting process, study the raw gem to decide whether to cleave or saw, based on the imperfections and the chances of achieving the desired results. Generally, after a crystallographic examination, you will cut the initial shape (cube, octahedron, or *dodecahedral rhombus*) in two halves.

Cleaving is a sharp blow oriented along a plane of exfoliation. In general, use a saw on the thickest part of the diamond, partly because of the risk that cleaving involves; but in many instances, it's more desirable not to separate the diamond along the exfoliation planes.

In contrast to what many people may think, diamonds are not perfect. They have imperfections caused by irregularities in their crystalline structure, inclusions and crystallographic tensions, as well as bits of

various horizontal spinning disks made of different materials that hold the abrasive diamond dust. First create the table, and then polish it so it can serve as a guide in creating the other facets of the gem; this is the facet through which the light enters and is reflected back. Varying abrasives are used to polish the table, depending on the type of gem; for quartz, a methacrylate disk is used as a support, along with *cerium oxide* powder.

After the table is polished, attach the gem to the end of a metal rod, using an adhesive that allows it to be manipulated. The rod is referred to colloquially as the *dop.* It's very important for the table to be perfectly centered with respect to the axis of the dop so that the subsequent facets will be perfectly symmetrical.

Secure the dop in the faceting machine, and do preliminary polishing on the girdle by holding it against the spinning abrasive wheel; next, adjust the angle of the facet on the machine, and press the gem against the wheel again. Proceed in this order to create all the facets on the top part of the gem. Afterward, turn the gem and secure the completed top part to the dop, exposing the culet for faceting.

Polishing and Buffing

Faceting produces a precise finish that has to be completed with careful polishing. Even with good material and an exceptional job of cutting, the brilliance will not be satisfactory if the surface is not polished properly. Very hard crystals take a better polish, and therefore have better brilliance. Very fine-grit diamond disks, and copper or metal alloy disks coated with different abrasives, are used for polishing; the most common and traditional examples include *chromium oxide*, cerium oxide, and *aluminum oxide.* To check that a facet is perfectly polished and brilliant, reflect light off the surface and examine any detail reflected in it. To polish large facets, use leather chamois disks of different diameters saturated with cerium oxide.

carbon that are commonly tiny garnets. These appear black because the *refraction index* of these stones is inferior to that of diamonds. The garnet produces a crystallographic tension in the diamond, and that may cause the saw to stop cutting when it encounters the carbon. Worse yet, when a sharp blow is administered in the cleaving process, it may not produce a clean break into two halves, but rather create a multitude of pieces.

After sawing or cleaving (step 2), next round the two halves that result from the division. The process is *bruting*, and it's performed in a different, specialized workshop. Bruting produces a girdle around 90 percent of the table or main facet (step 3).

Faceting is done after bruting. First, trace four facets in the form of a cross on the upper part, or the *bezel*, and also on the lower part, the *pavilion* (step 4). Once the cross has been created, there are eight quadrangular facets or comets on the same angle as the previous ones; they form the perimeter of the table. From this point on, grind the triangular facets on the bezel, known as stars (step 5). Next, grind the median facets, spherical triangles that go from the vertex of the star to the girdle, around the shape of the comets of the main facets (step 6). Do the faceting and polishing simultaneously on a porous cast-iron disk known as a *scaif*, which should be coated with diamond dust. Eight basic facets should be ground first in the culet; a pair of comet facets is made on each one, for a total of 16 (figure 1).

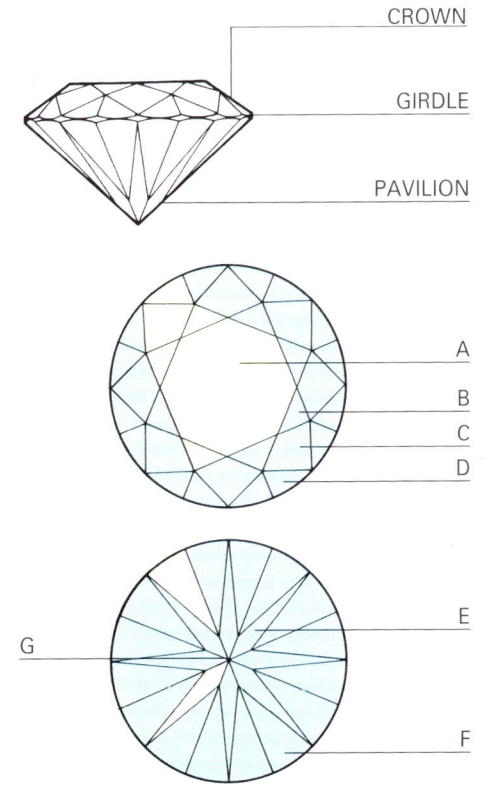

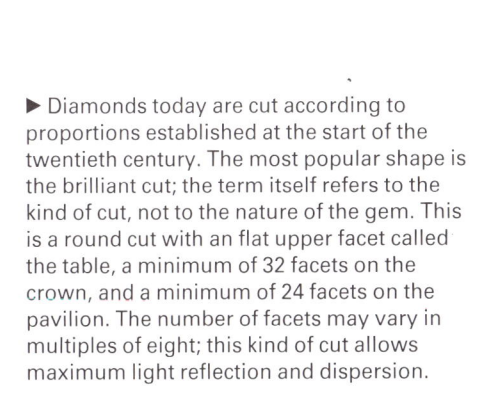

▶ Diamonds today are cut according to proportions established at the start of the twentieth century. The most popular shape is the brilliant cut; the term itself refers to the kind of cut, not to the nature of the gem. This is a round cut with an flat upper facet called the table, a minimum of 32 facets on the crown, and a minimum of 24 facets on the pavilion. The number of facets may vary in multiples of eight; this kind of cut allows maximum light reflection and dispersion.

▲ Diamond cutting follows precise rules because the stones are so hard; this is a costly and complicated technique. The process of faceting a diamond on a turning abrasive wheel is illustrated in the photo.

▶ In general, it's slower and more costly to saw a diamond than to cleave it. Sawing a one-carat diamond takes about eight hours—barring problems—with constant vigilance by specially trained people. The photo shows the process of sawing a diamond; workshops where sawing is done have large collections of saws that use high-speed phosphorus copper disks for cutting. The cutting edge of each disk is coated with a paste of oil and diamond dust.

▼ Figure 1. **Crown:** Table or main facet (A); eight star facets (B); eight quadrangular bezel facets (C); and 16 upper girdle (triangular or half) facets (D).
Pavilion: Eight pavilion (basic, lower) facets (E); 16 lower girdle (triangular or half) facets (F); and 1 culet (G).

▼ Phases of diamond cutting

▲ Step 1    ▲ Step 2

▲ Step 3    ▲ Step 4

▲ Step 5    ▲ Step 6

Bernd Munsteiner, Master Gem Cutter

Since gems are obtained from crystals, they are costly, unique materials with physical properties that require special handling by experienced artisans. Today, most cutting processes are mechanized and automated. This often leaves little room for the creative individual, whose goal is to preserve as much of the gem's weight as possible and extract from it all possible brilliance and color.

Quartz, beryl, and all other gem-quality crystals behave differently from other types of material. Cutting and endowing a gem with unique characteristics is quite complicated, requiring not only professionalism and experience, but also a special disposition and a certain creative spirit.

Bernd Munsteiner is one of the pioneers in a new type of gem cutting that departs from the norm. His professional path has given rise to a new artistic form of expression in this field; it has demonstrated a different interpretation of this speciality that breaks with old concepts. His work brings together the cutting of precious stones and the very values of the modern world, with criteria that are more artistic than material. This innovator demonstrates clearly how cutting precious stones is also a process of artistic creation; he is skilled in endowing his gems with a distinctive personality and identity, and this is a quality that's hard to find in the world of precious stones.

Munsteiner begins with a thorough observation of the nature of the material he will work. He investigates what's going on inside the crystal: its color, its purest areas, its inclusions, and its crystalline structure. He observes and finally decides on a shape for the crystal, but does so without imposing a predetermined idea on the work. Every work of his is based on a concept, and the execution is also excellent, a perfect melding of his refined aesthetic and workmanship. His philosophy motivates him and inspires him to cut, as he demonstrates in his most recent work. He calls this process "prism" cutting; described in the following pages, it's a method wherein the artist exhibits a deep respect for the very nature of the material with which he is working.

▲ Munsteiner interprets the inner nature of the material and makes it part of his cutting process, blending sensitivity and a profound knowledge of the material, resulting from his respect for nature. Above all, he succeeds in endowing the gems with a personality—previously, something that has been difficult to accomplish. In this photo, he is polishing *Metamorphosis I*, a rock crystal with shiny, needle-like rutile inclusions. Photo by Ludgar Grunwald.

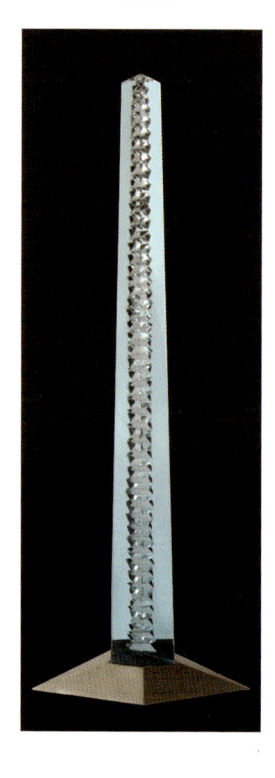

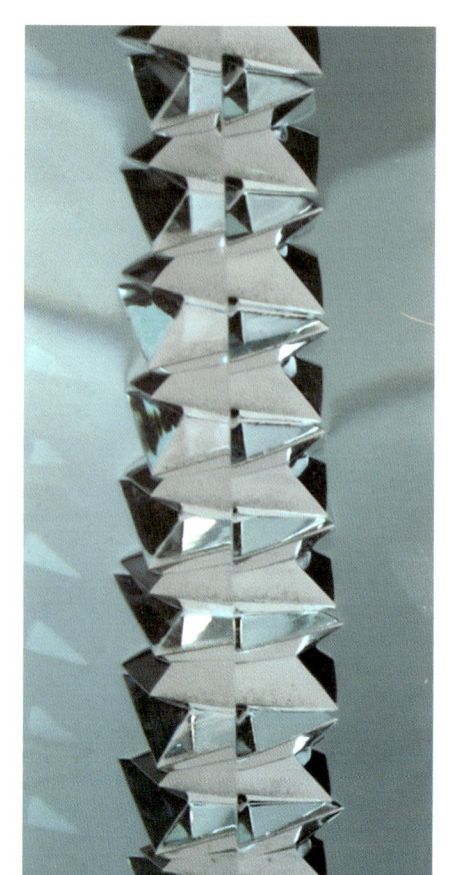

◀ He seems to have an intuitive way of cutting, as if he interprets the nature of the stone and combines it with the cutting process to achieve a perfect balance between the interior and the exterior.

◀ 355-carat aquamarine, mounted on platinum

◀ Detail of the sculpting at the rear of the aquamarine

Gems

▲ Some works are absolutely unmistakable compared to those that attempt to imitate it. Gilded beryl weighing 92.32 carats, cut by Bernd Munsteiner.

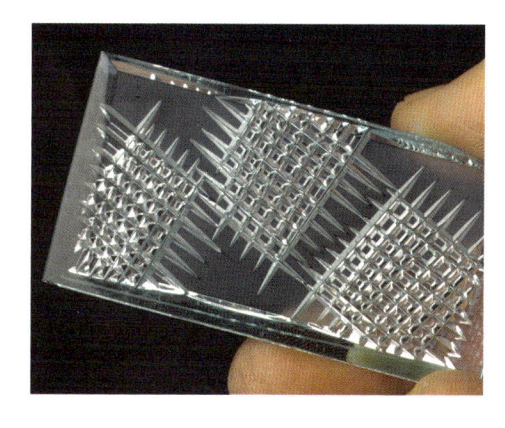

▲ Aquamarine weighing 134.07 carats

▲ Many inclusions in a gem are often considered defects that reduce its value, but for some gemologists, an inclusion can reveal a stone's identity and origin. Some lapidaries feel these flaws deserve to be respected and should be integrated into the work. Shown here, the renowned *Don Pedro* aquamarine, weighing 1072 carats, with a silver and jade base. Work sculpted in 1993 by Bernd Munsteiner.

▲▲ *Millennium Crystal Reflections*. 100 citrines mounted on aluminum and steel; one of his recent creations.

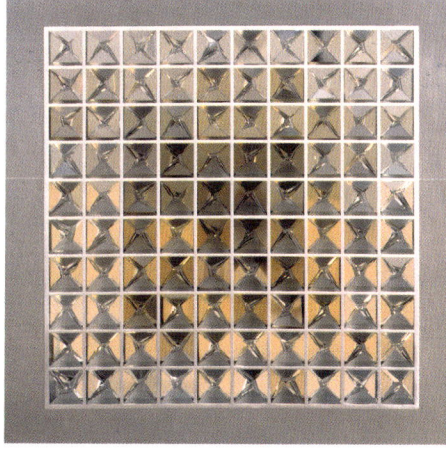

◀ *Tourmaline Reflection*. Brooch made by Munsteiner using tourmalines and peridots.

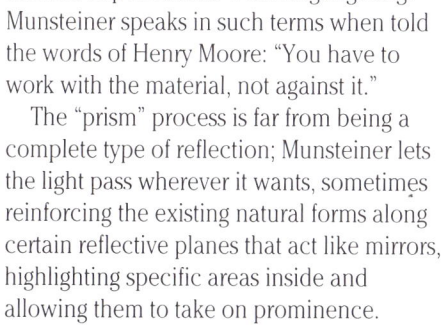

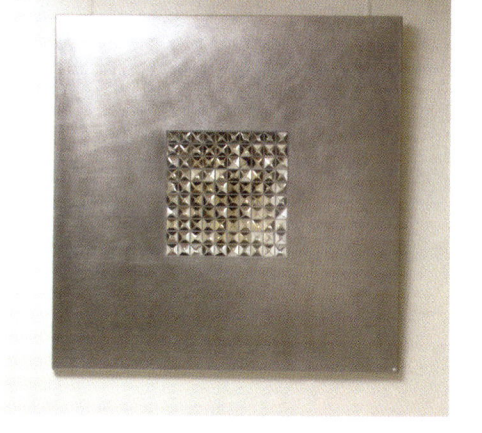

▼ Detail of the preceding work

"Prism" Cutting

In the following pages, Munsteiner demonstrates one of his recent processes, a philosophy of cutting that he designates "prism cutting." This method reflects contemporary values; it's a manual process that appears simple, but is indeed a synthesis of experience on the part of the artisan, in which the main consideration is clearly the nature of the stone itself. This process is based on the shape of the prism that occurs in nature, and that's the only shape that Munsteiner uses in cutting, sometimes using the internal lines that the material suggests to him.

As a system of cutting, "prism" involves a new interpretation of the crystal, one respecting the nature of a crystal that may include imperfections worth highlighting. Munsteiner speaks in such terms when told the words of Henry Moore: "You have to work with the material, not against it."

The "prism" process is far from being a complete type of reflection; Munsteiner lets the light pass wherever it wants, sometimes reinforcing the existing natural forms along certain reflective planes that act like mirrors, highlighting specific areas inside and allowing them to take on prominence.

A Demonstration of "Prism" Cutting by Bernd Munsteiner

Munsteiner has selected several sparkling quartz crystals from Brazil, which he will work simultaneously while he evaluates them, changing his work in response to what each crystal suggests to him at any time. This is a creative yet craftsman-like cutting process that involves no complicated systems of measuring and cutting—a process carried out intuitively and passionately, one that requires observation, sensitivity, and experience.

▲ Every cutting process requires careful selection of good material. Gems can be purchased in the country where the mineral originates, but sales may also take place in the workshop. A fair price is negotiated after studying the material.

▲ Although Tom and Bernd Munsteiner produce different results, they use the same criteria when they begin cutting. The process is decided on the studio table, in response to the needs of each cutter and the characteristics of the mineral.

▲ 1. Bernd Munsteiner knows what possibilities a certain crystal possesses before he begins cutting it. He takes several crystals, inspects them, rejects some, and chooses others in a process that involves a continuous examination of the crystal. He looks at the interior of the material and studies how it will relate and integrate with the entire gem once it's cut.

▲ 2. The first pass is cutting the material on saws. This is done with a large metal disk studded with diamonds 1 mm in diameter, constantly cooled in water so it's possible to saw great quantities of crystal. He secures the crystal firmly in a wooden clamp and presses it against the diamond wheel at a predetermined angle.

▲ 3. Here, Munsteiner has selected new clear quartz crystals that he considers appropriate for "prism" cutting because of their shape and internal attributes, and he makes more preliminary cuts in the material.

◄ 4. He works several crystals at the same time, cutting them in broad planes so he can better see inside the crystal. He makes a number of decisions as he continues to make ever smaller and more precise cuts.

◄ 5. Munsteiner now cuts these large crystals on a smaller and thinner diamond wheel than the one in the previous photo. This diamond wheel is about .5 mm thick, and is much more precise than the previous wheel. It's essential that he use a saw with a water reservoir to keep the disk constantly wet.

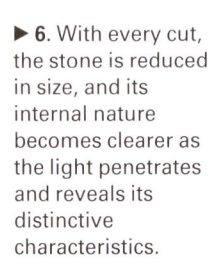

► 6. With every cut, the stone is reduced in size, and its internal nature becomes clearer as the light penetrates and reveals its distinctive characteristics.

▲ 7. With a smaller machine, it's not necessary to hold the crystal in a clamp; he cuts the material as he holds it by hand and presses it against the front of the diamond wheel.

▶ 8. Munsteiner looks into the quartz and applies his philosophy, a ceaseless process of observation, experimentation, and adjustment that he employs passionately; this is his intuitive way of working that breaks with the traditional cutting methods.

▶ 10. Successive cuts through the plane of the star more clearly reveal the inner nature of this stone and suggest the final cut. He executes the cuts with great care by exerting a regular and constant pressure on the wheel, since any lateral movement could break the crystal.

▲ 9. He works different quartz crystals at the same time; the nature of each one suggests how he should cut it. The discovery of a rutile star inside one of the pieces prompts a longitudinal cut with the saw.

◀ 11. It's difficult to reveal a star, and accomplishing it requires a certain amount of experience. It is necessary to do gradual, tentative cuts that safely allow access to the star. Munsteiner cuts away all the material that doesn't have the right transparency, so the star can be seen in its greatest splendor.

◀ 12. Now the star is clearly visible, but there's still a high risk of cutting through it. He will have to make more cuts to remove opaque areas and get even closer to the star inside.

Clear quartz is not a particularly expensive material compared to other crystals, such as aquamarines and topazes; with those minerals, it's preferable to seek out purer areas, and to cut more precisely to avoid unnecessary waste.

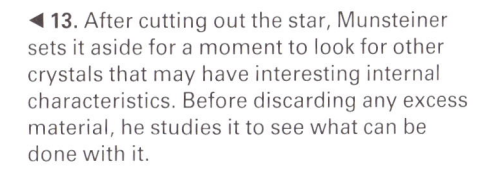

◀ 13. After cutting out the star, Munsteiner sets it aside for a moment to look for other crystals that may have interesting internal characteristics. Before discarding any excess material, he studies it to see what can be done with it.

◀ 14. He inspects several crystals at the same time, making it possible to work faster in the cutting phase. He is first attracted by the internal light and fire of the mineral.

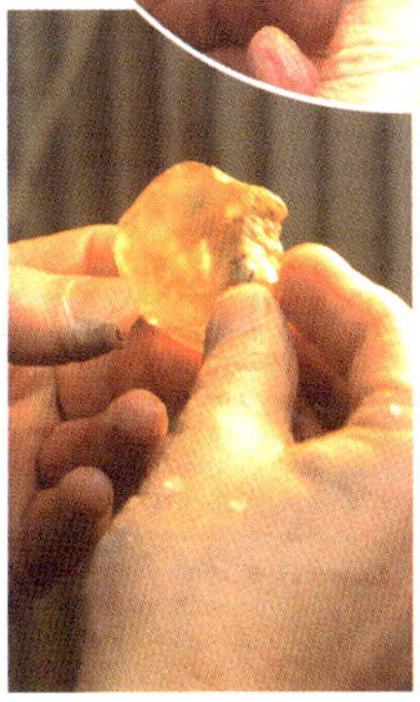

◀ 15. In one of these crystals, Munsteiner sees some crossed rutiles, which may be perfect for "prism" cutting. If so, the process will be the same: make several tentative cuts using the diamond wheel and prepare the crystal for the silicon carbide grindstone.

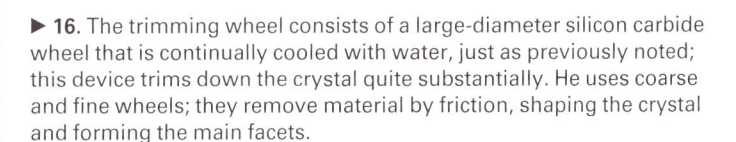

▶ 16. The trimming wheel consists of a large-diameter silicon carbide wheel that is continually cooled with water, just as previously noted; this device trims down the crystal quite substantially. He uses coarse and fine wheels; they remove material by friction, shaping the crystal and forming the main facets.

▲ 17. He holds the material against the wheel as shown in the photo. This type of wheel becomes clogged with material as it's working, so it has to be faced off to create a surface that's rough and even. Silicon carbide wheels can be faced off with black agate or highly vulcanized rubber.

▲ 18. Munsteiner continually monitors how the work is progressing; sometimes he discards the piece or decides to work on it later. In this instance, he is roughing out the first of the selected gems. It now clearly reveals its rutilated star.

▲19. The silicon carbide wheel creates the major facets of the "prism" cut; this is where the mineral is given its definitive shape.

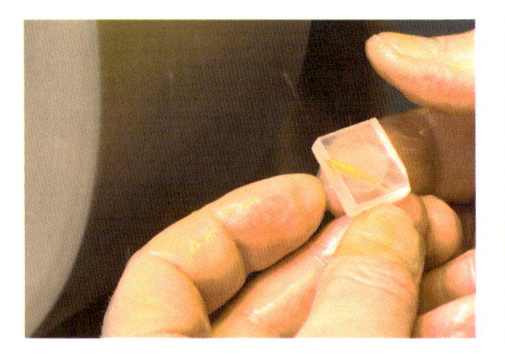

▲ 20. He shapes the various crystals successively and gives them different facets in what will become the definitive "prism" shape, illustrating that this type of cutting must be in balance with the internal nature of the mineral. By this time, he has created the main shape of the gem, and enough material has been removed to allow the stone to be brought to its final form.

▲ 21. Large circular wheels produce slightly curved faces, and these faces have to be perfectly flat and polished. For this step, he secures the stone in dop wax or pitch and smoothes it on a disk made from an alloy of tin and lead. This disk revolves slowly, using a silicon carbide or diamond paste as an abrasive, depending on the hardness of the gem being shaped. To attach the stone, he uses a special dopping wax that softens with heat and hardens at lower temperatures; this facilitates the smoothing of the stone and the creation of the facets.

◄ 23. A perforated surface supports the opposite end of the dop and provides the proper centering and angle to create the different facets of the gem.

◄ 24. During this operation, he uses his sense of touch to check that the face of the gem is perfectly flat; this assures a good polish in subsequent stages and an excellent final polish.

▲ 22. Now, Munsteiner switches to a disk made of copper alloy, to which diamond paste and water are applied. This new disk is used on the main facets created in the preceding step to give the crystal a much finer finish.

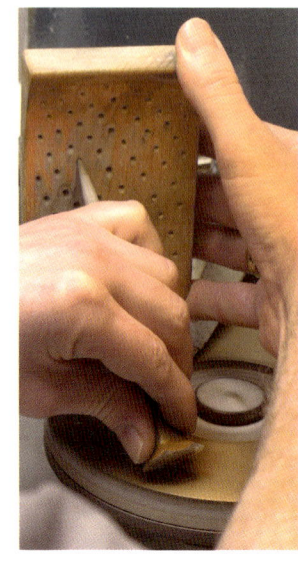

► 25. He uses the same process on each of the facets, so that they are completely flat before proceeding with any further cutting.

Gems

▲ 26. Now he examines the stone, and designs a series of carvings or facets. He may choose to leave certain facets unpolished to allow light to escape without reflecting.

▲ 27. Munsteiner now creates the cuts that are characteristic of his work—facets that reflect light much like mirrors and highlight the internal qualities of the stones, lending a personal touch to his gem cutting.

▲ 28. He creates these shapes using a sintered diamond disk; in this case, the wheel has a thin edge. This type of wheel comes in various shapes and edges; the tool always requires constant cooling with water, as previously mentioned.

▲ 29. Some gems are faceted by making flat surface cuts on the back, a series of brilliant facets that reflect light and contrast with the back of the stone without polishing. This work is also done on a much finer sintered diamond disk that polishes the most recent cuts.

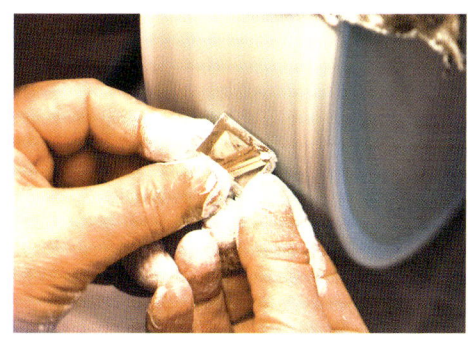

▲ 30. He polishes the facets of some gems on large wheels, which are generally made of felt or leather. Different types of polishing agents are used depending on the hardness of the material being worked; usually, the substances used are cerium oxide and aluminum oxide.

▲ 31. A detailed view of a felt wheel in the polishing machine. The most delicate polishing operations are done on small polishing motors.

◄◄ These photos shows the culmination of Munsteiner's new concept of "prism" cutting. This cutting procedure is based on his personal philosophy and applies a creative concept that respects the essence of the stone.

▼ Here's the final transformation of the rutilated quartz crystal into a 15.38-carat gem. Munsteiner doesn't see this process as the imposition of a shape onto the gem, but rather as an intimate and personal interaction with it.

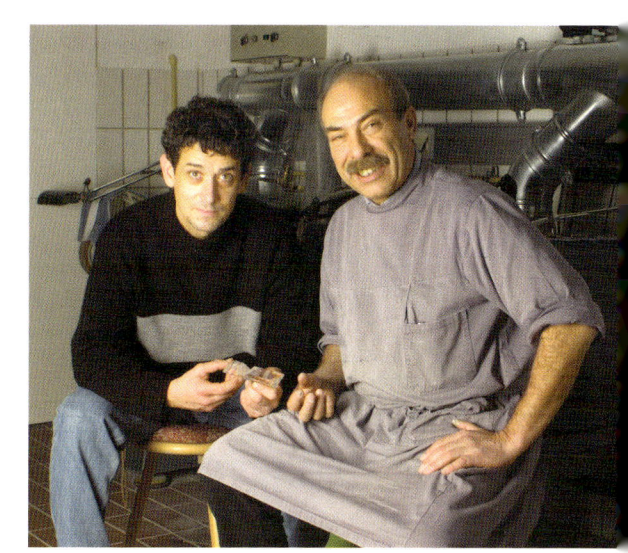

▲ Bernd Munsteiner, right, with the author, after shaping the gems in Munsteiner's workshop in Stipshausen, Germany.

Concept
and Image

Each creative process generally involves a struggle and an interplay among various factors, including decisions regarding color, shape, composition, materials, technique, and so on—thought processes that require the human quality called *creativity*, which varies in response to different objectives. The first part of this chapter is devoted to four different ways to approach this craft. Jewelry making can be understood and interpreted from very different points of view: commercial jewelry, contemporary jewelry, and costume jewelry, for example. The teaching of jewelry making, too, has its unique perspective. You can work creatively in any of these areas, if you employ the contemporary awareness promoted in this book that is evident in the following four sketches.

In the second part of this chapter, some crucial information that is often neglected by many goldsmiths is discussed, namely, creating an image and marketing your work, including the use of photography.

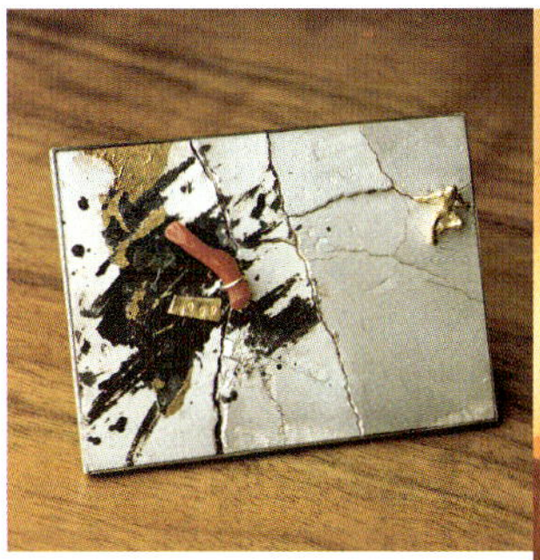
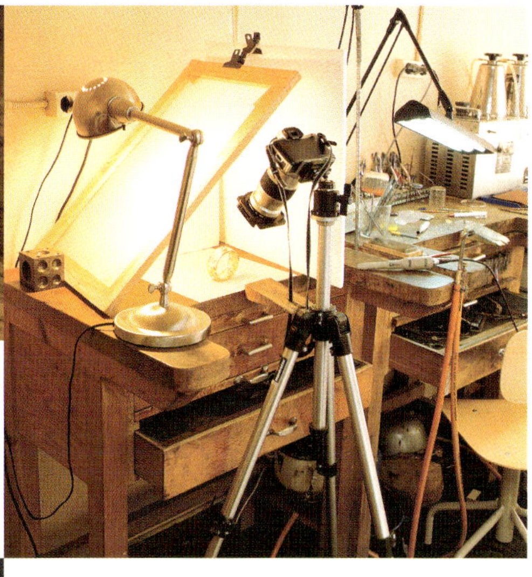
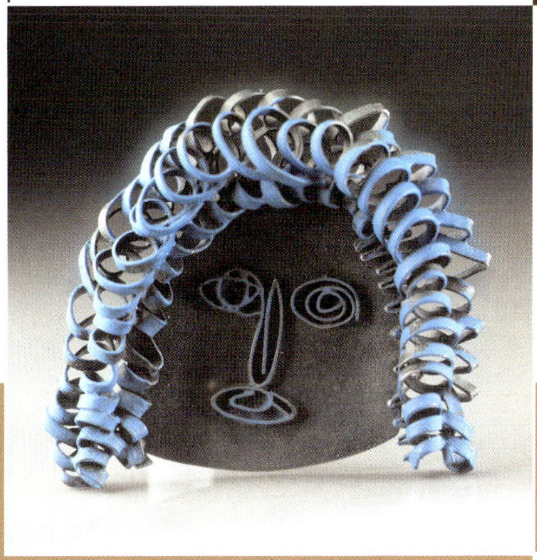
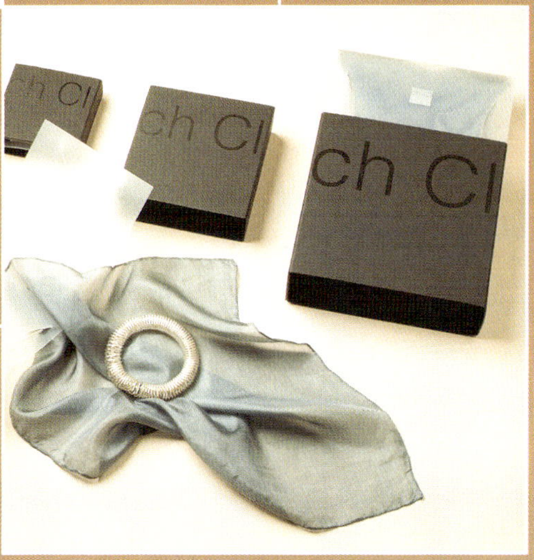
ch Cl
ch Cl
ch Cl

Four Concepts of Creativity

The following section will present four unique ways of understanding and interpreting the reality that is the jewelry business. Here are four distinct concepts—based on different assumptions with different objectives—which nonetheless have in common a clear, creative focus. All four are part of the same craft, using the same resources and some of the same tools. Some of their creations, consciously or not, evoke themes associated with a specific place or culture.

Bagués Jewelers

Bagués Jewelers is a company with a long family tradition that has succeeded in adapting to a varied and competitive market place. It has developed a dynamic management style, and it has introduced collections of jewelry that can be marketed to the broad public without sacrificing any of the company's personal identity. Their success is based on teamwork in the production of distinctive items, developed through a study of culture and history.

Their jewelry collections blend artistic expression with cultural influences that are in line with the company's sales objectives. They developed a sound marketing strategy to get the product into the hands of consumers. This melding of product and marketing approach is underscored by their belief in the uniqueness of the product.

This group of products honors the influence of Catalan art, which is the basis for developing these collections of jewelry. Some specific qualities are taken from this art form, such as the use of color, austerity of shape and movement, and a characteristic treatment of light, which is unique to the Mediterranean region. These are elements that are clearly different from those of other countries and cultures; they are values that are manifest in the very evolution of all aspects of Catalan art, especially in the Romanesque, Gothic, and Modernism movements.

▲ Façade of the distinctive jewelry manufacturer Bagués, located on the lower levels of the historic Amatller House in the center of Barcelona, Spain.

▲ Ring made of yellow gold with enamel, mother-of-pearl, and rock crystal inlays; part of the *Vitralls* collection in tribute to Frank Lloyd Wright.

▼ Pendant/brooch with translucent enamel done in plique-à-jour and basse-taille techniques using diamonds and a pearl; from the *Masriera* collection.

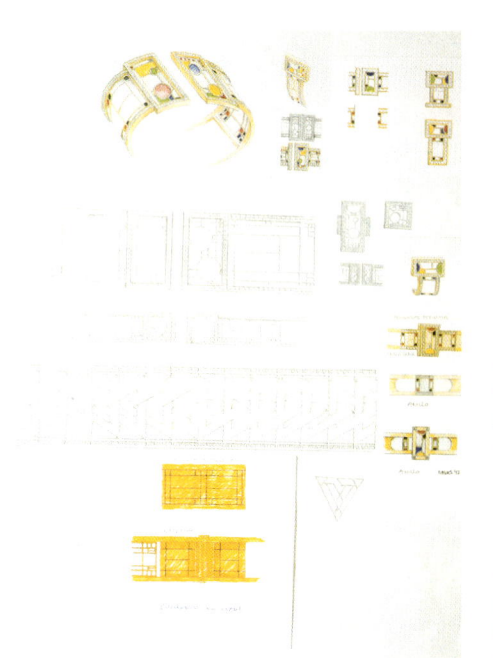

▲ Earrings made of yellow gold with translucent enamel, created with the plique-à-jour technique. These pieces are part of the *Xarxa* collection.

◄ Sketches for a collection inspired by the stained glass designs of the renowned American architect Frank Lloyd Wright (1867–1959).

Concept and Image

Ricard Domingo

Often designers who are finishing their studies try to establish themselves by learning a trade. Some might try to adapt designs and ideas to metropolitan life and street reality, but Ricard Domingo has never done that, mainly because his work and life are the very essence of the street. His career is the perfect expression of the spirit of the modern city life that formed him; it is provocative and sometimes disrespectful, influenced by the urban cultural aesthetic in which he is immersed.

When he finished his studies at the Massana School, Domingo created a small company to sell his jewelry. He soon figured out that one person can't handle every aspect of the business—creating displays, selling, purchasing, designing—and do a professional job of it. He now devotes himself to what he does best: creating a product and its image. Domingo is a nonconformist who works as a freelancer in collection design, and also as an image consultant for prestigious firms in the industry. This work is based on his analysis of the company and a study of the project; then he devises a set of basic premises that allow him to create an up-to-date and coherent image for any given product, in accordance with the needs of the marketplace.

▲ "My work is personal; it's based on a study of the company's image and its prospects. It's the product of a profound knowledge of the marketplace and its evolution."

▲ "One opportunity came from the Adorno Company, a division of the firm Joi d'Art. Here, the challenge was to create a product that adhered to the concepts discussed during the client briefing."

▶ "My packaging designs are intended for the jewelry world; this sector is still a little behind other areas of design, such as the technology and electronics sector; the innovative furniture industry; but especially, the wonderful packaging for the perfume business."

◀ Rings and vase from the summer 1998 collection for the Adorno Company, by Ricard Domingo.

◀▼ One of the first and most representative works by Domingo, a collection of retail items that displays his nonconformist and daring style.

◀ "You have to position a product in the marketplace, decide on a system for displaying the pieces, and sell it without losing sight of the taste, preference, and economic level of the consumer."

Ramón Puig Cuyás

Ramón Puig Cuyás considers jewelry to be a highly personalized art form. Far more than mere ornamentation or a mundane form created in a factory, he considers jewelry to be the ideal medium; it allows him to experience the profound pleasure of using his own hands to give material form to his dreams and desires.

Every one of his pieces of jewelry is the culmination of a long physical and emotional process that attempts to make tangible something indefinable; it's a process for giving expression to his very consciousness.

A memory, a subject, a shape, or a word can be the catalyst for a new work. He begins with a drawing; the drawing explores the various elements, seeking harmony or contrast, balance or tension, and each drawing uncovers the potential of many other possibilities. During this relentless process, Cuyás eventually abandons the drawing and begins working directly with the different materials. This is a most important moment, when he places the material—metal, stone, plastic, etc.—into a relationship and each element has its place in the composition. Then, his goal is for these common objects to cease being inert and acquire a life of their own, revealing something undefined, yet desired.

▲ "What drives me to begin each new work is the need to respond to a challenge, to convert a passing thought into a real feeling. Thinking while working with our hands, in an intimate dialogue with the materials and shapes, humanizes us and helps us find the necessary harmony between ourselves and the world around us."

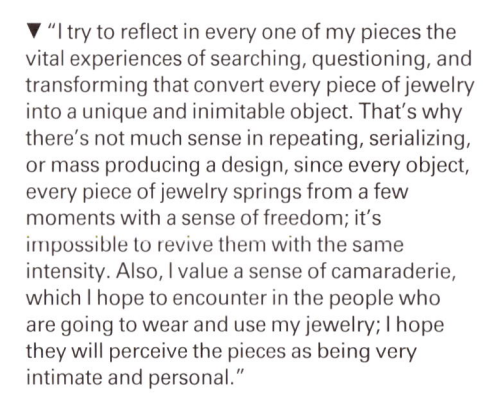

▼ "I try to reflect in every one of my pieces the vital experiences of searching, questioning, and transforming that convert every piece of jewelry into a unique and inimitable object. That's why there's not much sense in repeating, serializing, or mass producing a design, since every object, every piece of jewelry springs from a few moments with a sense of freedom; it's impossible to revive them with the same intensity. Also, I value a sense of camaraderie, which I hope to encounter in the people who are going to wear and use my jewelry; I hope they will perceive the pieces as being very intimate and personal."

▲ "I try to make every one of my works a metaphor, a poetic form of expressing things that can't be communicated rationally, and these metaphors arise in relation to my most immediate surroundings, to my daily landscape, the sea. The Mediterranean, with its light and its smell a constant in my life, is the great inspiration for my poetic language. Also, the horizon, the roads, the sky, the night, the constellations…and voyages, direction, and the discovery of new worlds…all these are a reflection, a poetic allusion to the fascinating voyage of exploration that is creation and life itself."

▼ "In general, I prefer to forego the traditional metals and stones of conventional jewelry, since for me any material can assume the stature of preciousness; this communicates that the value of a piece of jewelry lies more in the emotions and feelings that we project onto it than in expensive materials."

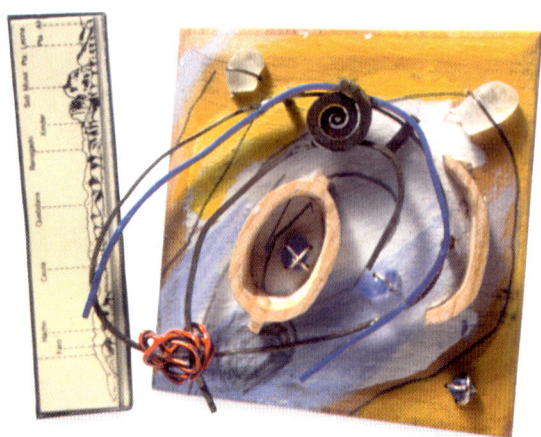

◄ "All of my creations are like the pages of a travel diary, and the people who use them are invited to write their own memories in them."

Joaquim Capdevila

Joaquim Capdevila combines mastery of the trade and a long family tradition with the innovative aspects of contemporary jewelry. His works have evolved from geometric mastery to the creation of more organic shapes and forms with Mediterranean colors and hues. He is a creative artisan who's capable of giving visual expression to his personality, his thoughts and emotions, in a piece that is small enough to fit into the palm of the hand.

He thinks of jewelry as a means of expression that uses his trade as an artistic technique; this allows him to communicate his emotions and passions to his contemporaries, while at the same time suggesting new ideas and concepts, new ways of understanding life. For him, jewelry can cause people to rethink their habits, their traditions, and indeed, redefine their whole way of thinking.

Capdevila believes that all professionals working in an expressive artistic medium have an obligation to be honest with themselves, and they must create projects that they consider worthwhile. This expression advances human progress.

There should be no limits on utopian and daring ideas, because they become the means for investigation and experimentation, capable of opening up new avenues to unforeseen possibilities. Some of these new works may appear useless, but there will always be a few that are not, and the latter are the ones that validate the experiment.

Capdevila likes to make jewelry on commission because he thinks this establishes a human contact that motivates him to create new projects. He accepts a commission as he accepts a relationship with a friend or a client, and the results are varied and enriching, involving a stimulating exchange of ideas and experiences.

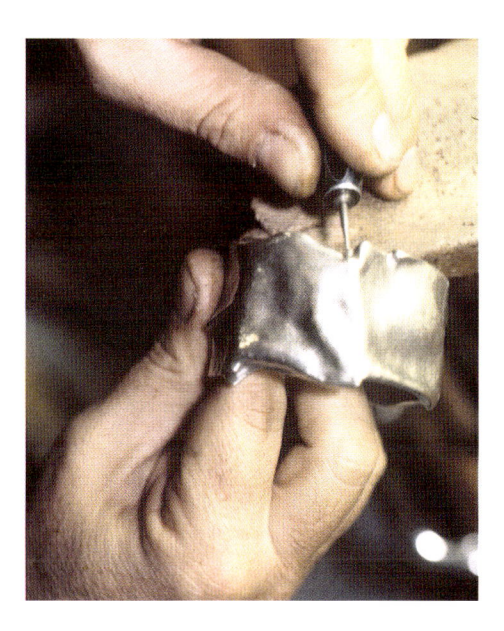

▲ "The hand is the instrument of the mind."

▲ "Look for the cause of things, go back to the origin to rediscover what we were, what we are, and what we hope to be." Photo by Ramon Manent.

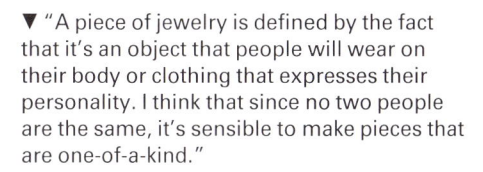

▼ "A piece of jewelry is defined by the fact that it's an object that people will wear on their body or clothing that expresses their personality. I think that since no two people are the same, it's sensible to make pieces that are one-of-a-kind."

▲ "The senses, especially touch and sight, are an inexhaustible source of knowledge. The use of textures, shapes, material, colors, and forms in the conception of these unique objects give us the possibility of communicating, feeling, and being vibrant." Photo by Ramon Manent.

▲ "The complex process of conception and design for a building is applied to constructing a single product. Artists also do paintings that are unique; so why should a piece of jewelry be made more than once, if we consider that it's intended for just one person, far more than a building or a painting is? I can understand making series of pieces, whether on a small-scale or industrial basis, only for objects that do not pretend to make an impact on the user's personality."

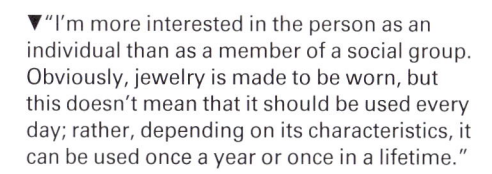

▼ "I'm more interested in the person as an individual than as a member of a social group. Obviously, jewelry is made to be worn, but this doesn't mean that it should be used every day; rather, depending on its characteristics, it can be used once a year or once in a lifetime."

Image and Business

Most artists instinctively create for pleasure; they are motivated to produce items that provide them with personal satisfaction. This perfectly legitimate mindset appeals to many contemporary creators of jewelry. However, if what in fact satisfies the jewelry maker is having other people buy and wear his or her products, then certain business considerations must be taken into account. It's not enough to go out to the marketplace and try to sell a product; to be a successful jeweler, you must identify the market segment for your products and produce works that satisfy the needs of the consumers who compose it. You must develop a sound business plan to achieve success in the marketplace.

▶The display case for jewelry can be simultaneously original and practical. In the photo, a display unit in the Galeria Forum Ferlandina.

Method and Procedure: Client Briefing

Designing a product and creating an image for it (brands, logos, displays, promotional photographs, ads, catalogs, stands, display samples, and packaging), whether for your own work or for someone else's, involves a challenge equal to any other design project. Plan the marketing strategy with your client in a brief.

During this briefing, you and the client should thoroughly discuss the product; this meeting should provide valuable direction for you, the jewelry maker, and have a direct influence on the results.

You should analyze the company placing the order and study the visibility of the project before beginning work. Also, scrutinize the brand's résumé and find out if other designers have done any previous work for the company, and consider the impact your work will have on the company. For example, if you plan a display case, you should find out how they have been made in the past. Check into the availability of human and material resources, yours and the company's, including outside investment, professional level of the employees, technical resources such as machinery, technology, and so forth, since all of this will have an impact on the success of the product. It's also very important to determine the number of pieces in the proposed collection to assure a volume of profitable billing, based on how often the collection will be restocked each year.

Another important factor to consider is the customer for whom the product is destined. It's important to analyze the nature of the shops that will sell the product—for example, are they wholesalers or retailers, jewelry stores or gift shops (which ones, and what kind), and are there any other types of stores that may be appropriate. The product position in the marketplace, the geographic location of the customer base, and the display and sales system will help resolve any doubts about the ultimate design of the product. Use all of these factors to define a target clientele or set of end users to which you will direct the work. It's essential to know the final price of the product and the profit structure, since this has a tremendous effect on the size, complexity, and production method of the resulting pieces.

There are also other factors to be considered, such as the marketing plan; this is of course crucial to the success of the collections. This plan includes such things as the presentation of the samples, the representatives who will market the work, and the product's presence at regional trade or technology shows and on the Internet. Other external factors are market evolution, which can have an effect on future production, and fashion trends that can dictate such things as size, color, and finish of the objects.

Analyzing all these factors is very useful, and should serve as a guideline that can help change and improve the company's strategy, if necessary.

▼ Trade fair display booth belonging to the D'Argent company; coordination and consultation by Ricard Domingo

▶ Wooden case for displaying his silver rings, by Andronikos Sagianos

Product and Marketing

In this new millennium, the ability to access a great quantity of information and communicate conveniently and quickly has become routine. Our society tends to place increasing value on leisure and services, yet still places importance on things that contribute to self-fulfillment in the workplace. As a result, any creative person really needs to be innovative in producing works and products destined to satisfy the needs of the new consumer, who is faced with many choices in a global culture grown increasingly large.

To be innovative and appeal to this wide audience, you can revive traditional knowledge of crafts and incorporate these ideas with contemporary techniques, and new materials can be combined with traditional ones. Work a project on a different scale, or create pieces that are functional as well as symbolic, explore new ergonomics, or produce abstract or figurative works. Above all, however, you must produce contemporary, high-quality works. Today's marketplace is extraordinarily competitive; thousands of inventive products compete with one another, so it's really difficult to excite the consumer's interest. To do that, it's wise to carefully consider two basic factors: strategy and specialization.

All enterprises, from sole proprietorships to huge multinational companies, need a strategy that matches their product—how to produce it, what type of clientele to target, and how to get it to this customer base. This strategy is applied with the same coherent philosophy used to create the brand, the packaging, the advertising, and the sales methods. The approach will vary as a function of the available resources; keep in mind that in many instances, good, original ideas are more useful than large investments.

Consider the production process, which again depends on technology and resources, as well as the organization and capacity to manufacture the work. All of this has an effect on the quality and ultimate price of the pieces.

To sell jewelry successfully, conduct a meticulous study of the market sector to determine how to satisfy the needs of most of those consumers. Explore how to reach that segment of the market with your products and analyze the client profile—how the customers choose their purchases, their tastes and interests, their purchasing power, the kinds of shops they frequent, and so forth. This information will allow you to determine the correct price for your work, the most effective distribution channel for your pieces, as well as how and where to sell the products. This type of research also helps resolve any doubts about the market image to be created for the work.

Image and Brand

After your ideas have taken shape in the creation of a series of high-quality pieces, you must determine what else it needs to sell reliably, including creating a favorable public image through things such as packaging. This involves extending the design work beyond the creation of the object or piece of jewelry to the entire marketing strategy, including the production processes and the distribution channels; the creation of a solid and distinctive image; and the use of new and creative sales methods. All these factors should be in harmony with the products that have been created.

▲ Simple and effective way to display and wrap a gold necklace, handmade by Ulla and Martin Kaufmann

▶ The typical jewelry display cases can be arranged to harmonize perfectly with the overall image of the store. The photo shows various glass display cases in the Barcelona shop of Joaquín Berao.

▶ Examples of applying the same logo to different types of jewelry display materials, from the company of Enric Majoral

Creating an image for your work begins with a brand name; it's a good idea to get professional advice with this step. The brand needs to identify you and reflect the distinctive personality of the product; simultaneously, it needs to correlate with the sales strategy and the image created for your product. Lastly, it needs to communicate all of that adequately.

Thus, you should create a specific product philosophy along with a distinctive image for it. The packaging you choose should reflect the design of the product, as well as the image, the price, and the merchandizing. It should project a clear, unique, and recognizable image of your company and your products. Packaging should generally incorporate your name and logo. The brand has to be represented in all forms of communication regarding the product: business cards, letterhead, invoices, packaging, promotional material, displays, and so forth.

◀ Display window outside the jewelry shop of Joaquín Berao in Barcelona. The light and the simple displays inside, plus a pleasing arrangement of the product, guarantee an effective display, even though diverse pieces are exhibited in the same space.

▲ There are many ways to exhibit jewelry other than traditional display windows. Here is Beatriz Würsch in her Forum Ferlandina Gallery, putting necklaces on a cardboard mannequin.

▶ A modern display, for a watch with a red horsehide band and a string of diamonds around the crystal. From the Alfex firm.

▼ A good portfolio for the collection is essential in making a presentation to a businessperson, a representative of the press, a manufacturer, or a marketer. As stated before, the packet needs a coherent theme. Here is a good example, created for the *Al dente* collection by Ricard Domingo.

▼ This packaging creates anticipation before the recipient discovers the piece of jewelry. Project designed by Duch Claramunt.

Concept and Image

▲ It's important to highlight the product inside the display window so it is clearly visible and attracts attention.

▼ Box for high quality rings by the Piaget Company. These packages are characterized by fine materials worked in a singular manner.

▲ Felt pockets for silver pieces from the D'Argent Company, designed by Ricard Domingo; the color and the use of the logo on all the elements make this packaging distinctive.

◄ Cardboard box from the Nova ring collection by the Saymor Company; its distinguishing feature is the manner in which the box opens and displays the ring.

▼ Sample of a box from the Platamundi Company, made of recycled and embossed cardboard; it's designed to contain moderately priced merchandise.

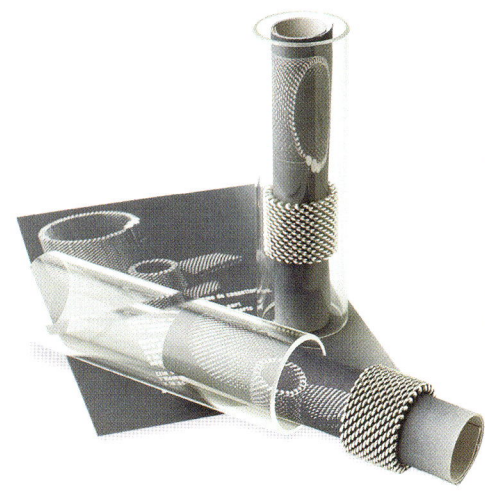

◄ Great ideas are a good substitute for large expenditures of money. Graphic image and packaging made of glass and printed cardboard by Igor Siebold.

▼ Judith McCaig, *Eternal Flame,* 1988. Unique piece in which the box and the piece of jewelry form an integrated sculptural work.

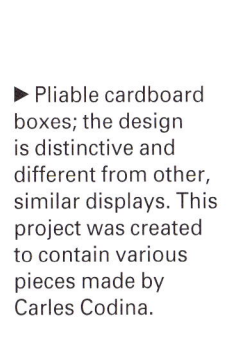

► Pliable cardboard boxes; the design is distinctive and different from other, similar displays. This project was created to contain various pieces made by Carles Codina.

Photography and Jewelry

The primary technique used to photograph pieces of jewelry is *macro photography*. This particular application of close-up photography requires special lighting conditions and much preparation, and sometimes the necessary photography equipment can be expensive. Photography is a complex medium that will be only briefly discussed in the following chapter, since it can require considerable professional experience. The following pages will instead focus on techniques used by most hobbyists who have mastered the basics of this craft, explaining some concepts that will help in doing this type of photography.

Equipment

Use a *reflex* camera for macro photography, one that allows you to view the actual image through the lens, not through a separate viewfinder. Thus, it's best to avoid using rangefinder cameras for this type of work. Four megapixel digital cameras can also be used; these high-resolution cameras have a LCD screen for viewing the image.

You can photograph moderately sized pieces like necklaces or bracelets with most normal lenses, but for small pieces such as earrings and rings, the image needs to fill the whole frame while staying in sharp focus. Otherwise, the photo will have to be enlarged so much that clarity will be sacrificed. So, you will first need to determine that the camera can be held close enough to the piece of jewelry to produce a good image.

With reflex cameras, you can use a macro lens, or you can attach an *extension tube* that extends the lens-to-film distance on a normal lens to provide closer focusing. Whether you use a film or digital camera, it's more economical to buy a *supplemental close-up lens* of three or four diopters that screws into the regular lens than to purchase a macro lens itself.

If possible, it's preferable to use a lens with a focal length between 70 and 100 mm. This range is also an advantage because it produces less distortion and allows you to position the camera a little farther away from the piece; that's helpful in setting up screens, lights, and other equipment you'll need for the shoot.

▲ Gold bracelet with diamonds; this photo is the work of Joan Soto, who contributed much of the photography in this book.

◀ 35 millimeter single-lens reflex camera with zoom lens and extension tube.

◀ Digital cameras can be held close to the object, especially if they have a macro function. In addition, you can instantly view the results on a small screen built into the camera.

Framing, Focus, and Exposure

Photographing small objects such as pieces of jewelry involves focusing at a very short distance from the object and working with a greatly reduced depth of field. To increase the depth of field, and thus achieve the sharpest focus for the image, the f-stop needs to be closed down to a high number, such as f/22. For proper exposure, you then compensate by decreasing the shutter speed. To keep the image from being blurred, it's a good idea to mount the camera on a tripod and use a cable release.

With a close-up lens or an extension tube attached to your lens, it's a little awkward to use the focusing ring, since you are often so close to the object. You can compensate for this by moving the tripod a little or placing the object onto a surface like a piece of cardboard, moving it back and forth until you get the proper focus.

▶ Example of a supplementary close-up lens

▲ A tripod is essential; it's tremendously helpful in framing, setting up the right distance from the object, and eliminating any involuntary movement or vibration in the camera.

Background

Cylindrical gold and silver pieces such as rings and bracelets reflect everything in their surroundings, especially if they have a highly polished surface. This includes the bottom and sides of any material on which they are placed; as a result, instead of a dark background, it's preferable to use a clear one that reflects luminosity onto the piece. For example, if you intend to photograph a round, polished gold ring, and place it onto a dark surface, the lower half of the ring will reflect the dark background and the upper half will reflect the rest of the surroundings. Therefore, a dark background is not a good choice to best display this piece of jewelry.

If you want to photograph a thin, flat piece such as a medallion, it will hardly be affected by a reflection from the background, so a dark background can be used.

Photographing certain polished, spherical pieces is difficult, because they tend to reflect everything in their surroundings. Pieces with a satin finish are always easier to photograph, as are flat pieces with a matte finish, since these will not reflect the environment; rather, they will have a surface area on which the reflection of light can be controlled.

Illumination

For taking good photos of jewelry, appropriate lighting is an absolute necessity. You have to regard the piece as an object that is capable of reflecting the light of its surroundings, and you also must consider all the nearby objects that may be reflected and thus captured by the camera lens.

The built-in flash that many cameras have is designed to illuminate spaces and large bodies at a medium distance, like rooms and groups of people. This type of flash is not suited to photographing pieces of jewelry, though, because of the close distances at which the photographs have to be shot; the piece would not be illuminated evenly. It is better to use separate lighting to photograph jewelry.

◀ A highly polished convex piece may reflect its entire surroundings in a fish-eye effect. These are very difficult to photograph, because the photographer's lens is always visible.

Photographing a Piece of Jewelry

It can be easy to photograph a piece of jewelry in the workshop if you follow the right steps. In the following section, Joan Soto demonstrates how to achieve high-quality photographs using resources available to any enthusiast.

It's possible to produce fine photographs using natural light, but you have to choose the right time of day. When the light appears filtered on a slightly overcast day, the diffused light can be excellent for producing images with great light qualities. All you have to do is place a matte crystal next to a light-colored wall and photograph it as described in this chapter.

In taking photographs outdoors, use a film for natural light; conversely, for indoor photography it's best to provide halogen illumination and use type L tungsten film with an ISO of 100 or thereabouts. If you use a print film, you may have some control in the darkroom that's not available with slides or transparencies.

Digital cameras have the advantage of repeating the shot until you get a satisfactory image, which you can monitor on the LCD screen. With this equipment, it's necessary to adjust the white balance and interior light as required.

▲ Set up a small arrangement like this when you are shooting with existing light. Make a light-diffusing tent from a soft, white sheet; place the tripod and camera at the edge of the opening, and use the techniques described in this chapter.

◀ Photographing precious stones requires a different type of light than that used for metals. Metals need a soft light, whereas a bright, direct light is better for gems. This piece of mossy quartz was photographed by Joan Soto against a background of rusted iron.

Concept and Image

Working with Reflectors and Lamps

It's very difficult to describe a general method for illumination, since every piece requires special conditions that should be taken into account. Study the piece and experiment with it, looking at it with just one eye and changing the camera angle, light, and reflectors in that order, until you achieve a composition that has the desired quality of light, where there is no preponderance of glare or shadow.

To eliminate undesirable reflections on the piece and control the light that reaches it, use small boxes stuffed with aluminum foil or pieces of matte white material such as poster board or polystyrene foam. These panels reflect light so it falls on the object in the appropriate manner, softening and adjusting the light to create the image you desire.

▶ Most pieces of jewelry can be photographed using a simple setup on a tabletop background, lateral light, and a diffuser at the appropriate distance from the light source. This diffuser was made from polyester tracing paper; its translucency can be a factor in the appearance of the piece. It's crucial to observe the piece and understand how it reflects light. It's possible to influence the image by varying the distance between the source of light and the diffuser, and by varying the distance between the diffuser and the piece of jewelry. Adjusting these factors, along with changes in the reflectors in the rear, will produce the desired image. It may suffice to place two or three reflectors closely above, behind, and to the right of the piece; they will act as matte mirrors, and can be made from small pieces of light, white poster board.

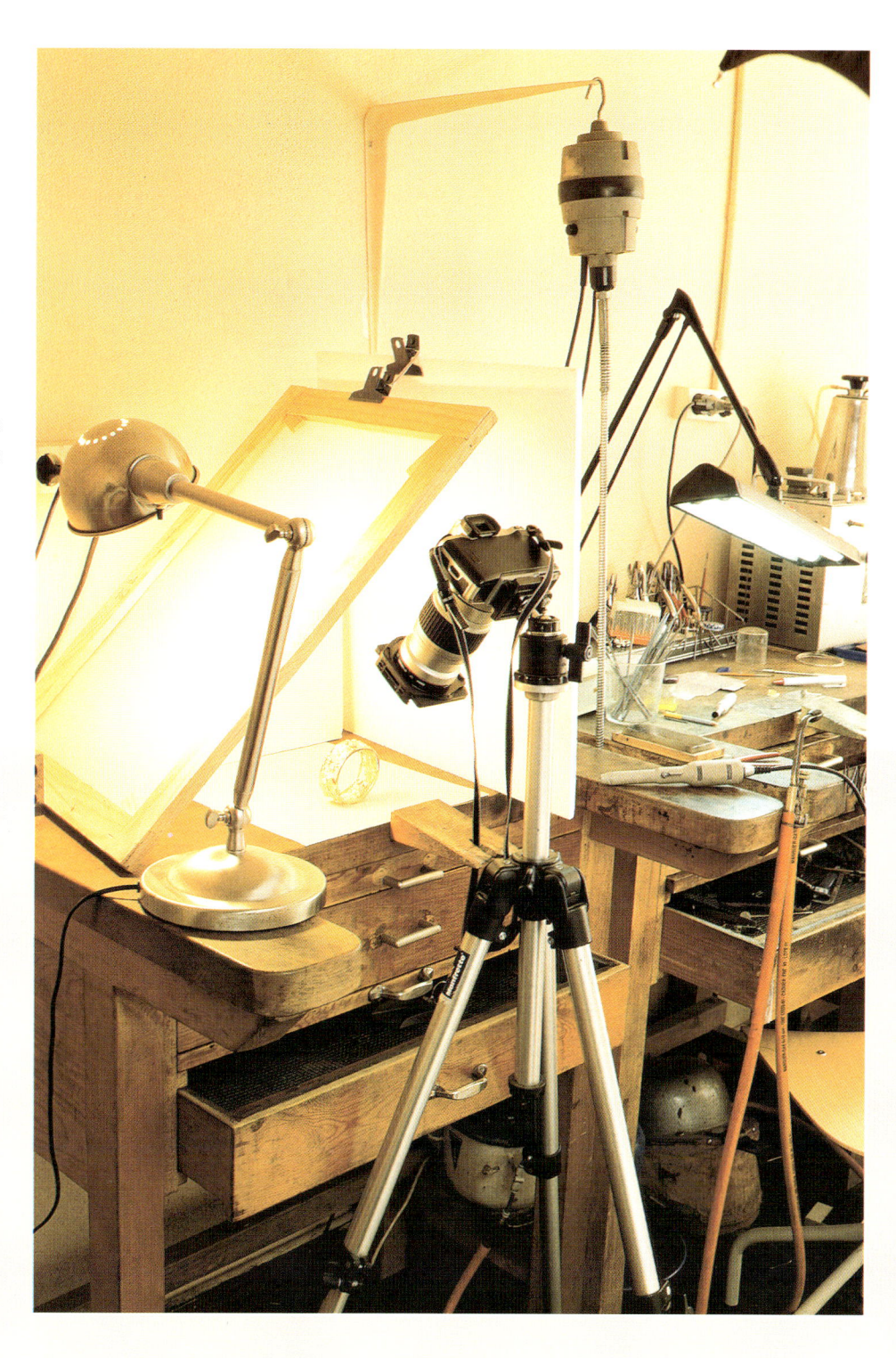

▲ Low illumination from reflectors causes brilliant light, but creates a series of dark areas.

▲ Proper illumination

▲ In this photo, the piece is surrounded by too many reflectors, giving it a matte appearance.

Gallery

◄ Carles Codina i Armengol. Brooch with niello and Kum Boo.

▲ Aureli Bisbe. 23 x 12 cm. Silver teakettle with rubber handle.

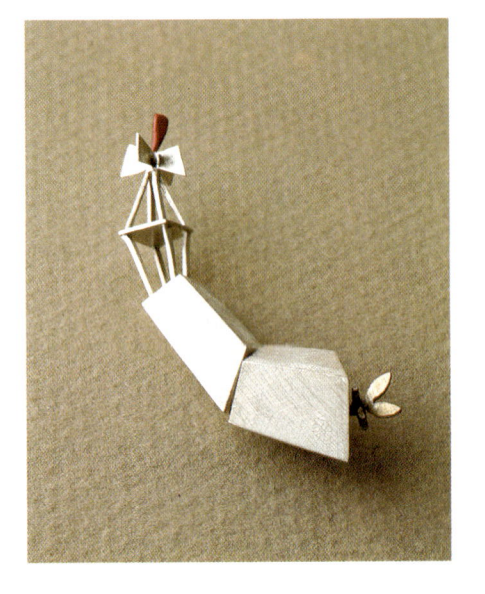

▲ Jimena Bello. Silver pendant.

◄ Kerstin Östberg. Personal diary, hand engraved on copper.

▲ David Huycke, *Stripped Bowl,* 1998. 18.5 x 18.5 x 7 cm. Silver.

◄ Carmen Amador, *The Argonaut.* Patinated nickel (German) silver and gold.

▲ Enric Majoral. Silver and lichen brooch.

▼ Carles Codina i Armengol, *Ring for the Royal Coronation,* 1995.

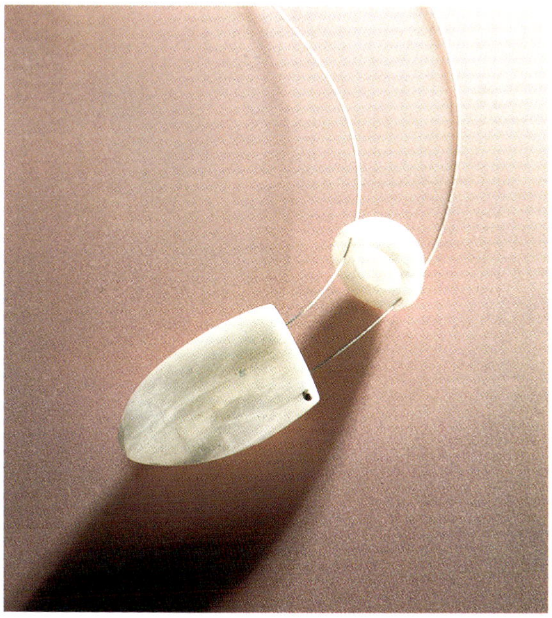

◄ Tanja Fontane. Pendant made of alabaster.

Gallery

▲ Carmen Amador, *Night*. Patinated and chased nickel (German) silver.

▲ Carles Codina i Armengol, *Protected Species* series, 1995. Ring made of oxidized silver.

▲ Silvia Walz, *Reproducer*. Silver, methacrylate, brass, and wax.

◄ Carles Codina i Armengol, *Poor Charles, 1995*. Wood, paper, and cactus core.

▲ Ramón Puig Cuyás, *Twings,* 2001. Silver, nickel (German) silver, plastic, and calcareous fragment.

▲ Silke Knetsch. Silver rings, fine gold, and precious stones.

▼ Joaquim Capdevila, *Girl with a House,* 2000.

▲ Xavier Doménech. Brooch from the *e-motions* collection, 2000.

▶ Judith McCaig, *God Faunus,* 1993. Acid engraving, chased and patinated.

111

Gallery

▲ Karin Wagner. Handmade felt bracelet.

▲ Kay Eppi Nölke. Rings made of industrial felt.

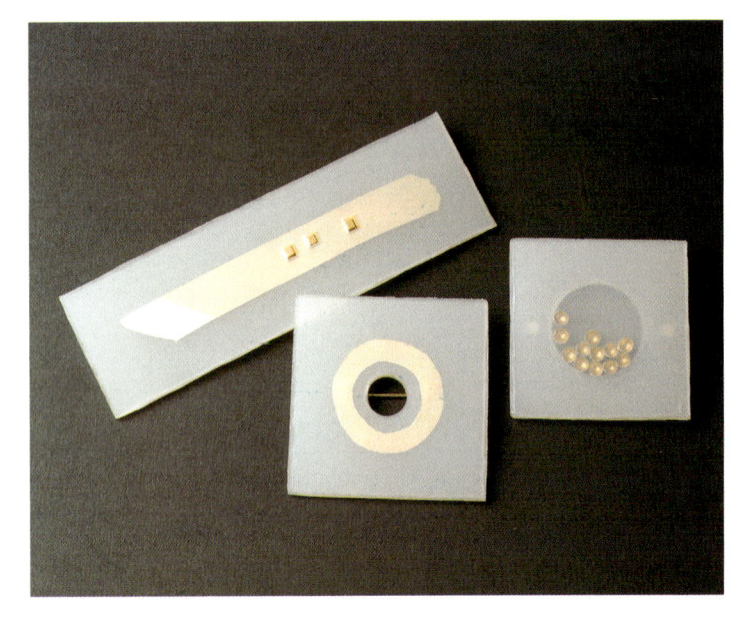

◄ Tanja Fontane. Plastic brooches with silver and gold laminations.

▼ Estela Guitart. Silver bracelet with Japanese lacquer.

▼ Christian Streit. Rings and brooch made of silver, fine gold, copper, and onyx.

112

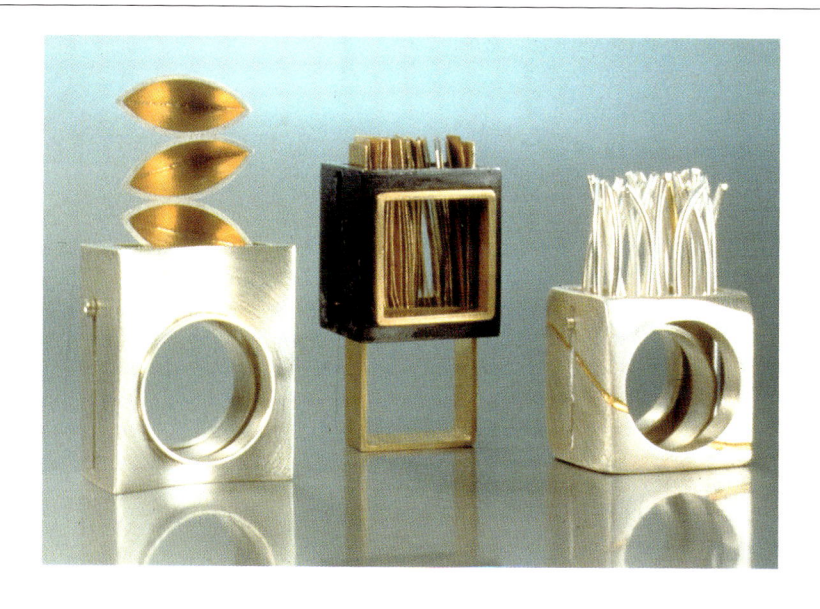

▲ Solveig Ihle. Rings.

▼ Ika Bruse. Pendant.

▶ Ana Hagopian. Paper bracelets.

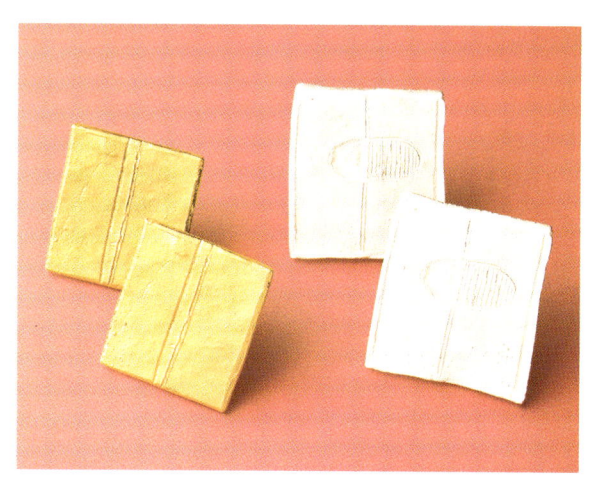

◀ Beatriz Würsch. Cast gold and silver earrings.

▼ Carles Codina i Armengol. Brooch made of silver, niello, and fine gold.

113

All learning requires a certain amount of practice, including numerous attempts—even mistakes—that are important to the educational process. Jewelry making is no different, but because of the high cost of the materials, mistakes can be very expensive. Be very careful in your work, and continually check to decide if it makes sense to continue, or to correct a project that wasn't planned or executed properly. This chapter shows a series of projects, some of which are presented in their entirety. The accompanying photos illustrate the most important processes in each project; they are valuable learning tools in making each piece of jewelry. You will also learn some workshop tricks and special construction techniques.

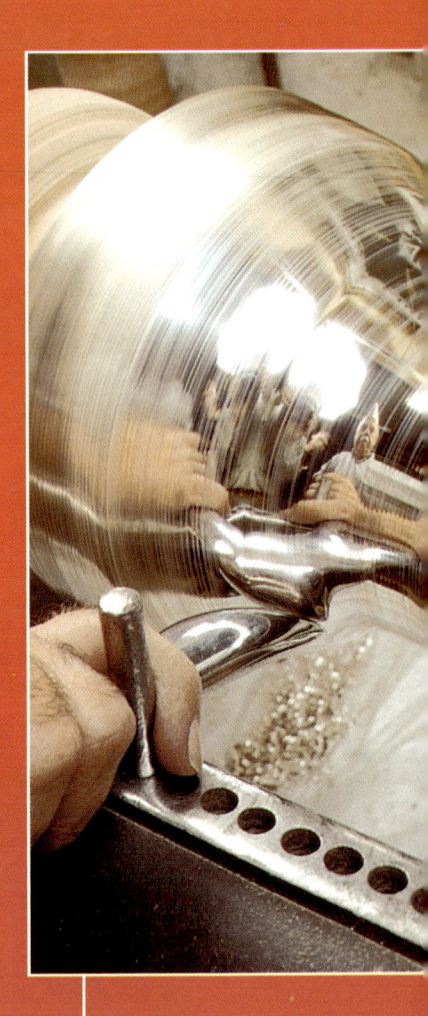

Step by Step

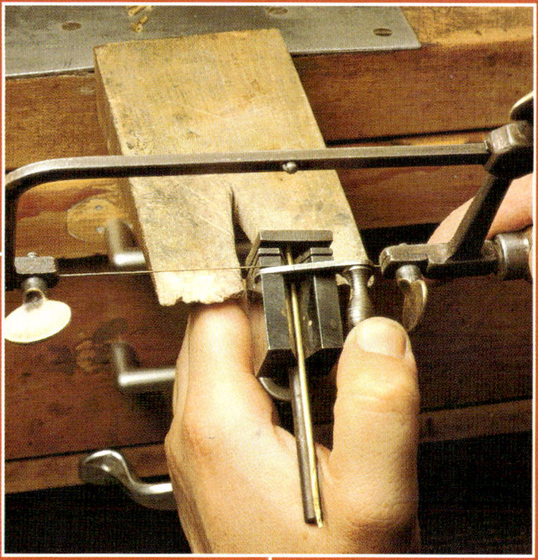
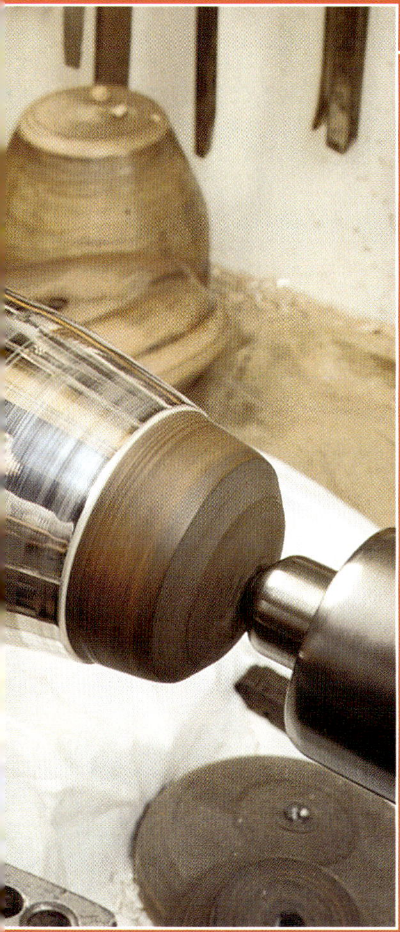
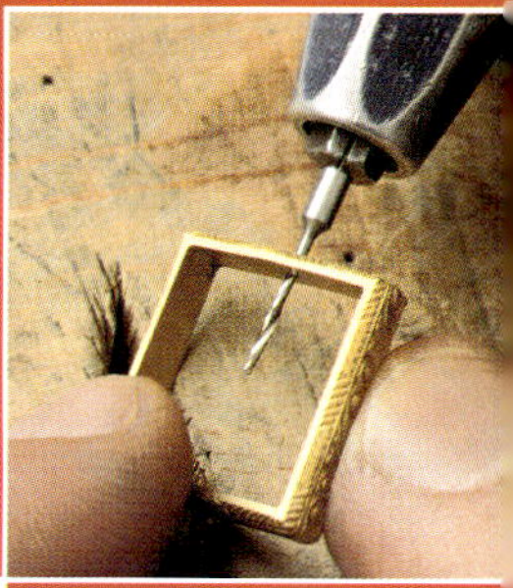
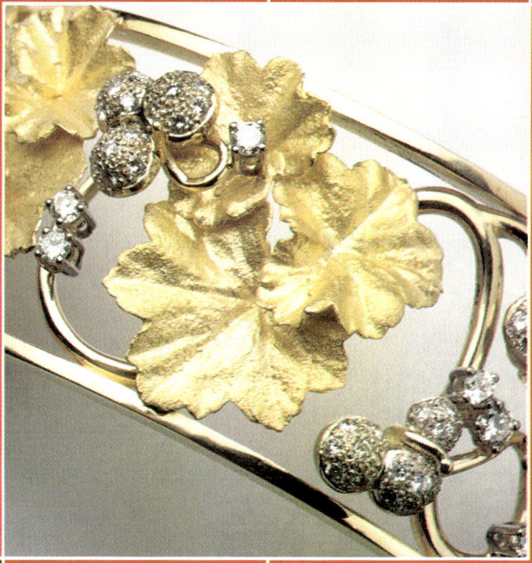
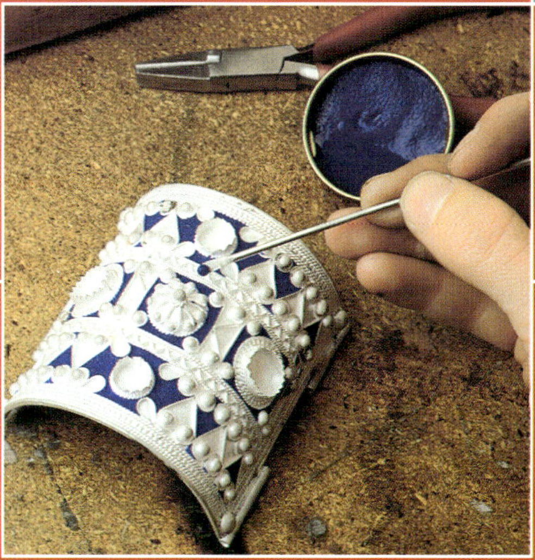

Coffee Service

The following project involves making an original coffee service, with a coffeepot and six cups and saucers. This is a complex project that requires the expertise of several different professionals. Every jeweler should be familiar with the following procedure, even without an immediate application for it. This project will show how silver behaves when it's worked in a larger project, including the tensions in the metal. It will also demonstrate the art of spinning metal on the lathe, how to apply the final finish to a piece made of silver, and introduce a series of concepts and techniques that meet the special demands of working with silver.

The Spinning Lathe

The lathe is an ancient tool that was used as early as the Middle Ages; first it was turned by a pedal, and later on, with waterpower. The metal-spinning lathe is based on the structure of the wood-turning lathe; it's been slightly modified to shape metal sheets and disks on wooden *chucks*, or *patterns*, to create precious silversmithing objects.

Essentially, the lathe consists of a fast-spinning motor that transfers its speed to a spindle by a belt. A metal disk is attached to the spindle along with a wooden chuck (in the shape desired for the finished piece); the assembly turns quickly while you hold a spinning tool against the work for cutting or forming, depending on the nature of the project. This creates hollow pieces such as cups, plates, and countless other objects, all from metal disks, as shown in the following section.

▲ Metal spinning is a technique that demands a certain amount of experience. The lathe is a tool that requires smooth, delicate, and very precise movements. Contrary to what people may think, the metal is controlled with the body loosely strapped to the lathe's toolrest; light, gentle body movements are transmitted through the hands to the ends of the polished spinning tools of the expert turner pictured here, Raimundo Amorós.

▲ Detailed, full-scale plans are essential for all sizeable silver work that involves several processes and different professionals. Drawing by Josep Carles Pérez.

Step by Step

Making a Cup

The first step in every forming process is making a wooden chuck out of well-seasoned maple; this wood is a good choice for projects like this because of its hardness. Once the wood is clamped in the *headstock*, the shaping can begin. This requires precision and a certain amount of experience, as mentioned before. An expert turner is able to use small body movements to transfer any shape or decoration to the silver, and to increase or decrease the thickness of the metal by displacing it precisely wherever it's needed.

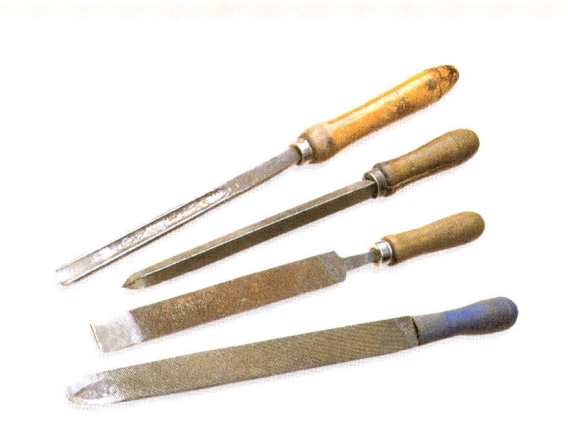

▲ First, prepare the wooden chuck by turning it on the lathe. In this process, use wood chisels for roughing out, turning, and hollowing. Sometimes these tools can be made from old files and special steel. The main tools shown here are the roughing gouge, the square-nosed scraper, and the parting tool.

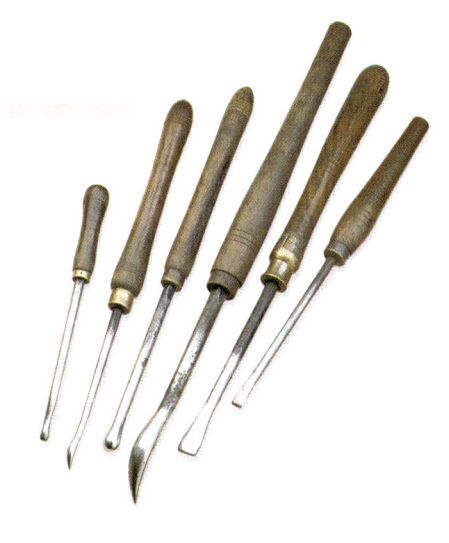

▲ The metal will be spun over the wood after the wooden chuck is shaped. Steel spinning or burnishing tools of different sizes are used in this process; they are also referred to as spoons. They must be perfectly polished on the surfaces that come into direct contact with the metal.

▲ 1. Start by centering the piece of wood and turning it to a perfect cyclinder; at this point it will still be quite rough. Be sure that the block of wood is held very tightly between the centers by applying pressure with the tailstock. Next, use a roughing gouge to make several passes along the cylinder to make it as uniform as possible.

▲ 2. Now, cut a narrow band at the tailstock end of the wood. Deepen this cut with a square-nosed scraper and round off a 2-cm section. Next, use a parting tool to cut the piece of wood to the dimensions specified in your design; make certain that the work piece has a flat end.

▲ 3. Change the setup, so the narrow band at the end of the piece is held in a four-jaw clamp. Using a standard twist bit held in the tailstock, drill a hole in the wood by running the lathe and feeding the bit into the wood. To control the depth of the hole, mark the bit with a pencil to indicate the desired depth.

▶ 4. Replace the drill bit with a tap. With the lathe motor turned off, turn the chuck with your left hand and hold the tap with a wrench to cut threads inside this end of the wood.

▶ 5. Insert a screw chuck into this threaded hole, and from this point on, do all the remaining shaping operations on this chuck.

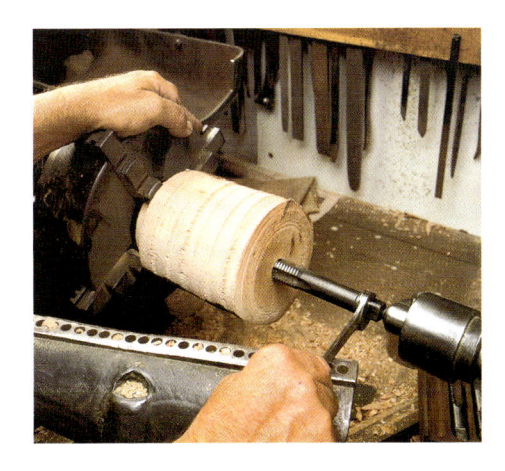

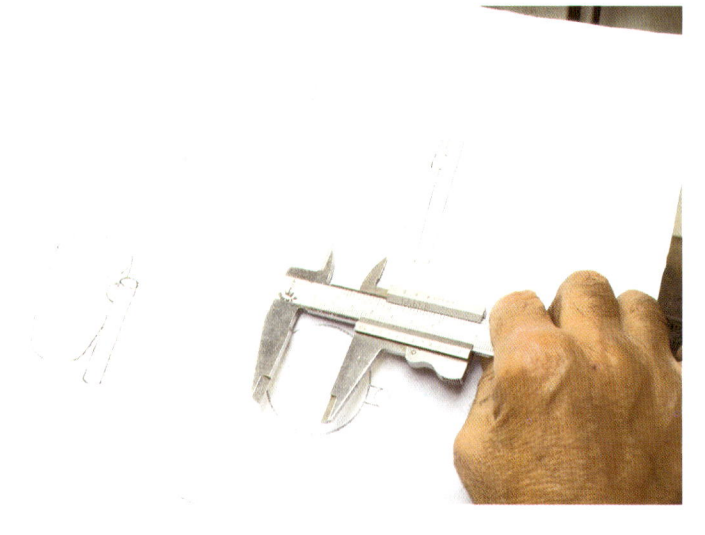

Coffee Service

▲ 6. Securely attach the screw chuck to the headstock; use this setup to finish the chuck and shape the metal.

▲ 7. Mark the diameter of the cup's base on the wood. First, take the exact dimensions from the drawing using calipers, so you can transfer them to the wooden chuck. At this point, it's essential to subtract twice the thickness of the silver sheet from the measurement on your calipers, so that the cup will have the precise dimensions specified in the drawing.

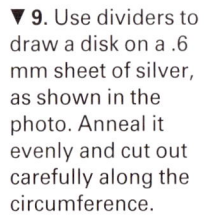

◀ 8. Now, transfer the measurement from the design to the block of wood. Start with the measurement of the base to make the preliminary chuck, and keep checking the diameter as you shape the wood, as shown in the photo.

▼ 9. Use dividers to draw a disk on a .6 mm sheet of silver, as shown in the photo. Anneal it evenly and cut out carefully along the circumference.

▼ 11. Take a parting tool and remove any high spots on the chuck, pressing gently until the silver disk is centered perfectly.

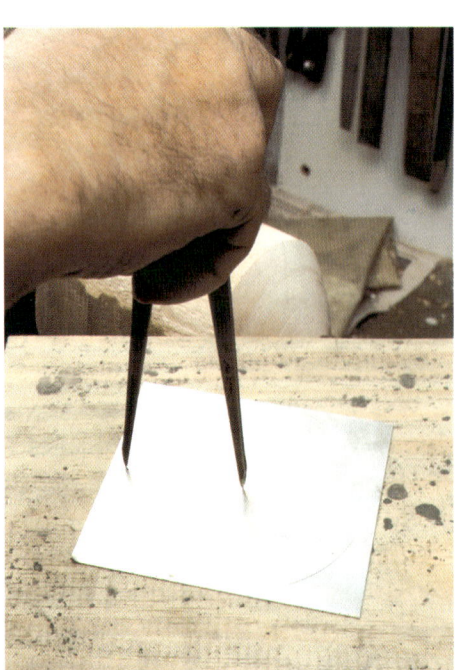

▼ 10. Press the disk between one end of the chuck and a follow block. This piece needs to be precisely the same diameter as the cup's base. The metal disk has to be held firmly in place between centers, located between the chuck and the follow block on the tailstock end of the lathe.

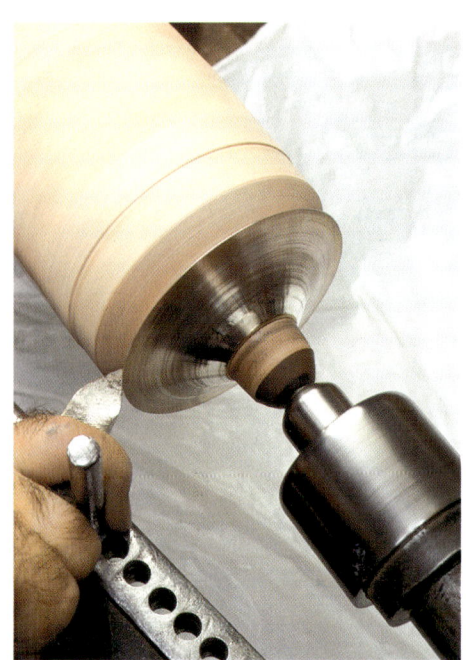

Step by Step

▲ **12.** Begin to shape the metal using a burnishing tool like the one in the photo; as you lean to the rear, press the metal disk from the center toward the outside, gradually forcing the metal over the chuck or template with a strong, continuous movement. During the process of shaping the metal, wipe a little light oil on the tip of the tools for lubrication.

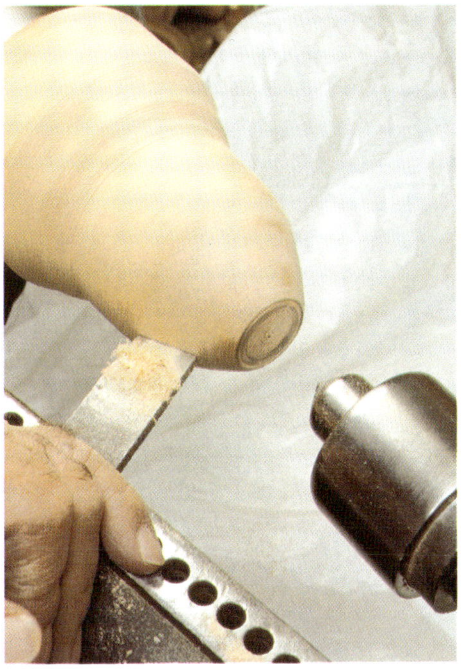

▼ **15.** The process continues as previously described. Use the spinning tool and press firmly and smoothly from the center to the outside.

▲ **13.** Use the square-nosed scraper to refine the chuck and bring it closer to the true size of the cup.

▶ **16.** Gradually form the metal onto the chuck, annealing the metal whenever it becomes too hard to shape.

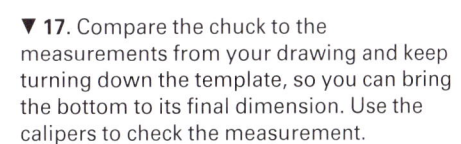

▼ **17.** Compare the chuck to the measurements from your drawing and keep turning down the template, so you can bring the bottom to its final dimension. Use the calipers to check the measurement.

▶ **18.** Now that the bottom part of the chuck is its final dimension, compact the surface of the wood with the same spinning tool you're using on the work piece. This burnishing technique produces a finer and smoother surface and makes it easier to remove the metal from the wood later.

▲ **14.** Because the silver becomes quite hard as it's worked on the lathe, anneal it and then clean in sulfuric acid or some other pickling solution.

119

Coffee Service

◀ 19. Now, use the scraper to refine the upper portion of the chuck so its shape fits the precise curve of the cup.

▼ 20. Measure the height of the cup on your drawing using a pair of dividers, then use the dividers to mark a groove indicating the height on the chuck.

▲ 21. Check the diameter of the chuck using the calipers, remembering to account for the thickness of the silver sheet, as in step 7.

▲ 22. Use the spinning tool once more to compact and burnish the chuck.

▲ 23. Finish up the chuck with a light pass using fine abrasive paper.

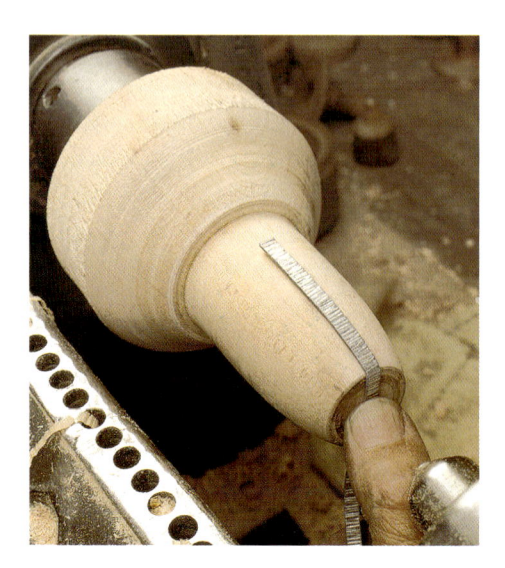

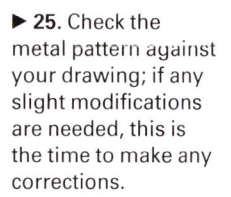

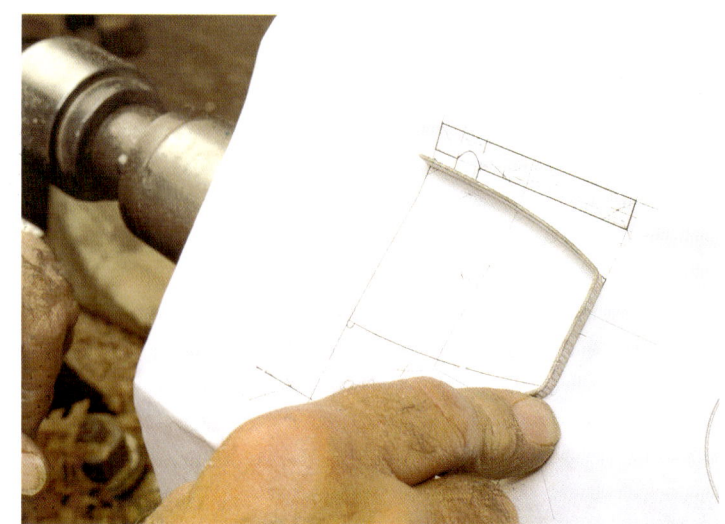

◀ 24. To make sure that the curve of the chuck is done to specifications, take a strip of lead or tin and bend it over the template, beating it lightly to reproduce its exact shape.

▶ 25. Check the metal pattern against your drawing; if any slight modifications are needed, this is the time to make any corrections.

Step by Step

▶ 26. Now that the chuck is perfect, put the annealed metal back into place, making sure it's centered correctly.

▼ 27. Use a larger spinning tool; starting with the point of the tool near the follow block at the base of the cup, press forcefully and evenly, moving the tool toward the rim. Make several passes in this manner.

▶ 28. Continue to shape the cup so it conforms perfectly to the chuck.

▼ 29. The base is a critical area, because it needs to be absolutely flat. Smooth this area with a flat spinning tool, pressing from the center and moving outward toward the edge.

▼ 30. The lip is made with a beading tool that has a rotating wheel with a concave profile. To form the rim, simply press on the metal to make the silver roll and close over on itself.

▼ 31. Rub the cup inside and out with a pad of steel wool. It's now ready to add the final elements; these steps will be shown on pages 126 and 127.

121

The Coffeepot

The coffeepot is a large item, but it's made on the spinning lathe using similar steps as the cup. The construction is somewhat different from the cups, since the final chuck is made to the exact specifications of the inner shape of the coffeepot, while the preliminary chucks are pre-existing ones that have been adapted to the project. Use thicker sterling silver sheet for the pot, about .8 mm thick.

◀ 1. Use the method previously described to make another wooden chuck for the coffeepot, exactly like the drawing; remember to reduce the diameter by twice the thickness of the silver sheet. Make a follow block to the precise diameter of the base; use this to press the silver disk against the chuck.

▶ 2. Start by making a preliminary chuck and press the silver disk between it and a follow block. Form the disk over the template using a large spinning tool, beginning at the end closest to the follow block. Next, anneal the silver to restore the ductility it needs for the work that follows.

▶ 3. Now, turn down the preliminary chuck and the follow block to continue forming the metal and closing up the shape. To help shape the curves, pivot the spinning tool against a pin in the toolrest.

◀ 4. Put the final chuck into place and shape the silver with the spinning tool, using it as a lever against the pin at the appropriate place in the toolrest. These operations require considerable force, and you'll need to use a long, sturdy spinning tool and keep the metal well annealed.

◀ 5. Use the flattest face of the spinning tool; with smooth, regular movements, keep closing the metal onto the chuck. Continue to anneal the metal.

Step by Step

▲ 6. Make increasingly longer passes, pressing against the metal with the broadest part of the tool; as stated before, the tool must be perfectly polished in order to assure a smooth, uniform surface.

▲ 7. Once the metal has been completely closed over the chuck, go over the surface with a pad of fine steel wool, and then remove the metal from the chuck. Sometimes the wood has to cool down completely before the metal can be removed.

▶ 8. The body of the coffeepot is complete. Next, attach the remaining features.

Construction

Soldering with silver is different from working with other metals such as gold; that's due partly to the nature of the metal, and also to the size of some silversmithing pieces. Silver has to be worked with great care, since it is prone to distortion when it's subjected to a direct heat source and rapid cooling. Because of its unique characteristics, it has to be handled, soldered, and polished with special care.

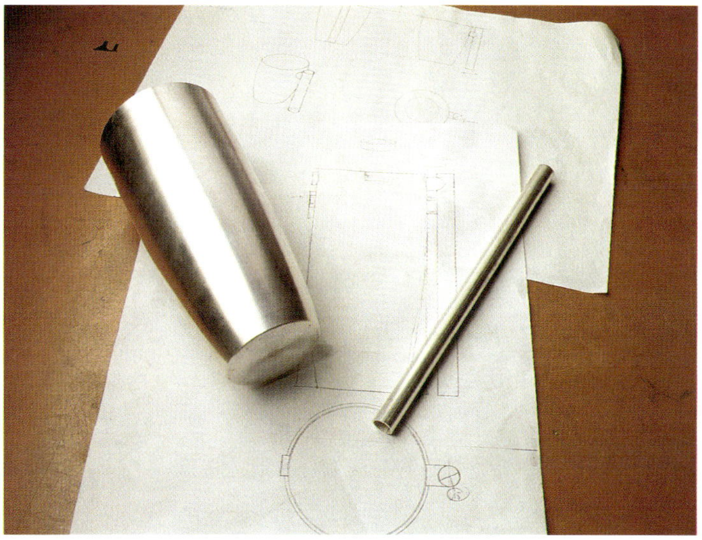

◀ 1. To fashion the handle, make a tube from a sheet of silver about 1.2 mm thick and join the seam with hard solder.

◀ 2. Solder a thick plate on top using hard wire solder. For the duration of the project, set the piece aside so it can cool slowly after each soldering process; any rapid temperature change may cause distortion.

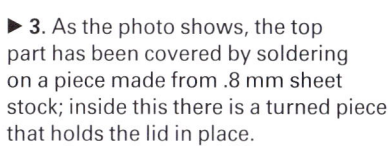

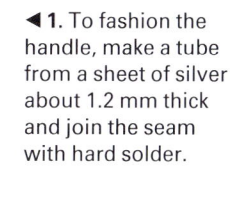

▶ 3. As the photo shows, the top part has been covered by soldering on a piece made from .8 mm sheet stock; inside this there is a turned piece that holds the lid in place.

123

Coffee Service

▲ 4. Close-up of the opening in the top

▶ 5. Use a wide file to remove the excess metal from the top edge.

▲ 6. To attach the tubing for the handle, use a round or half-round file to make a cut in a small piece of the same tubing.

▲ 7. Insert a piece of very thick sterling silver or a thick piece of cut-out sheet stock into the part of the tube where the cut was made in the preceding step; this is needed to support the weight of the coffeepot with the liquid inside it.

▲ 8. After this solid core of silver is soldered in place, drill and tap threads for a threaded shaft, preferably of brass or steel.

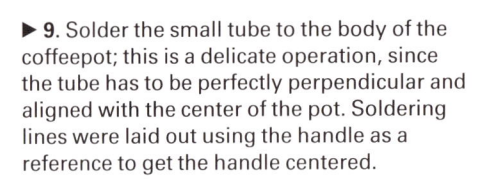

▶ 9. Solder the small tube to the body of the coffeepot; this is a delicate operation, since the tube has to be perfectly perpendicular and aligned with the center of the pot. Soldering lines were laid out using the handle as a reference to get the handle centered.

◀ 10. Now, cap the two ends of the handle with .8 mm silver sheet and file off the excess.

▶ 11. Polish the handle until only very fine scratches remain, using progressively finer grades of abrasive paper up to a grit of 1000 to 1200.

Step by Step

▶ **12.** Insert a threaded brass or steel pin into the body of the coffeepot; drill the handle and insert a tube with a wall thickness of about 2 mm. Solder this in place, file to remove any excess, and shape it to the profile of the tube.

▶ **13.** To make the handle more secure, make a small inner fitting of thick wire; drill a hole and insert the wire.

▲ **14.** Drill and tap female threads in a brass tube so it screws perfectly onto the threaded pin already inserted into the body of the coffeepot. Solder a brass piece with female threads into another silver tube that fits into the hole in the handle, and cap the end by soldering a thick sheet of silver in place. Create a notch in the sheet to form a screw. This is soldered and polished until the whole assembly fits inside the hole in the handle.

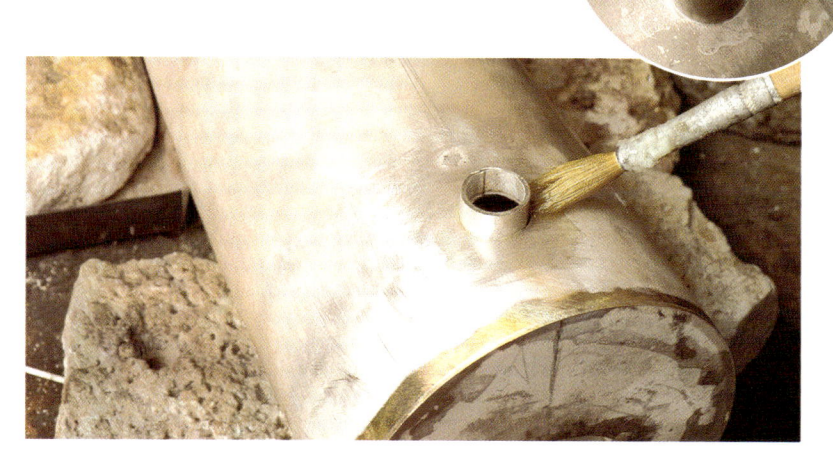

◀ **15.** Fashion the pouring spout on the other side of the coffeepot. A piece of tubing the same diameter as the handle is soldered on at the same level as the attachment point for the handle.

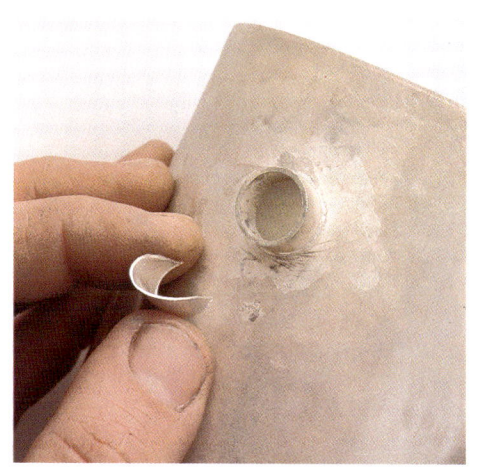

◀ **16.** Solder a small tongue inside the tube; this will help guide the liquid to prevent spilling. It's specifically designed to avoid dripping after the coffee has been poured into cups.

◀ **17.** To make sure the inner tongue is in the right position when it's soldered, you have to keep it from shifting. Silversmiths use very fine soldering clay to keep parts in place; this also keeps adjacent joins from melting or slipping when they are heated again during the soldering process.

◀ **18.** After soldering, it's a good idea to take off the handle and pickle the silver before polishing the parts with various buffs and strong abrasive paste. Next, sand extensively with very fine abrasive paper before using the buffing wheels.

▶ **19.** The coffeepot before polishing

125

Coffee Service

▲ 20. Use various buffs for the initial polishing on the wheel, applying some strong abrasives to remove the scratches and discoloration from the surface of the silver. Take care to avoid rounding the edges while polishing the piece. After this process is complete, clean the piece thoroughly and shine it up.

▲ 21. Give the piece another buffing. Primarily, use sewn cotton buffs or mops and a smooth rouge paste to produce a bright shine on the surface of the metal. When the polishing is complete, the piece should shine brightly, with no discoloration or matte areas on its surface. Go over the piece once again with the buffing wheel.

▲ 22. After they have been polished, bolt the coffeepot and handle together tightly.

▲ 23. Fit the handle and give the piece a final polish on the buffing machine before installing the features of the lid.

▲ 24. The spinning lathe was also used to fit the lid into the opening on the pot.

◄ 25. Make the handles of the cups by soldering a pair of 9 mm silver tubes perpendicular to one another.

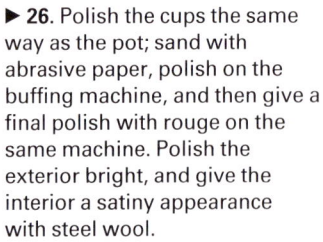

► 26. Polish the cups the same way as the pot; sand with abrasive paper, polish on the buffing machine, and then give a final polish with rouge on the same machine. Polish the exterior bright, and give the interior a satiny appearance with steel wool.

▲ **27.** To make the saucers, start with a series of disks, lightly worked on the edges so they appear rounded; this provides a nice consistency to the saucers and produces a better finish. To add a little height, solder three small pieces of wire on the underside to raise the saucer slightly.

▲ Close-up of the lid and top

▶ Since this handle screws on, it can be interchanged with others in different materials or shapes.

▼ The entire coffee service, designed by Carles Codina and fabricated by master silversmiths Joan Ferré and Raimundo Amorós.

Square Rings

The following projects demonstrate how to make two square rings using stamped bar stock created as shown in the section on metal stamping, pages 65 through 71.

The choice of an attractive and interesting gemstone is a crucial factor in the successful completion of any piece of jewelry; although the following projects use the same type of stock, the gems make each ring special. The cuts of the stones are different, but both projects share the common purpose of highlighting the color and asterism of the gems. In this section, you will learn to make settings or mounts for stones and how to construct square rings.

Rings with Blue Sapphires

The following project uses two blue sapphires weighing a total of 7.6 carats; they are two very special pieces that exhibit the characteristic and desirable asterism or star. In addition, there are some interesting transverse stripes inside them, and the gems have exceptional shine and depth. They are cut to an oval, slightly cabochon shape that emphasizes the star effect. You will learn how to make an oval setting or mount, and practice beveling and soldering to produce the square ring; this project should offer some techniques to facilitate further work with gold jewelry.

▲ **1.** Begin with a piece of stamped gold stock with some decorative designs; the same ring body could be made from a casting or any rolled wire stock of laminated or hammered gold.

▲ **2.** File and polish the edges; both sides should be perfectly parallel.

◀ **3.** Next, use the compass to mark off two lines that divide the body of the ring into three parts. Base the measurement on the length of one side of the square.

◀ **4.** Using a square file, very carefully make two V-shaped cuts on the two lines previously marked with the compass. Make the cuts as deep as possible without going completely through the stock; be sure that the angle is 90°.

▶ **5.** Anneal the metal before bending the stock; otherwise, it could break when it's bent. Then, pickle to remove the oxidation.

▶ **6.** After the metal has been rinsed in water and dried, bend the piece into 90° angles, using pliers with smooth, parallel jaws to avoid damaging the metal.

128

Step by Step

▶ 8. Use fine tweezers to place a small paillon or snippet of hard solder at each joint, and then apply heat from a gas torch. The flame needs to be a gentle, broad reducing flame that allows the solder to flow uniformly into the joints.

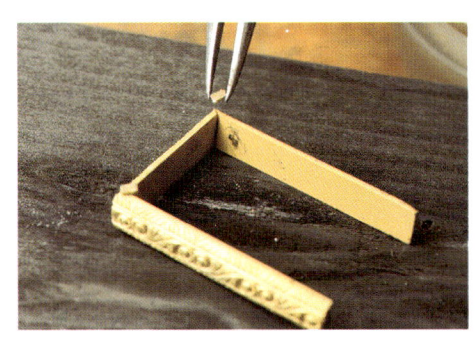

▲ 7. Apply soldering flux and place the ring on a charcoal block for soldering.

▶ 9. Once these areas have been soldered, repeat the process of beveling, bending, and soldering on the upper side of the ring to close it up completely and create the square shape.

▲ 10. With the sapphire nearby for reference, use flat/round nose pliers to hold a .8 mm or 1 mm rectangular wire and bend it to fit the outline of the gem.

▲ 11. Close up the setting entirely and solder the two ends together with hard solder. The pliers shown in the photo are the best type for this job.

▲ 12. Strike the setting in an oval bezel-forming punch set to give it the proper size and shape; strike on both sides to keep it straight and keep it from flaring.

◀ 13. Try to keep the solder invisible, especially if the finished piece will not be polished. Therefore, when you join the setting, try to keep the solder just along the edge. To begin this process, prepare a small sheet of .8 mm gold to serve as a base for the setting for the sapphire.

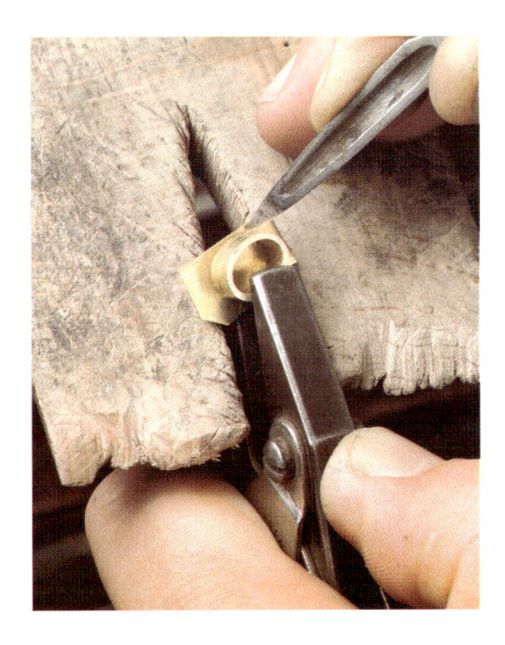

▶ 14. Next, use flat-nose parallel action pliers to squeeze the setting and the sheet together; next, scribe around the outside of the sheet, saw it out, and file and polish the outer edge.

Square Rings

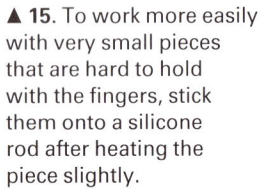

▲ 15. To work more easily with very small pieces that are hard to hold with the fingers, stick them onto a silicone rod after heating the piece slightly.

▲ 16. Dip the silicone in water until it's completely cooled.

▶ 17. Using a 5 or 6 mm rotary diamond bur, chamfer the entire inner edges of the setting to a 45° angle.

◀ 18. Use a flat file and go over the edge of the oval base to create a 45° angle; that way, the two pieces (the base and the sides) will match up with the same angle.

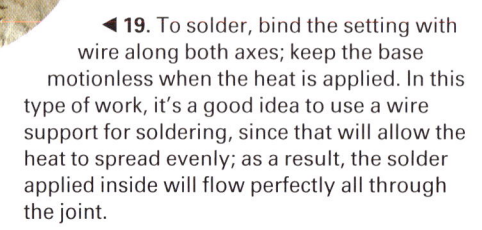

◀ 19. To solder, bind the setting with wire along both axes; keep the base motionless when the heat is applied. In this type of work, it's a good idea to use a wire support for soldering, since that will allow the heat to spread evenly; as a result, the solder applied inside will flow perfectly all through the joint.

▶ 20. Drill a hole in the center of the ring; then use a cylinder bur to widen the hole until the 1.4 mm round wire fits in perfectly.

◀ 21. Apply some flux and a tiny paillon of solder on the inside; next, solder it using the electronic water torch, since this is a very precise soldering job. Remove the excess wire from inside of ring shank; clean and pickle.

▶ 22. To serve as a temporary spacer between the body of the ring and the mouth of the setting, cut a small piece of silver or copper and insert it between the two elements in preparation for soldering, as shown in the photo.

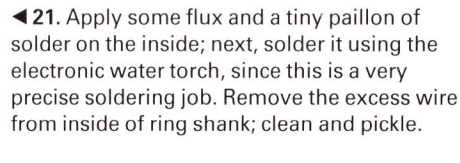

▶ 23. Apply some paste solder at the base of the wire inside the bezel and solder with the electronic water torch.

130

Step by Step

▲ **24.** Remove the temporary spacer. Solder the signature plaque to the inside of the ring.

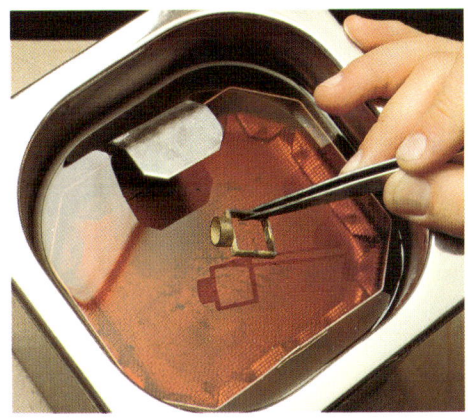

▲ **25.** Remove the superficial oxidation that takes place when the piece is soldered; then rinse in water and dry.

▲ **26.** Now you will prepare to set the sapphires into place. Secure one of the rings in a wooden ring clamp or dopping stick. Soften the setting pitch or wax by heating with an alcohol lamp.

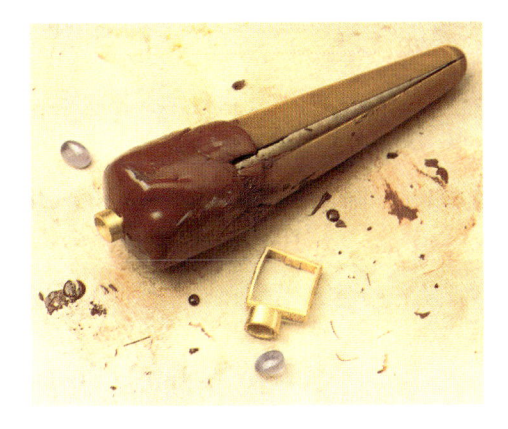

▲ **27.** Surround the setting with the softened pitch or wax. Then, dip the ring clamp into cold water, because the setting pitch must be cold before setting the stone.

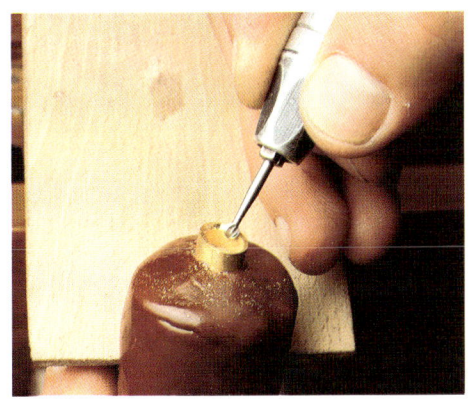

▲ **28.** Hold the ring clamp tightly against the bench pin. Remove the metal from the inside with a ball bur, because the stone has to fit and seat perfectly inside the setting.

▲ **29.** Do the final fitting with a half-round hand graver; chamfer the inner edge until the sapphire fits. The rim of the stone has to be secured in the setting a minimum of about 1 mm from the outside edge.

▲ **30.** Finally, press the stone into place all along the perimeter with a burnisher or bezel pusher, then with a hammer handpiece. File off any rough areas, and shape the contact area between the gem and the setting with a flat graver to eliminate any small burrs and even out the shine of the metal.

▶ **31.** Blue sapphire rings by Carles Codina

A Ruby Ring

This ring will highlight a stone with very special characteristics; it's a ruby cut in cabochon shape, with a pronounced star pattern. This project will be constructed with the same bar stock as the previous rings, with a setting or mount made from various laminated pieces. The following section describes the construction process and the fitting of the various parts of the ring, with special emphasis on constructing the setting.

◀ 1. This star ruby has a strong, characteristic pattern that is exhibited in the rutilated crystals that were absorbed and captured in the crystalline corundum network during its formation. The cabochon cut is not a random choice, since it's the cut that reveals this effect to best advantage; it must have the same orientation as the optical axis.

▶ 2. The basic components also include decorated bar stock that was stamped in a steel die. Prepare a .8 mm gold sheet and 2 mm round wire for the setting; use the wire to join the setting to the body of the ring.

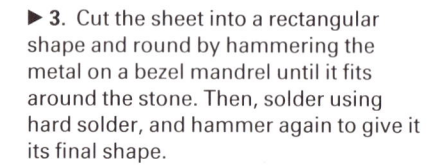

▶ 3. Cut the sheet into a rectangular shape and round by hammering the metal on a bezel mandrel until it fits around the stone. Then, solder using hard solder, and hammer again to give it its final shape.

▶ 4. As in the previous project, bevel the bar stock with a square file and bend into a 90° angle. Next, solder the bevels with hard solder, and then sand the inner surfaces and polish smooth; once the setting is soldered on, it will be difficult to get to this area with the buffing wheel.

◀ 5. Next, you will prepare the setting. Cut a circular bearing or seat from a piece of .5 mm sheet stock and fit inside the setting; secure it with binding wire and then solder it in place. Put in several paillons of medium solder and apply a broad reducing flame to make the solder flow completely around the perimeter of the bearing.

▶ 6. After the inner bearing has been soldered in place, solder a piece of .6 mm sheet stock into the base of the setting, taking care to bevel this piece to fit inside the setting so the solder joins will be hidden.

Step by Step

▲ 7. Using a 2 or 3 mm ball bur, make a lateral cut on both sides of the setting to receive the ends of the round wire and assure a strong, clean solder join. In this step, use medium solder in paste form and an electronic water torch.

▲ 8. After calculating the desired height, mark the bar stock and use a ball bur to create indentations that will accommodate the pins on the bezel. After binding the assembly together with wire, use soft solder, a gas torch, and a broad reducing flame for this soldering job.

◀ 9. After soldering on the signature plaque, polish the inside to eliminate scratches, first with polishing compounds, and then with rouge, to produce a final luster. When that's done, secure the piece into a ring clamp and setting pitch to begin the actual setting process.

▲ 10. To set the gem, reduce the inner wall, first with a ball bur, and then with a half-round graver, until the stone fits into place. Next, press around the outer edge with a bezel pusher and a hammer handpiece. The last step is to polish and finish the setting.

▶ 11. Here is the completed piece, by Carles Codina.

133

Prism

The following project involves an interesting pendant made entirely of 18-carat yellow gold, which involves some of the techniques presented earlier. This piece is begun by creating a rich textured sheet with a paper towel. This delicate surface can be neither filed nor sanded after it's made, so it will be impossible to remove any scratches. This texture is an important factor that influences the subsequent construction of the piece, as well as its final finish. While creating this pendant, you will learn to bevel sheet stock, bind it together properly with a section of wire, and solder a complex piece.

One item of note: In jewelry workshops it's sometimes necessary to make a custom tool, one needed for a particular procedure, as you will see in this demonstration. These tools can be made from special tool steel; however, in many instances a jeweler can modify old files or pliers and use them in new applications.

▶ **1.** It's possible to create many kinds of surface textures using unusual materials. To produce a rich and interesting surface for this project, run an annealed sheet of gold and a piece of common, textured paper towel through the rolling mill.

▲ **2.** To produce a uniform surface, keep the paper from wrinkling when it goes through the mill—however, you can also create some interesting results using very wrinkled paper.

◀ **3.** After rolling the metal to a thickness of .6 mm, anneal and pickle once again. This surface is delicate and it can be ruined when it's soldered or bumped. There is no way to file or polish out any scratches or defects without permanently marring the texture.

▶ **4.** Handle the construction of the piece very carefully from this point. Now, flatten the gold sheet, but avoid blows that could leave marks; instead of a steel hammer, use a nylon or plastic mallet.

Step by Step

▲ 5. To solder the different planes, you'll make a bevel and fold the gold sheet. You must make a special tool to create this bevel so the edges will bend crisply without leaving any marks on the surface. Take an old file and use a torch to anneal the tip; let it cool slowly on top of a soldering block. This removes the temper from the tip of the file so it can be shaped properly and then tempered again; this new tool will allow you to cut a bevel on the inside of the sheet stock.

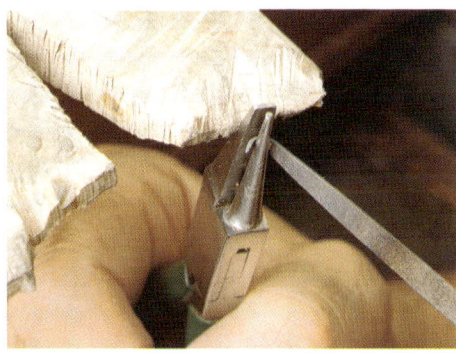

◀ 6. Bend the tip with pliers; then use files or a fine grinding wheel to create the triangular tip.

◀ 7. To create the proper cutting angle, use several types of grinding wheels; begin with a coarse wheel and then progress to a finer one; finally, use an Arkansas stone to refine the desired angle.

◀ 8. Once the shape is established, heat the tip of the file again to an orange-red and plunge it quickly into cold water to restore the temper.

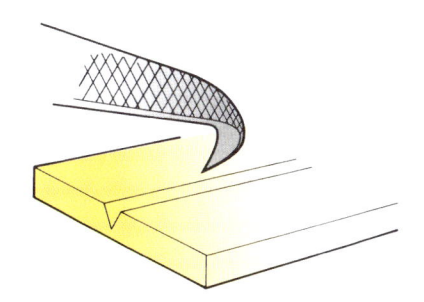

▼ 9. This is the desired shape of the cutting area of the tool.

▲ 10. Take two identical sheets of textured gold stock and saw them into rectangles, using a steel square to measure them as shown; file each side as necessary to correct the angle.

◀ 11. Use a steel rule to mark a line as a guide for the bevel. Then place the point of the tool at the farthest end of the line and draw the tool toward you with downward pressure; the metal rule will help you make a straight, controlled cut. Make several passes to deepen the cut as much as possible. The deeper and cleaner the cut, the sharper the corner will be after the metal is bent.

Prism

▲ 12. Before bending, it's wise to anneal the sheet again, so that the remaining bit of metal in the bevel doesn't break. Bend by clamping the piece in the jaws of a hand or bench vise, then hold the two parts of the sheet along their full length and bend them over cleanly in a single motion.

▶ 13. After making the bends, use a vernier caliper to check the dimensions of both pieces and confirm the two pieces will be a perfectly square tube when joined.

◀ 14. File the outside edges of each section to 45° so the solder will stay inside the shape when the two halves are joined together. Now, cut two squares of the textured gold sheet for lids on the top and the bottom.

▼ 15. Place the piece onto a revolving wire wig for the soldering procedure; this support is ideal for this type of join, since it allows the flame to reach every part of the piece and distributes the heat evenly. Apply a reducing flame so that the two walls reach an even temperature; at that moment, use tweezers to apply the hard wire solder.

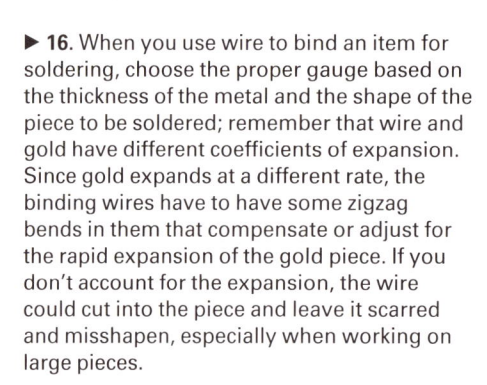

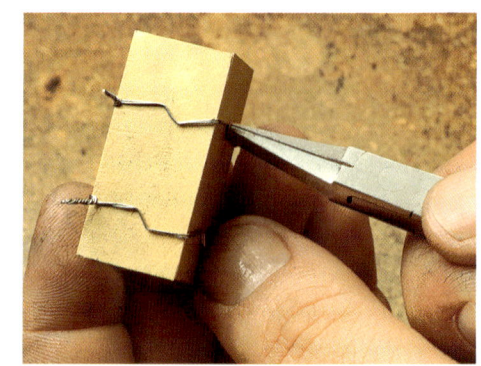

▶ 16. When you use wire to bind an item for soldering, choose the proper gauge based on the thickness of the metal and the shape of the piece to be soldered; remember that wire and gold have different coefficients of expansion. Since gold expands at a different rate, the binding wires have to have some zigzag bends in them that compensate or adjust for the rapid expansion of the gold piece. If you don't account for the expansion, the wire could cut into the piece and leave it scarred and misshapen, especially when working on large pieces.

▶ 17. After the two pieces are soldered together and the prism itself is finished, use a steel square or a vernier caliper to square up the top and bottom to 90°. Then, use a small three-square file to create a 45° angle around the entire inner perimeter of both ends of the tube, as well as the perimeters of the two squares that will serve as ends.

Step by Step

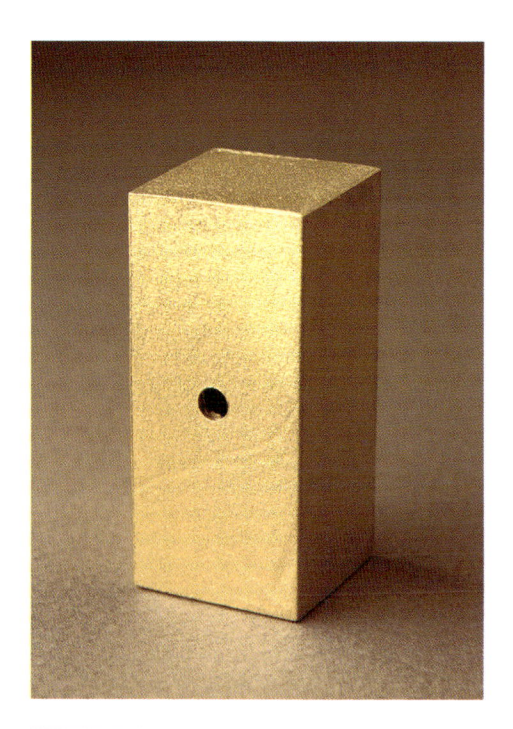

◄ 18. Solder on the ends by placing medium solder inside the bevels and apply a reducing flame that pulls the solder from the inside toward the outside. This method keeps the solder from running over the surface, which would spoil the texture and make unsightly blotches on the surface.

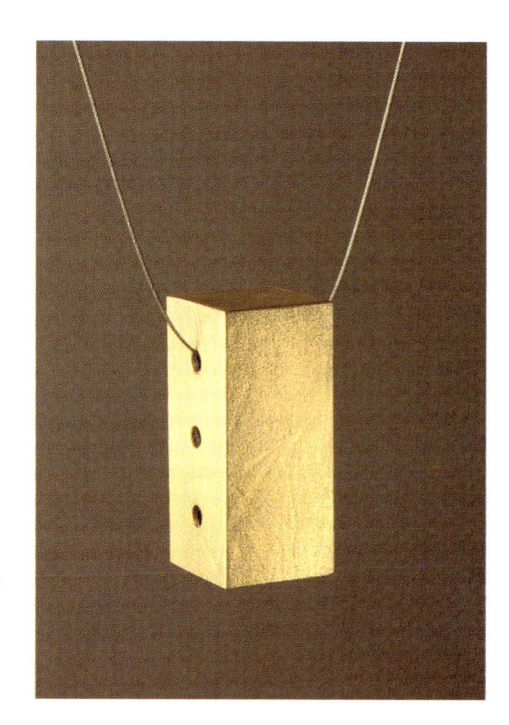

► 19. Proper execution can turn a simple piece into a thing of great beauty. To complement the attractive texture and pleasing shape, add three sets of symmetrical piercings to accommodate a chain.

▲ 20. To give the jewelry some symbolic content, add figures representing a father and a daughter who are undertaking a long journey. Create these elements by direct metal casting and then solder them to the top of the piece.

► 21. Give the piece a light sandblasting, and a last bath in acid to provide the final finish. Then, engrave a special message to impart particular meaning to the piece. Carles Codina created this basic yet beautiful shape.

Earrings

This section demonstrates different tools and techniques for constructing and setting jewelry, plus offers some tricks and advice that make it easier to create any type of jewelry.

The foundation of this project is a stamped sheet of metal, which is used to create a pair of earrings with omega clips. Various small elements are made separately and then added to the body of the earrings. Stampings made from a steel die are used here, but it's possible to make similar earrings in other shapes and to add small pieces fashioned with other techniques, like repoussé-formed or cast pieces. In this project, these pieces are created in 18-carat gold, and require gallery wire for the settings or mounts that's a little longer than normal; the earrings also have seven cut diamonds with a total weight of 0.50 carats.

◄ **1.** Here are some of the elements for this project. Begin with a motif that is first die-stamped and then sawn out with a jeweler's or piercing saw. The pieces that form the base or front of the earrings are stamped in a circular pattern. In addition, you will need .3 mm sheets that are rolled, polished, annealed, and cleaned.

▶ **2.** After the motif has been cut out, file the base and polish with abrasive paper to level the surface before soldering. Polish the mating surface and apply liquid flux; evenly distribute some small paillons of hard solder around the entire perimeter of the piece. Place the whole assembly onto a wire soldering wig and apply a broad reducing flame to melt the solder and join the pieces.

▶ **3.** Pickle the piece and then create the hollow motif by sawing along the entire perimeter with a jeweler's saw; file and polish the outer edge.

◄ **4.** Make a round tube from a piece of .4 mm sheet stock; join it with hard solder along the entire length of the seam. Later, this will have to be soldered to the body of the earring with medium solder.

▲ **5.** Use a round drawplate to size the diameter of the tube to about 2 mm.

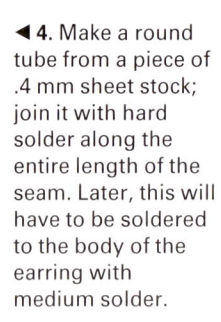

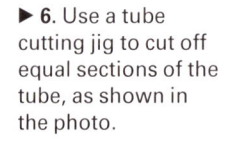

▶ **6.** Use a tube cutting jig to cut off equal sections of the tube, as shown in the photo.

138

Step by Step

▲ **7.** The tube cutting jig used in step 6 presets a measurement to cut off identical pieces of the tube.

▲ **8.** Using a steel square, trim the sheets for the base so that all the angles are 90°. Repeat for the sheets that will be used for the back of the earrings; then, use a vernier caliper to measure all the pieces and file them to exactly the same dimensions.

▲ **9.** Trim the two back plates even, then draw and mark a design with a steel scribe. To keep the traced design symmetrical, glue these two plates together with cyanoacrylate glue and saw both pieces at the same time.

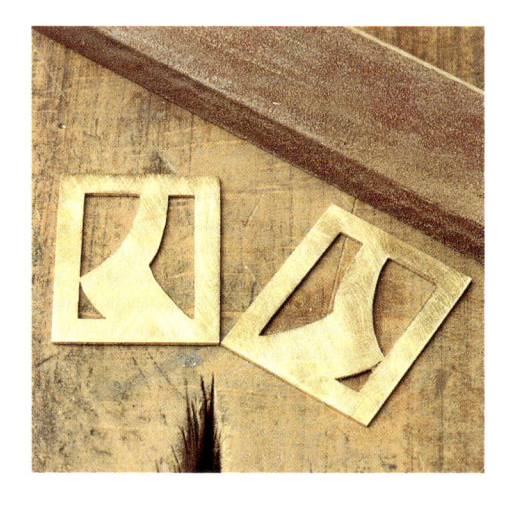

▲ **10.** As this photo shows, the sawn pattern is in perfect symmetry and has an outside border of about 4 mm. Leave some metal in the center to solder on the base of the omega clip and the post.

▲ **11.** Clean the parts. Then, place the tubes on the inside of the back plate as shown in the photo. Apply a small drop of cyanoacrylate glue to secure them. Using glue replaces a long and complicated preparation using plaster, but be sure to avoid breathing the fumes as the glue burns.

▲ **12.** Next, apply paste solder to the contact point at the top of each tube; set the front sheet in place and bind it with wire under light pressure.

◀ **13.** Place the piece onto a charcoal block and use a broad reducing flame to solder the plate for the front of the earring. The wire should have a slight bend as shown in the photo; as discussed previously, this technique prevents distortion when the piece is heated.

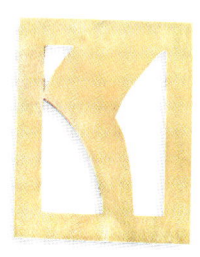

▶ **14.** Now, repeat the process to solder on the back of the earring. Apply solder to the other side of the tubes. Bind it all together again and solder as before.

139

Earrings

◀ 15. After soldering, file the entire outer edge of the body of the earring.

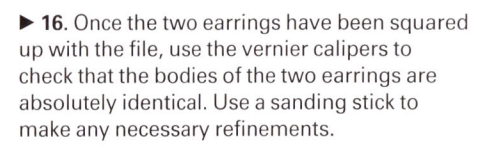

▶ 16. Once the two earrings have been squared up with the file, use the vernier calipers to check that the bodies of the two earrings are absolutely identical. Use a sanding stick to make any necessary refinements.

▲ 17. Now the main body of the earring has been soldered, and you will prepare to solder on the surface elements with soft or medium solder. Use an electronic water torch for the medium solder.

▲ 18. Always solder the largest objects first. Fit all of them, except for the settings, with a small stud to help position them; these studs also contribute to the quality and strength of the join—an essential characteristic in high-quality pieces.

◀ 19. These complex earrings are made of very fine sheets that have already undergone quite a bit of soldering. Every time a new element is soldered on, protect the existing ones with heat-shielding paste to keep them from coming loose when they're heated again during subsequent soldering.

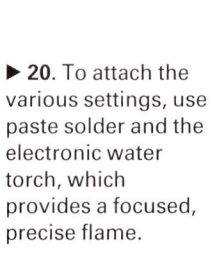

▶ 20. To attach the various settings, use paste solder and the electronic water torch, which provides a focused, precise flame.

140

Step by Step

◄ 21. Solder the omega clip onto the back starting at the base; then measure about 8 mm from the base and drill a .9-mm wide hole and solder in a .9 mm round wire for the post.

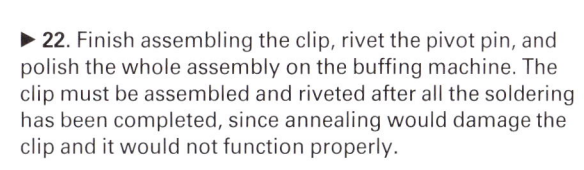

► 22. Finish assembling the clip, rivet the pivot pin, and polish the whole assembly on the buffing machine. The clip must be assembled and riveted after all the soldering has been completed, since annealing would damage the clip and it would not function properly.

◄ 23. Treat the outer face of the earring in the sandblaster to create the final finish; this machine creates a fine texture on the surface depending on the grit of sand used. To achieve the best results, though, the surface should be polished with abrasives in the polisher first and then sandblasted; this process eliminates any possible scratches.

► 24. After placing the piece in setting pitch or wax, use a bur to simultaneously notch each prong of the setting to the shape of the girdle of the diamonds.

▲ 25. Place each diamond into its setting and use a prong pusher to gently press each of the prongs over the stone; then file away the excess from the outside of the prong with a fine barrette file and a cup bur. Remove the setting pitch by boiling the piece in ammonia. Then, clean and dry the piece.

► 26. Here are the finished earrings by Carles Codina.

141

Hinged Bracelet

The hinged bracelet featured in this section is sometimes referred to as a slave bracelet. This project requires some mastery of basic construction techniques, especially soldering. Since this piece is rather complex, be precise in every one of the steps, and be critical of your work; don't continue if there's any doubt about having done the preceding steps correctly.

Geranium leaves are the decorative motif for the bracelet; they are cast using the technique explained in Casting and Sanding on pages 63 and 64. Other than the technique from the earlier chapter, this section demonstrates the entire process of constructing this bracelet, starting with the casting of the fine metal and ending with the final polishing. Special emphasis is placed on the different methods of soldering and putting together this elaborate piece. This is a complete project that involves making everything from a blind or concealed hinge to a clasp; ultimately, these are processes that should be familiar to every jeweler.

Preparing and Casting the Metal

The first step involves alloying about 100 grams of 18-carat gold, although the piece won't end up with this weight; always prepare more material than the piece will actually contain. This metal will be used to construct the body of the bracelet, which has to support the various decorative features, in addition to the clasp and the hinge.

Since 18-carat gold is composed of 750 parts of fine gold and 250 parts alloy, this 100 grams of gold will contain 75 grams of fine 24-carat gold and 25 grams of alloy. The latter is composed half of copper and half of silver—12.5 grams of each.

▲ **1.** Alloy 100 grams of 18-carat gold. The alloy has to contain 750 parts of fine gold and 250 parts of the alloy composed of half copper and half silver, as stated previously. To modify the color and the hardness of the metal, change the composition of the alloy, but retain the ratio of 750 parts of gold per 1000.

▲ **2.** Prepare the crucible by melting a layer of flux to fill the pores of the fireproof crucible material. Melt the fine gold first, and then add the alloy and a little more flux to promote a better and faster melt.

▶ **3.** Once the metal is molten, pour it carefully and quickly into an ingot mold. Part of the metal cast will be rolled into sheet form for constructing the clasp and the various tubes that will form the hinge.

▼ **4.** After the sheet is cast, make two billets in the wire mold; use these to make the rectangular outline of the bracelet. Remember that once the metal is cast it has to be pickled, rinsed in water, and dried well before proceeding to draw it down in the rolling mill in the next section.

Step by Step

Making the Framework

The main feature of this piece is its framework, which will hold the ornamental elements; in this project, a series of cast leaves and a structure of hammered wire will subsequently be added to the piece.

The framework has to allow the bracelet to open at the middle and fit the shape of the wrist, so it's important that the framework be fitted to the person who will wear it. Therefore, measure the wrist before bending the framework to shape.

▶ **1.** To create the outside profile, run the billet through the wire rolling mill and then draw it to shape using a rectangular hole drawplate. You can also create this shape by running the billet through a rolling mill for sheet stock. For this project, use a section 1.3 mm thick and 3.5 mm high.

▶ **2.** Take the rectangular sections that have been cut to the proper dimensions and annealed, and use a plastic mallet to shape them on an oval bracelet mandrel. Hammer these on a flat anvil too, since they also need to be completely flat. The two pieces have to be absolutely identical, with the soldering joins lined up.

▲ **3.** Make a tube for the hinge from .9-mm thick straight sheet stock. This diameter of the tubing is chosen carefully, for this piece is used to fashion the blind hinge that will make the bracelet open and close properly.

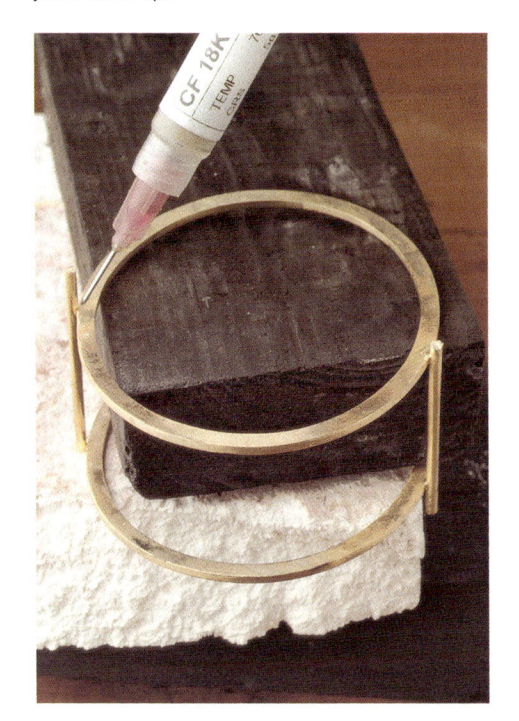

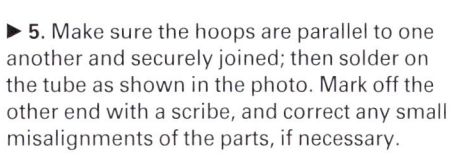

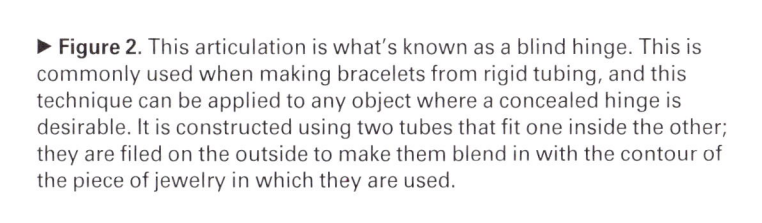

◀ **4.** Decide how wide you want the bracelet to be and solder some perpendicular bars between the two rims. These temporary bars will be removed later; they will serve to set up the alignment for the blind hinge and the clasp, and reinforce the framework before soldering on the decorative motifs.

▶ **5.** Make sure the hoops are parallel to one another and securely joined; then solder on the tube as shown in the photo. Mark off the other end with a scribe, and correct any small misalignments of the parts, if necessary.

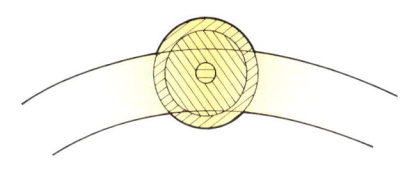

▶ **Figure 1.** Here's how the hinge should be positioned within the framework of the bracelet.

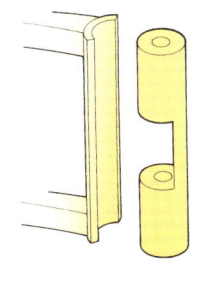

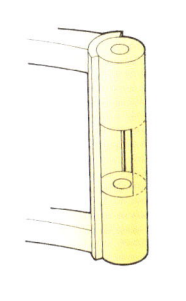

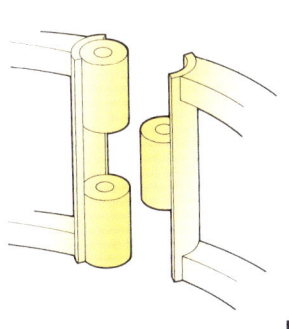

▶ **Figure 2.** This articulation is what's known as a blind hinge. This is commonly used when making bracelets from rigid tubing, and this technique can be applied to any object where a concealed hinge is desirable. It is constructed using two tubes that fit one inside the other; they are filed on the outside to make them blend in with the contour of the piece of jewelry in which they are used.

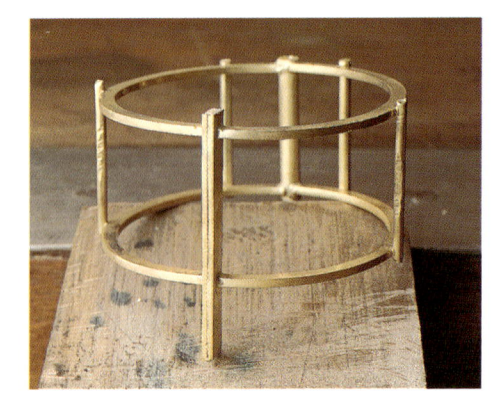

▲ **6.** Take a gold sheet 1 mm thick and bend it in the middle. Then hammer it flat on an anvil until both sides are parallel, and use hard solder to solder this piece onto the opposite side of the bracelet from the hinge, as shown in the photo.

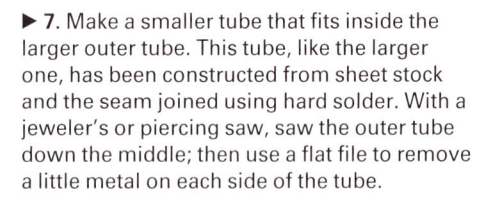

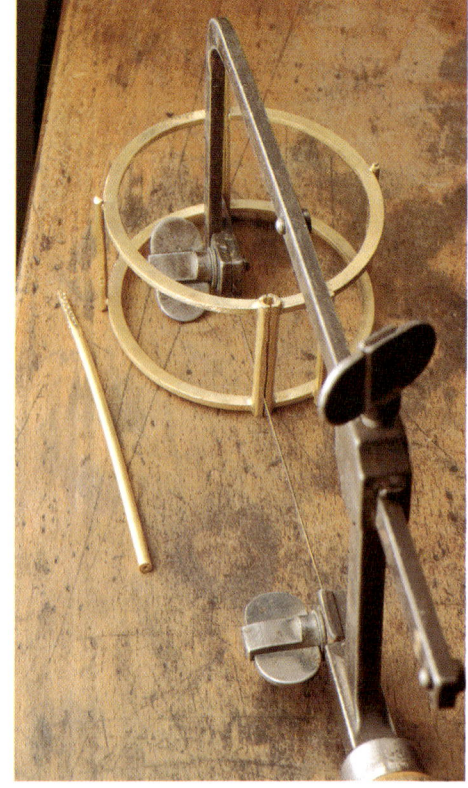

▶ **7.** Make a smaller tube that fits inside the larger outer tube. This tube, like the larger one, has been constructed from sheet stock and the seam joined using hard solder. With a jeweler's or piercing saw, saw the outer tube down the middle; then use a flat file to remove a little metal on each side of the tube.

▲ **8.** Divide the tube into three parts, with the middle section slightly longer than the two end sections. Then, saw away half of the middle section, leaving a small connecting segment that will keep the tubes perfectly aligned until they are soldered in place. An additional center section of tubing that will complete the closure is also shown in this photograph.

▲ **9.** Place the longer tube in position for soldering so the solder stays on the inside; the connecting piece should be on the outside where it will be easier to remove. Apply liquid flux and protect the existing joins with a heat-shielding product. Then bind everything together with wire; position a couple of small paillons of medium solder and solder.

▲ **10.** Remove the connecting piece with the jeweler's saw; then solder the center piece of tubing to the other half of the bracelet using medium solder, making sure that it fits perfectly inside the cutout. To keep this tube centered, put a small piece of broken saw blade or a needle between the two sides of the hinge to aid in centering the tube relative to the rest of the framework. This also keeps the two halves of the bracelet separate.

▲ **11.** After the soldering is completed, insert a wire pin into the hinge and use a file to remove a little metal as shown, preserving the curved oval of the piece.

▶ **12.** Here's the finished framework; it can be embellished with any type of ornamental feature. It should open properly, and the ends should match up precisely when it's closed.

Adding the Leaves

The following steps aren't difficult from a technical standpoint, but they require strict attention. The delicate task of arranging the cast leaves on the inside of the framework must be completed before soldering them to the main structure and making the clasp. The arrangement of the leaves demands sensitivity and a keen observation of nature; the composition has to provide a sense of lightness and highlight the natural elements that make the piece attractive. For a design like this one, look to nature and decide on the type of motif you want to use. You will probably want to avoid effects like a high polish and obvious symmetry, which would detract from the spontaneity of the piece; instead, emphasize the curves and the intentional imperfection in the arrangement of the shapes that lend expressiveness to the piece.

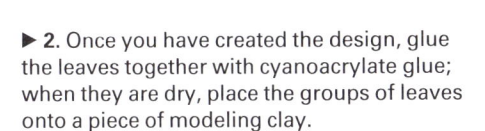

▲ Here are the geranium leaves that have been prepared and cast, using the technique explained on pages 63 and 64.

▲ 1. Put the leaves into the modeling clay to create the design; the leaves will also hold the settings for the diamonds, so keep that in mind as you work.

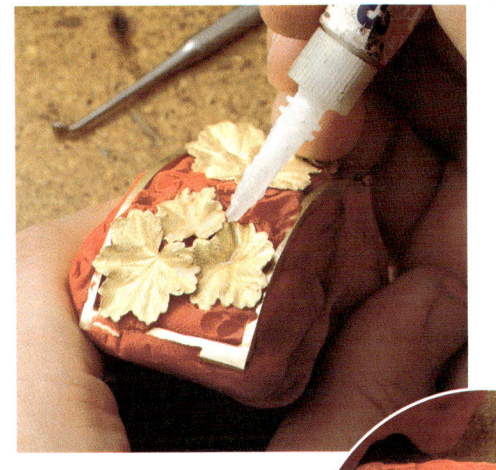

▶ 2. Once you have created the design, glue the leaves together with cyanoacrylate glue; when they are dry, place the groups of leaves onto a piece of modeling clay.

▶ 3. Using a small wax tool, fill in the hollows beneath the leaves with modeling clay to keep the plaster from getting into them.

▲ 4. Make some walls for the mold using the same modeling clay, and pour some fairly thick plaster into the mold.

▲ 5. When the plaster is dry, remove the modeling clay. Clean the plaster mold and add some paillons of solder.

▶ 6. Next, solder the leaves together. Soldering requires a hotter flame when plaster is used, especially if you're using a propane torch.

145

Hinged Bracelet

◀ 7. Ultimately, the various groups of leaves will be soldered in the same positions in which they were placed onto the modeling clay.

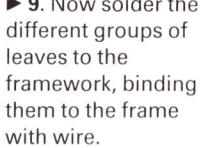

◀ 8. If you want to add a smaller feature, you can use a variation of this technique; fill the framework with modeling clay, arrange the leaves on the clay, and pour plaster over them. Then, remove the plaster and solder the elements together.

▶ 9. Now solder the different groups of leaves to the framework, binding them to the frame with wire.

▼ 10. As the groups of leaves are soldered into place, remove the temporary supports that have been providing rigidity to the framework.

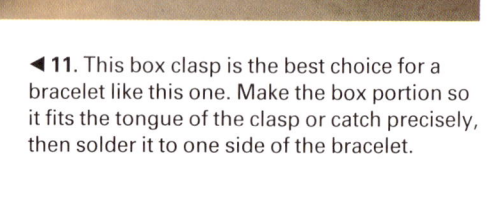

◀ 11. This box clasp is the best choice for a bracelet like this one. Make the box portion so it fits the tongue of the clasp or catch precisely, then solder it to one side of the bracelet.

▼ 13. Solder a pin onto the tongue of the clasp and make sure it works properly.

▼ 12. On the other side of the bracelet, prepare a support for the tongue portion of the clasp; make sure that the two pieces fit together and line up perfectly.

146

Step by Step

Settings for the Diamonds

The leaves on the frame also provide support for the diamonds that adorn the bracelet. Create these settings by forging and bending wire into asymmetrical shapes like those found in nature. Make irregular stems, and solder on the galleries at random.

▲ 1. To begin, cast a billet and run it through the wire rolling mill to create a final diameter of about 3 mm; then anneal and pickle it.

▶ 2. Use a hammer to forge the billet and thin it unevenly toward the ends. Anneal the metal several times in this process.

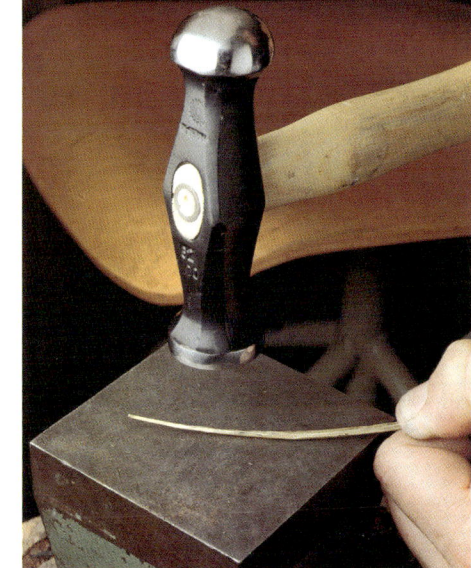

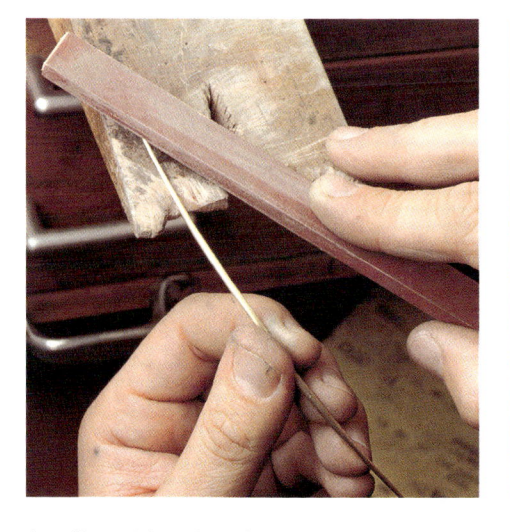

▲ 3. First with various files, and then with abrasive paper, work the wire down so that it's thinner at the ends.

▲ 4. Shape the wire using various types of pliers; keep your final design in mind and remember that these features will hold the diamonds that are interspersed throughout the bracelet.

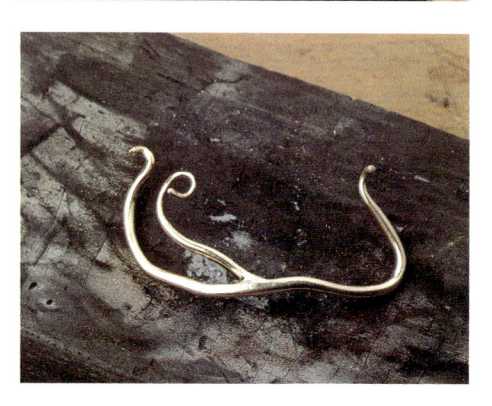

▲ 5. Solder additional pieces of wire onto some of these structures to create more elaborate shapes.

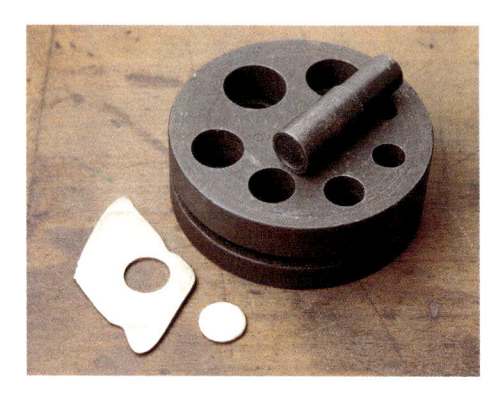

▲ 6. In general, commercially set diamonds look more brilliant when their settings are made of white gold and plated with rhodium. In this project, create the pavé setting as a representative motif. First, cut out various disks from a sheet of .9 mm white gold.

◀ 7. Make the disks in a domed or hemispherical shape; use a die and various rounded punches for this procedure, annealing and punching until the right shape is obtained.

▼ 8. File the flat edges of the hemispheres to make them level, and then carve with a rotary cutting bur so they will fit together in irregular clusters.

147

Hinged Bracelet

▲ 9. Next, solder the groups of domes together onto a .6-mm thick sheet of white gold.

▲ 10. Now, saw them out from the metal sheet, and file and sand the outlines. Fashion an opening in the back to allow light to pass through; this will also make it easier to clean the gems later on

▼ 11. To facilitate the arrangement, it's a good idea to fill the inside of the framework with modeling clay and then put all the elements into place, modifying the composition and adjusting features as needed.

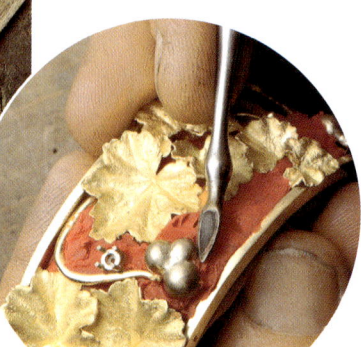

▲ 12. Solder the groups of domes to the structure by putting them on the gold wire supports; this assures a strong connection with the framework while simultaneously appearing to be light.

▲ 13. Make settings of white gold for the individual diamonds, and solder them to the existing framework into indentations made on the wires with a cylindrical bur.

▲ 14. Bind the supports for the gems to the main framework and apply paste solder to the joints. Protect the adjacent joins with heat-shielding paste before you solder.

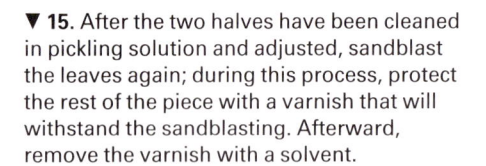

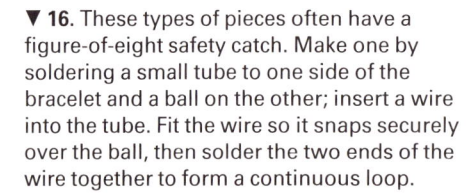

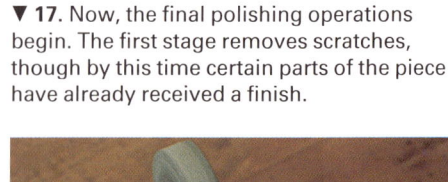

▼ 15. After the two halves have been cleaned in pickling solution and adjusted, sandblast the leaves again; during this process, protect the rest of the piece with a varnish that will withstand the sandblasting. Afterward, remove the varnish with a solvent.

▼ 16. These types of pieces often have a figure-of-eight safety catch. Make one by soldering a small tube to one side of the bracelet and a ball on the other; insert a wire into the tube. Fit the wire so it snaps securely over the ball, then solder the two ends of the wire together to form a continuous loop.

▼ 17. Now, the final polishing operations begin. The first stage removes scratches, though by this time certain parts of the piece have already received a finish.

148

Step by Step

▶ 18. Coat the parts of the bracelet that won't be polished—specifically the leaves that have been sandblasted—with a synthetic lacquer that will protect them from small errors or slips in the polishing process. The lacquer is easily removed later with acetone.

▶ 19. This piece has many areas that are hard to reach with normal polishing tools. It's necessary to thrum the piece using thick cotton string impregnated first with tripoli compound, and then with polishing paste. The piece must be thrummed with the string until all the hard-to-reach areas have been completely polished.

▼ 20. Set the diamonds by making a seat with a small ball bur inside the claws of the settings and closing the remaining metal over the stones.

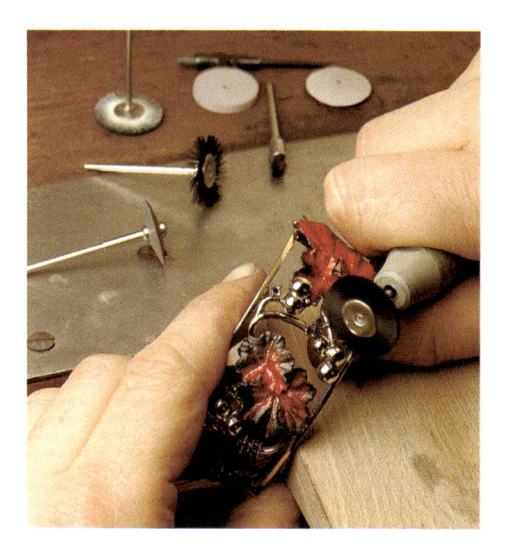

▼ 21. Make a pavé setting on the domes by raising small bits of metal with the onglette graver and curling them over each stone.

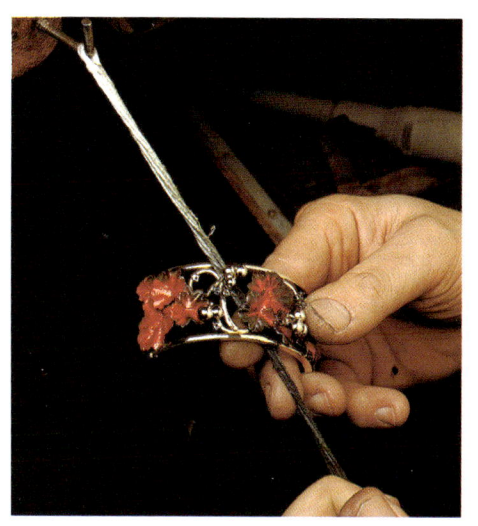

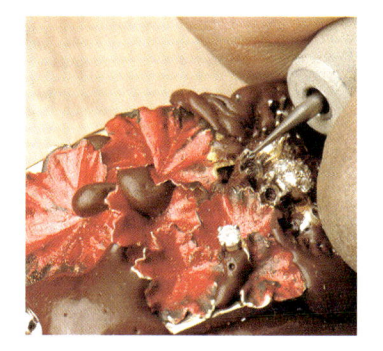

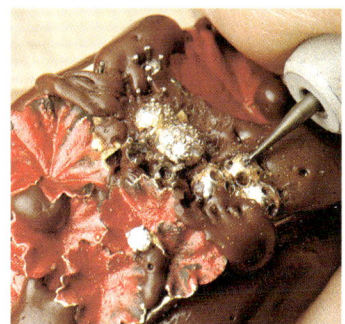

▶ 22. After setting the diamonds, remove the setting pitch by boiling the piece in ammonia, and polish once again. Finally, insert an annealed wire inside the knuckles of the hinge and peen the ends.

▲ There are 134 grams of 750 yellow gold and 5.87 carats of exceptional brilliant cut diamonds in this bracelet.

▶ The finished bracelet by Carles Codina

149

Brooches

The next project suggests a method of working on the metal in a very direct and intuitive way—an expressive process in which intuition counts more than rigidity of technique. This procedure involves a combination of decorative techniques, such as Kum Boo and niello, as well as some special types of finishes.

Start with a thick sheet of prepared silver and strike it forcefully when hot until it produces some interesting and unexpected metal fractures; after proper selection and arrangement, this material can be made into a series of attractive brooches.

▲ **1.** Use a series of sterling silver sheets with a minimum thickness of 2 mm; make several sheets so you can choose the most interesting ones after they are hammered. Place the sheets a small distance apart on a hard, clean refractory block. Heat them with a gas flame to a bright orange-red.

◀ **2.** Be sure to wear safety glasses for this step, in case the metal becomes airborne. When the silver reaches this orange-red color, strike it briskly with an old hammer, right in the center. It will be difficult to control the fracture, so the results will be unpredictable. If this is done correctly, the silver will break like glass and form some attractive and interesting fissures.

▼ **3.** Choose a piece from those produced in the previous steps; reinforce it if necessary. Solder a clasp onto the back before applying Kum Boo and niello, for once those are applied further soldering is impossible.

◀ **4.** Add an acid etching and then some Kum Boo, if desired, as shown in these examples.

▶ **5.** Add niello in an irregular pattern on top of the Kum Boo, then heat it and spread it out with various steel spatulas. Be sure to wear a respirator and work in a properly ventilated space when using this technique.

Step by Step

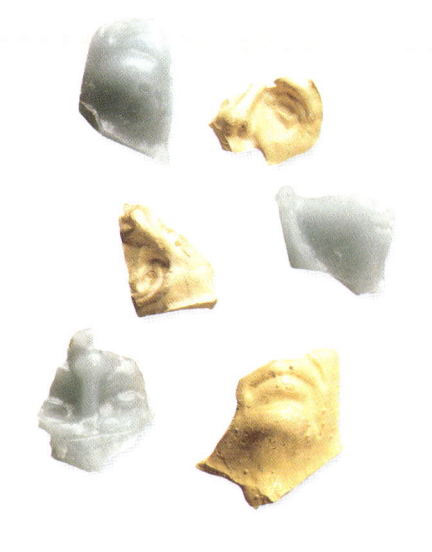

▲ 6. Add features to the surface that are modeled in wax and cast using 18-carat gold.

▶ 7. Since no more soldering can be done, rivet the decorative elements on through the back.

▲ This work features a piece of cactus that was cast directly; made by Carles Codina.

▲ This brooch includes a set garnet cabochon; it has been riveted in place through the back of the piece. Work by Carles Codina.

◀ This is a very simple piece; it has a single fracture and a nicely textured surface. Brooch by Carles Codina.

▶ Carles Codina, *Constellation*.
The surface of this piece was acid etched, and a repoussé-formed figure was added.

North African Bracelet

Here is a tribal bracelet made by Salima Saïd El Hadj and Oukali Saliha, two goldsmiths from the Kabylia region of Algeria. They have created a beautiful traditional piece that revives some of the classical elements of Berber goldsmithing, including the use of borsade filigree, calottes, and coral. This project is noteworthy for its execution of the ancient technique of filigree; this is a different style from that used in Europe and America, but it shares the same roots. Filigree originated in Mesopotamia and it was spread throughout the entire Mediterranean area by the Greeks and the Phoenicians. This work is very craftsman-like in its conception; its execution is very demanding, and it's constructed according to a tradition transmitted through the generations.

THE BERBER CULTURE

The land that is now known as Algeria was originally inhabited by the Berbers (or *Amazigh*). These people have lived in northern Africa from time immemorial; there were already references to them in ancient Egyptian and Greek documents dating from 3000 B.C. During the first millennium before the Christian era, the Berber society was organized into tribes. Before the arrival of the Phoenicians they had already developed a true civilization, with a cohesive social structure composed of principalities governed by a sovereign who bore the title of *Agnellid*, or military and political chief.

For many centuries, the Berbers occupied the entire northern African coast from Egypt to the Atlantic Ocean. They continued living there until the seventh century A.D., when the Arabs conquered northern Africa and drove many Berbers to the interior of the continent, the Atlas Mountains, and various parts of the Sahara. Today, the Berber or Amazigh live in northern African nations; they make up as much as 40 percent of the population of Morocco and 30 percent of the population of Algeria, and a much smaller portion of Tunisia. They are distinguished less by their facial features and their religion than by their spoken language with its many dialects. The use of the Berber languages is declining as the people adopt the language and culture of the majority population, which is Arab.

Kabylia is a mountainous and craggy region in northern Africa, located in northeast Algeria. Its coastline on the Mediterranean is one of the most beautiful in northern Africa. The region is in the middle of a mountain chain and extends from Algiers to Djidjelli. It is divided into two parts: Great or Major Kabylia to the west, and Small or Minor Kabylia to the east; the latter is lower in elevation and more open to the sea.

◀ The artisans of this project, Salima Saïd El Hadj and Oukali Saliha, are pictured here with author Carles Codina.

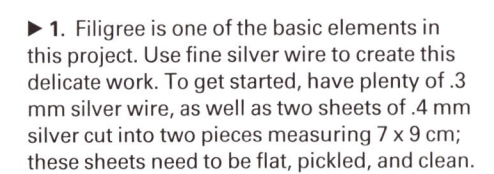

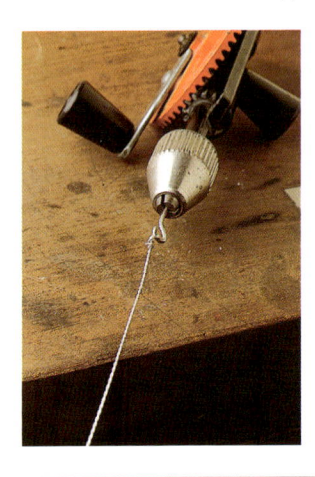

▶ **1.** Filigree is one of the basic elements in this project. Use fine silver wire to create this delicate work. To get started, have plenty of .3 mm silver wire, as well as two sheets of .4 mm silver cut into two pieces measuring 7 x 9 cm; these sheets need to be flat, pickled, and clean.

◀ **2.** You will decorate the two halves of the bracelet. To begin, take a thin round wire; bend it in the middle and make a loop on one end; then slip the loop onto a hook clamped in the chuck of a hand drill. Turn the chuck slowly and the lengths of wire will wind smoothly around each another into a braid.

▼ **3.** Anneal this braided wire a few times during the construction process to ensure an even braiding. After you anneal the wire the last time, stretch it by pulling tightly on both ends.

▼ **4.** Cut all the wires into equal lengths; these will be placed on the far outside of the rectangle for decoration.

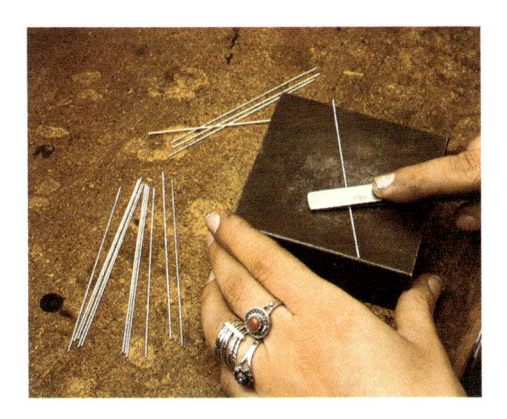

Step by Step

▲ 5. To keep the wires straight, flatten them by rolling on a steel anvil while exerting downward pressure with a flat object.

▲ 6. Dip all the wires in liquid flux and arrange them as shown in the photo. Insert some wire with a different decoration if desired.

▲ 7. Once all the wires are in place, use the torch to heat the whole piece so that the liquid flux secures the wires, keeping them in place the next time heat is applied.

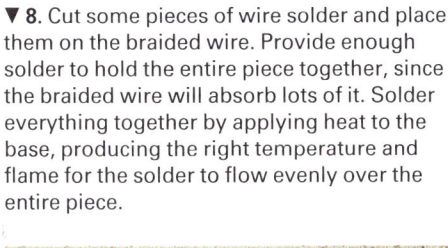

▼ 8. Cut some pieces of wire solder and place them on the braided wire. Provide enough solder to hold the entire piece together, since the braided wire will absorb lots of it. Solder everything together by applying heat to the base, producing the right temperature and flame for the solder to flow evenly over the entire piece.

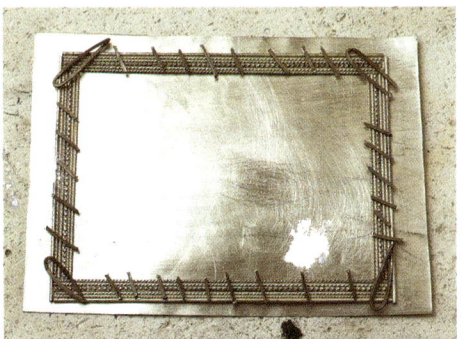

◀ 9. For the filigree, take a round wire and flatten it a little in the rolling mill. Take this wire and create the shape shown in the photograph using round-nose pliers.

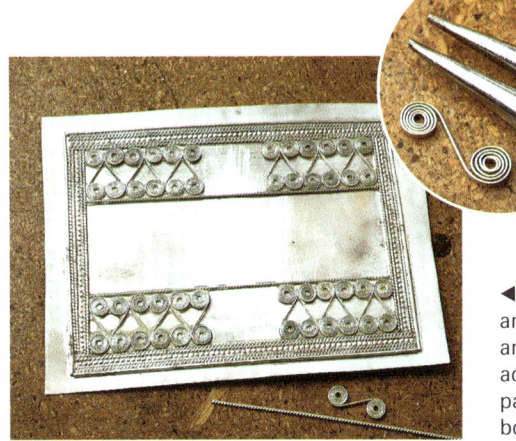

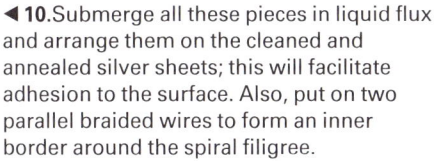

◀ 10. Submerge all these pieces in liquid flux and arrange them on the cleaned and annealed silver sheets; this will facilitate adhesion to the surface. Also, put on two parallel braided wires to form an inner border around the spiral filigree.

◀ 11. Put solder dipped in liquid flux on top of the filigree.

▲ 12. As in step 8, apply the flame to the base of the piece to equalize the temperature throughout the plate and cause the solder to flow evenly over the entire assembly.

▶ 13. Produce the wave-like features by feeding annealed silver wire through the gears of a hand drill; these are easy to make.

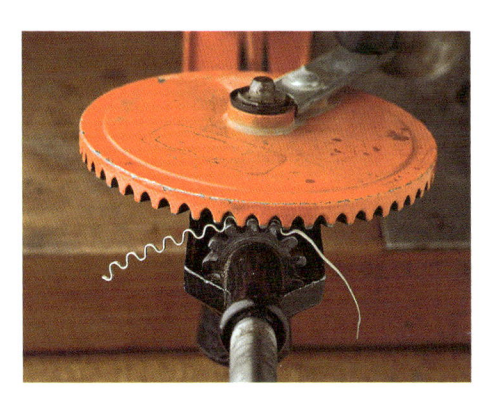

▶ 14. Place these decorative elements on the silver plate, and then solder in place.

▶ 15. Add two braided wires and additional motifs.

153

North African Bracelet

▲ 16. To make the settings or mounts for the stones, take several sheets of .5-mm thick silver and cut a toothed edge with the tip of the hand shears, as shown in the photo.

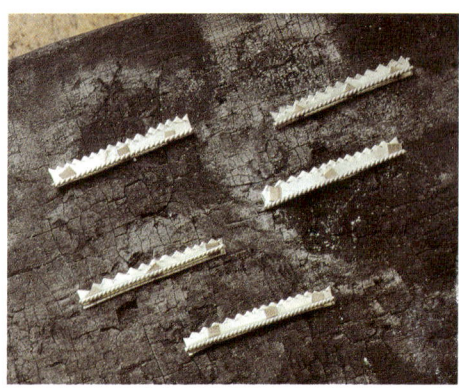

▲ 17. Flatten these pieces and then solder on a section of braided wire, using plenty of solder.

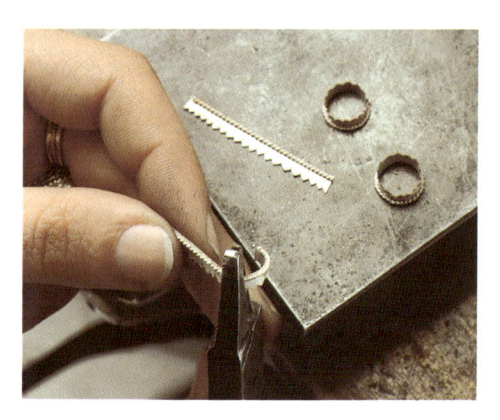

▲ 18. Use half-round pliers to bend the pieces into the right shape and size to hold the red coral gems they will hold in place.

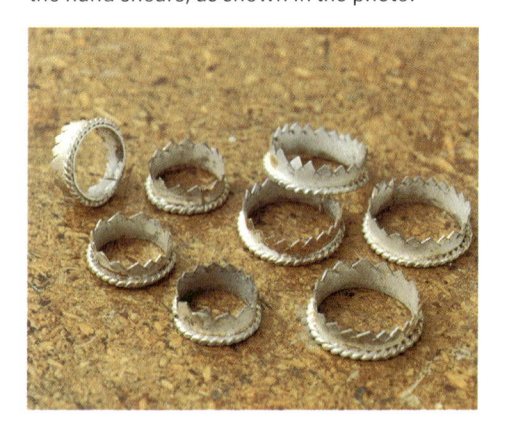

▲ 19. If you wish, you can hammer the settings lightly on a ring mandrel; that way they will be more round and even.

▲ 20. Then, enhance the decoration with a few more rings made from the braided wire; place these around the settings and solder in place.

▲ 21. Begin to create the central decorations of the bracelet by soldering together some teardrop-shaped wires, as shown in the photo.

JEWELRY FROM KABYLIA

Algeria has an extraordinarily rich cultural heritage, which includes goldsmithing. This means of artistic expression is not well known in other countries, yet it's craftsmanship that illuminates many essential values of the Mediterranean culture. Algerian jewelry speaks more eloquently about the history of its people than does perhaps its wars and its monuments. Through their talent and dedication, the artisans express the soul of the people in the bridal trousseaux and the various forms of the gold jewelry that are given as gifts in their region. The jewelry of the women of Kabylia, such as the bracelet being created in this section, expresses the value of these objects that reflect a trade and a culture that have existed for many generations.

The jewelry of Kabylia has great social significance; generally it is given to a young woman at the time of her marriage, and it is bought using the dowry that the parents of the groom receive. Some of the symbolic jewelry from Kabylia includes the *Thasabt,* diadems or pieces to be worn on the head, which are symbols of the union between the families. Another example is the large round pin known as *Thabzimt,* which is offered by the husband to his wife upon the birth of their first child. The large necklaces or *Thazlaith* are composed of many pendants of different sizes. The distinctive features of jewelry from this region include work on both faces of each piece, the colors of the enamels, the use of red coral, and the characteristic decorations that are present on all pieces of jewelry, from a simple ring to a large necklace.

◄ Perhaps the best-known part of Kabylia is Beni Yenni, a group of seven towns famous for their gold and silver jewelry. The photo shows a pin and a necklace from Great Kabylia.

▼ Women in Kabylia wear bracelets throughout their lives; they are worn in pairs, one on each wrist, while performing daily tasks. They are frequently mentioned in traditional songs and poems. Here are some bracelets from Beni Yenni, Great Kabylia.

Step by Step

▲ 22. Place the various shapes next to one another to form a flower. Throughout the entire construction process of the bracelet, remember to be sure the surfaces are even so all the elements of the piece will solder properly.

▲ 23. After the pieces are soldered together, very carefully form them in a steel dapping block.

▲ 24. Place the piece on top of a silver dome made in the dapping block, and set various silver balls inside the flower motif.

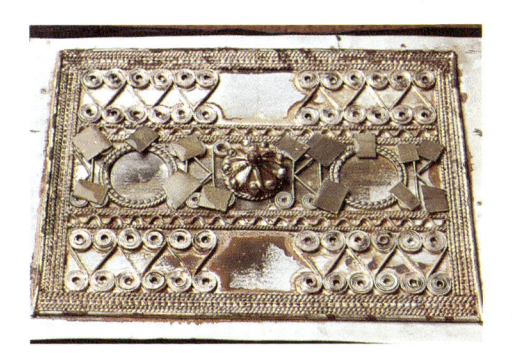

▲ 25. Put all these elements on the plate coated with liquid flux, and place several large pieces of solder on top of them.

▲ 26. It's very important to apply solder properly and uniformly in this type of construction. You have to create good contact between the surfaces to be joined, so they have to be cleaned properly in advance. Use a broad reducing flame so when the solder melts, it flows freely and blends in with all the previous work so it is soldered evenly throughout.

▲ 27. Spheres or balls are a feature that's commonly used in this type of jewelry. To make these, melt small silver loops on a hard refractory surface, such as an old piece of crucible. When you use this type of surface, the spheres remain flat on their undersides; to create perfectly spherical pieces, use a ball bur to make indentations in a charcoal block.

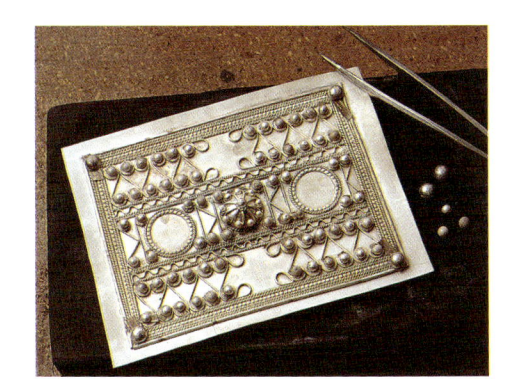

▲ 28. Dip the spheres or balls in liquid flux and set in place where desired; apply a broad flame to pull the previously applied solder to the base of the spheres. No new solder is required for these joins.

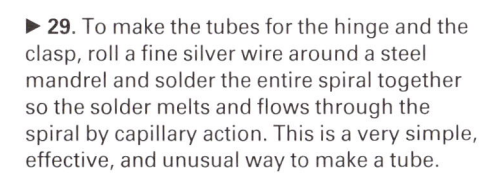

▶ 29. To make the tubes for the hinge and the clasp, roll a fine silver wire around a steel mandrel and solder the entire spiral together so the solder melts and flows through the spiral by capillary action. This is a very simple, effective, and unusual way to make a tube.

▲ 30. Cut the spiral tube into three pieces; two of these are soldered at the ends of one edge of the bracelet, and the remaining piece is soldered to the middle of the opposite, corresponding edge.

North African Bracelet

▲ 31. Now, take the settings for the coral that you made in steps 16 to 20 and solder them to the base plate.

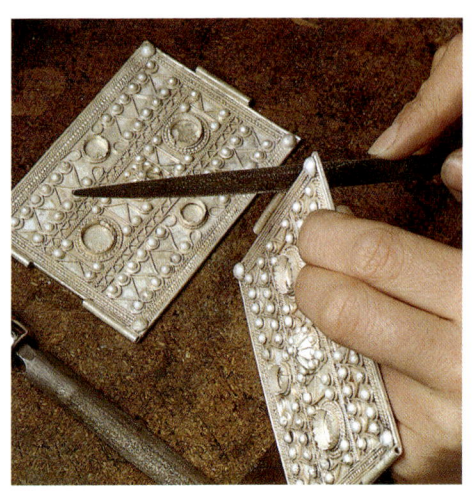

▲ 32. Use a file to carefully make the final adjustments to the hinge; try to get the knuckles to fit together as precisely as possible.

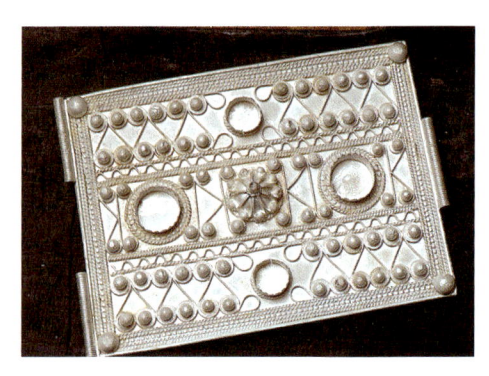

▲ 33. With all the soldering complete, the piece must be heated and cleaned in pickling solution before applying the enamel. Repeat this process until there is no new oxidation; after each pickling operation, the plates have to be cleaned thoroughly with water and baking soda to remove all traces of oil.

▲ 34. To give the bracelet the proper shape, bend it by hand around a bracelet mandrel, and then hammer with a plastic mallet.

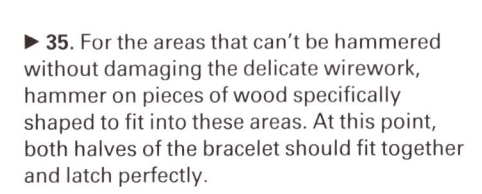

▶ 35. For the areas that can't be hammered without damaging the delicate wirework, hammer on pieces of wood specifically shaped to fit into these areas. At this point, both halves of the bracelet should fit together and latch perfectly.

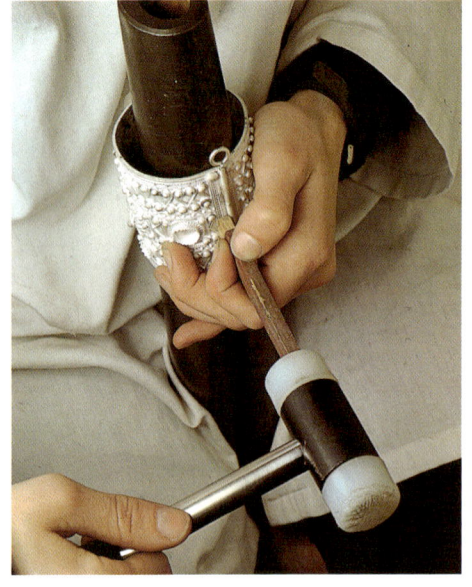

▲ 36. Grind the enamel with a mortar and pestle and then clean. Once it's moistened, apply it directly onto the metal with an artist's brush or a steel spatula. In this project, the blue enamel will uniformly fill specific areas of the bracelet, particularly the central portions where various settings are located.

▼ 37. Use the green enamel next, applied in the same way as in the previous step.

▲ 38. Finally, apply the yellow; allow the piece to dry so that there is no more moisture in the enamel.

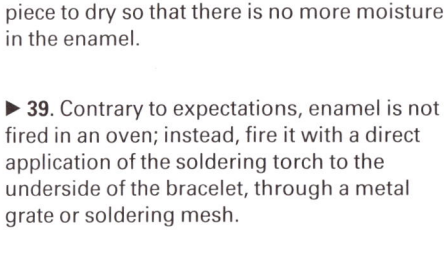

▶ 39. Contrary to expectations, enamel is not fired in an oven; instead, fire it with a direct application of the soldering torch to the underside of the bracelet, through a metal grate or soldering mesh.

156

Step by Step

▲ 40. After the enamel has cooled, insert an annealed round wire into the tubes of the hinge; peen the ends of this pin over using a hammer and a steel anvil.

▲ 41. The clasp is a length of round wire with one end bent into a loop so it's easy to insert and remove; this opens and closes the clasp. The wire acts like a door bolt, keeping the two halves of the bracelet together when it's slid into the three aligned tubes.

▲ 42. To give the piece an aged appearance, dip it into a silver oxide bath and heat slightly to fix the oxide onto the surface of the silver. It's important to do this step in a well-ventilated area; protect your hands with rubber gloves.

▲ 43. Before setting the gems into place, put a little bit of damp paper inside the settings. Add the red corals to their respective settings; the gems in the photo were cut by hand.

▲ 44. As you press on the coral with your thumb, use pliers to gently squeeze the metal of the setting over the gem until the coral is held solidly in place.

▲ 45. Set all the pieces of coral in a similar manner, and remove any excess enamel.

▲ 46. Polish in the traditional way, first removing any possible scratches and the superficial oxidation from the piece. Continue with a second polishing using red jeweler's rouge.

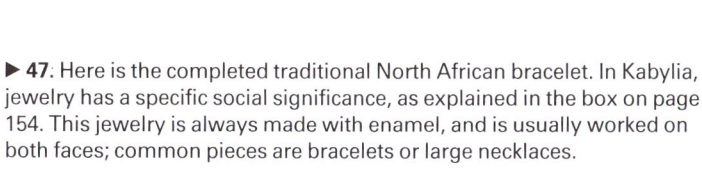

▶ 47. Here is the completed traditional North African bracelet. In Kabylia, jewelry has a specific social significance, as explained in the box on page 154. This jewelry is always made with enamel, and is usually worked on both faces; common pieces are bracelets or large necklaces.

Glossary

Angstrom. Unit of length used to measure radiation wavelengths; it is equivalent to one hundred-millionth of a centimeter.

Annealing. Action of heating metal to cherry red and then letting it cool. Annealing restores malleability to the metal after it has been subjected to a mechanical process, such as rolling or hammering.

Arkansas stone. Abrasive stone used to sharpen the hand gravers used in engraving and setting gems.

Atom. The smallest part of a chemical element; it remains essentially unalterable in chemical reactions. Even though atoms are considered to be neutral, they comprise electric charges of different types such as electrons, protons, and neutrons.

Birefringence. The double refraction that results when a ray of light passes through a crystal and divides into two unequally transmitted rays.

Borax. Vitreous paste that helps solder flow and dissolves metallic oxides when it melts.

Brilliance. The light-reflecting property of a stone; it depends on the nature of the surface, its refraction index, and light absorption.

Burnish. To polish a surface by rubbing it with a tool, generally made of steel, hematite, or agate.

Carat. The unit of weight measurement for gems, equivalent to 200 mg.

Carbon. The naturally abundant element that occurs in all organic compounds; sometimes visible as a black inclusion inside diamonds, which are pure refractive crystallized carbon.

Chisel. Tool used for shaping wood on a lathe. Lathe chisels have sharp cutting edges and come in several shapes, from half-round (gouges) and square (scrapers) in cross section to thin and pointed (parting tools).

Chuck. A one- or two-part wooden form over which metal is shaped during the metal spinning process.

Crystal. Material with an atomic structure that's identical among members of the same family.

Culet. The part of a cut stone that lies below the girdle; on a brilliant-cut gem, the flat face at the bottom of the stone.

Durability. The resistance of a mineral to loss of brilliance or polish due to physical and chemical agents.

Facet. A flat face on a cut stone.

Fissure. Fracture or exfoliation that occurs in gems.

Follow block. A small piece of lathe-turned wood, used in conjunction with the tailstock to provide pressure to a metal disk being shaped on a lathe.

Girdle. The outermost rim of a cut stone, generally the point at which it is held in the setting.

Graver. Pointed steel tool used by engravers to cut designs into metal; also called a burin.

Hardness. Resistance of a mineral to scratching.

Headstock. A fixed head on the lathe that holds the work piece and spins it for turning. Used in conjunction with the tailstock for metal spinning.

Join. The place where two or more parts are fitted together, *after* the soldering process; see joint.

Joint. The place where two or more parts are fitted together, *before* the soldering process; see join.

Karat. Unit of measurement for the quantity of pure gold included in an alloy.

Knot. An imperfection in the crystalline structure of a diamond.

Lapidary. The professional who cuts, polishes, or engraves precious stones.

Orient of pearl. The iridescence on the surface of a pearl; this causes a characteristic interplay of colors due to the interference of light on the fine layers of nacre.

Paillon. Small piece of solder used on a project; also called a snippet.

Pickling solution. Acid-based solution used to remove the oxidation produced on the surface of metal after annealing or soldering.

Refraction. The turning or bending of light rays when they pass through mediums with different optical densities.

Spinning tool. A tool with a highly polished surface used for shaping metal disks on a lathe.

Synthetic. Designation for man-made stones created in a laboratory; these materials have the same composition and structure as natural gems.

Tailstock. Movable part of a lathe opposite the headstock, used to secure a metal plate for spinning.

Index

acknowledgments, 160
annealing, 11
Ayoreita mines, 75
Bagués Jewelers, 96
Berbers, 152
bibliography, 160
binding with wire, 12, 19
bracelet projects: hinged, 142–149; Kum Boo, 37; North African, 152–157
brass, in solder, 11
brooch projects: aniello, 150–151; Kum Boo, 150–151; soldered, 24; wire, 26
burin. *See* graver
business, 100–107
Capdevila, Joaquim, 99
casting: ashanti, 50–51; ceramic shell, 56–59; cuttlebone, 52; Delft sand, 53; investment, 10; natural models, 63–64; natural stone, 54–55; room temperature vulcanizing mold , 62
chain project, 25
clasp projects, 29
cutting precious stones, 84–86
damascening. See inlay
diamonds: about, 80–82; cutting, 86–87
dies, 69–71
Domingo, Ricard, 97
earring project, 138–141
electroplating, 44–46
electropolishing, 46–47
engraving, 38–41
fire stain, 12
flux, 10, 18
frame project, 23
gems: about, 74–78. *See also* precious stones, synthetic gems
glossary, 158
graver, 38, 39, 41
imitation gems. *See* synthetic gems
inlay, 41
inlay project, 42–43

investment casting, 10, 50
join, 11, 12
joint, 12
Kabylia, 152, 154
Kum Boo, 34–36
lathe, 15, 116
mandrel, 15, 25
moissanite, 81–82
Munsteiner, Bernd, 88–93
oxidizing, 11–12
paillons, 12
pearls, 82–83
pendant projects: frame, 23; hollow tube, 22; prism, 134–137; soldered, 21
photography, 104–107
pickling, 11–12
platinum, 30–31
polishing, 46–47
precious stones: about, 74–78. *See also* gems
prism cut, 89–93
Puig Cuyás, Ramón, 98
repoussé, 11
ring projects: baguette ring, 60–61; hollow, 20; square blue sapphire, 128–131; square ruby, 128, 132–133; wedding ring, 61–62; wire, 27
sandblasting, 47
silver, about, 10
silversmithing, 10
silversmithing projects: bowl, 13–14; centerpiece, 15–17; coffee service project, 116–127
snippets. *See* paillons.
solder: gold, 18, 19; platinum, 31; silver, 11, 12
solder seam. *See* join
stamping, 65–68
sterling silver, 10
stringing, 28
synthetic gems, 79
tarnish, 12
wire, working with, 25
zirconite, 81–82

Bibliography and Acknowledgments

Evans, Chuck. *Contemporary Design and Technique.* Worcester, Massachusetts: Davis Publications, Inc., 1983.

Guía de piedras preciosas. Barcelona: Editorial Grijalbo, 1986.

Munsteiners. Joyeras Publications, Inc.

Untracht, Oppi. *Jewelry Concepts and Technology.* London: Doubleday, 1987.

Vitiello, Luigi. *Orfebrería moderna.* Barcelona: Ediciones Omega, Inc., 1989.

Webster, R. *Piedras preciosas.* Barcelona: Ediciones Omega, Inc., 1987.

The information in this book is based on notes and information generously provided by many friends and collaborators. Much of the knowledge presented here comes directly from the professionals, who demonstrated the techniques just as they learned them from previous generations.

I have learned that in any activity, the journey—including the means of travel, the traveling partners, and the sharing of experiences—is far more satisfying and valuable than the end result. One of the keys to completing these two books on jewelry has been the emotional and human element, including choosing the right people to include as collaborators. Sometimes I selected these people based on my personal relationship with them; other times, I simply stumbled upon them. These are people with whom I have shared both books, and also a small part of my life; they are all true professionals, but especially, they are good friends who have given character to this work. In fact, I knew from the beginning that in order to start a journey of this magnitude, I needed to select good companions with whom I enjoyed a friendly, personal relationship; they needed to be people I could communicate well with, colleagues who would help me share new knowledge about this craft of jewelry making.

I was right in all of that, and the special vision with which I began Handbook of Jewellery Techniques has been carried through to Jewellery and Silversmithing Techniques; it has surely been the key to the success of these books.

Joan Soto's pictures, as well as his personal involvement, have made this work possible. I also thank my patient editor, María Fernanda Canal, and the team at Parramón Editions for the high expectations they had for this second project.

Thanks also to my good friends and companions for their selfless collaboration and kind support, which was the product of countless conversations and many photo sessions: To Ricard Domingo for his chapter on image and business, as well as to Pilar Cotter and Jaime Díaz for the information on casting—we really had fun. To Silvia Walz and Maike Barteldres, for their interesting, amazing casting and stamping techniques, as well as to Hans Leicht, for the section on inlaying, and once again to Joan Soto, for his chapter on photography. To Ramón Puig Cuyás, Joaquim Capdevila, Joan Oliveres, and Ricard Domingo, who contributed their personal vision of this craft. Also to my friends Xavier Doménech, Xavier Ines Monclús, Joaquim Benaque, and Juan José López, as well as to my friend Estela Guitart, who all collaborated generously and freely on several chapters in this book.

It was a great learning experience to work with Salima Saïd El Hadj and Oukali Saliha on the Kabylia bracelet, which is an unforgettable contribution to my book.

Thanks also to these master goldsmiths and tireless collaborators: Joan Ferré, Raimundo Amorós, and Jesús Pérez Matamoros. To my friends Bea Würsch and Tanja Fontane at the Galería Forum Ferlandina in Barcelona, as well as Xavi and José María de la García Bonilla and Josep Sánchez-Lafuente ("Pitu"), for their advice, help with the text, and passionate collaboration through countless conversations about precious stones.

Thanks to Bernd Munsteiner and his family, for their generous collaboration and kind hospitality.

Thank you to all who have helped by generously showing me your work, offering opinions, supporting me, and inspiring me in this task; I stress the help of the Sanjuán family, as well as the collaboration of Clara Inés Arana, Jimena Bello, David Huycke, Kerstin Östberg, Imaz, Josep Carles Pérez, Sivillà, and the Touiza-Solidaritat Association.

Finally, I thank my wife Montserrat and my children Joan and María for the patience they have shown me during the past year.

Thanks to all for making this possible.

Carles Codina